The Best Laid Scher

The Best Laid Schemes

SELECTED POETRY AND PROSE OF ROBERT BURNS

Edited by

ROBERT CRAWFORD AND
CHRISTOPHER MACLACHLAN

Polygon

This edition published in 2009 by
Polygon, an imprint of Birlinn Ltd
West Newington House
10 Newington Road
Edinburgh EH9 1QS
www.birlinn.co.uk

ISBN 978 1 84697 094 8

9 8 7 6 5 4 3 2 1

British Library Cataloguing-in-Publication Data
A catalogue record for this book is available
on request from the British Library.

Typeset in Great Britain by Antony Gray
Printed and bound by Bell & Bain, Glasgow

Contents

REDISCOVERED POEMS

PROSE

Acknowledgements

In addition to other libraries and collections named in the text of this volume we would like to extend special thanks to David Hopes of the National Trust for Scotland's Robert Burns Birthplace Museum at Alloway and Kenneth Dunn of the Department of Manuscripts at the National Library of Scotland for their generous help, especially with regard to the rediscovered poems in this book. We would like to thank, too, the staff of St Andrews University Library, particularly Dr Alice Crawford, Mrs Rachel Hart, Ms Moira Mackenzie, and Dr Norman Reid. Though the texts of the poems and prose have been re-edited from manuscripts and early printed sources for *The Best Laid Schemes*, like other readers of Burns we are especially indebted to James Kinsley's three-volume edition of *The Poems and Songs of Robert Burns* (Clarendon Press, 1968) and to the two-volume edition of *The Letters of Robert Burns* by J. De Lancey Ferguson (Second Edition by G. Ross Roy, Clarendon Press, 1985) – both for many years the standard collected editions. The *Definitive Illustrated Companion to Robert Burns* (2004) edited by Peter Westwood has been of great assistance, as have the digital resources of the Eighteenth Century Collections Online (ECCO) database, the National Burns Collection (whose catalogue is available at www.burnsscotland.com) and SCRAN (Scottish Cultural Resources Access Network). Lastly, warm thanks are due to Hugh Andrew at Polygon who commissioned this book and to Neville Moir, who guided it through the press; to Jonathan Meuli, whose skilful copy-editing allowed us to make several improvements; to a patient agent, Sophie Hoult at David Godwin Associates; to our colleagues in the School of English at the University of St Andrews; and to our families for accommodating yet more Burns work.

Robert Crawford
Christopher MacLachlan
St Andrews

Textual Note

Most of the texts of the poems in this book are taken from editions of his work which Burns saw through the press and with which he was closely associated. This allows readers to experience the texts that Burns's early readers read, and which made the poet's name. Many of our texts are taken from the 1786 Kilmarnock edition of Burns's *Poems, Chiefly in the Scottish Dialect* or from the expanded 1787 Edinburgh edition of that collection. A number of songs are taken from the *Scots Musical Museum* whose contents were substantially shaped by Burns.

The most obvious difference between the poems as they appear here and the form they took for Burns's readers is that our texts have line-by-line glossing of Scots words. Burns recognised that some glossing was desirable, and from the very first Kilmarnock printing he provided a glossary of Scots words at the end of his book. Some nineteenth-century editions began the practice of having line-by-line glosses beside the poems themselves, since this makes the reading experience more immediate, avoiding any need to turn to the back of the book in mid-poem. Though it is labour-intensive from an editorial point of view, we believe this way of presenting the poems is the one that is most helpful for a modern international audience. Poems have been glossed individually, so that it is not assumed the reader should remember the meaning of a Scots word simply because it has already been glossed fifty pages earlier. Readers can dip into the book anywhere, and be confident that they will find sufficient line-by-line glossing.

In the interests of readability, the eighteenth-century 'long s' (which looks very like an 'f' to modern readers) has been modernized to an ordinary 's'; we have expanded some words left blank (sometimes for political or religious reasons); some inconsistencies in indentation and capitalization have been silently corrected, and numbering of stanzas has been omitted; we have numbered Burns's own footnotes rather than using asterisks; and we have modernized the use of quotation marks. Otherwise the punctuation and spelling of the original texts have generally been maintained since, though it does not always make for absolute consistency, and in some cases Burns's usages are unconventional by present standards, this lets modern readers relish a flavour of the pauses, hesitations, and emphases which Burns's early readers experienced. Where a poem was not published in editions of his work which Burns supervised or in the *Scots Musical Museum*, we have printed a version from a Burns manuscript or from a reliable printed source. This is not a variorum edition, so we have listed alternative manuscript or printed readings only in a very small number of especially interesting instances; however, in the case of the poetry and the prose we have tried to make it clear in our notes which text we are following and where any substantial editorial modification has been made. A separate and more detailed note about the rediscovered poems and fragments which are published in this book appears later. Bearing in mind that it does not list most textual variants, we hope this edition provides texts that are clear, well glossed, reliable, and allow readers to get a good sense of the vivacity of Burns's work.

Introduction

Tender, humorous, sly, sometimes stinging, Robert Burns is one of the world's greatest love poets. His vernacular tone of address can have a beguiling intimacy about it at the same time as sounding cheekily egalitarian. In tone and tenor Burns, not Shakespeare, is the representative poet of modern democratic cultures. In his work a warmth and a radical political alignment, a bonding of poetry to the causes and traditions of 'the people', are immediately apparent and engaging. Though his politics are complex, even at times contradictory, recent writing has reshaped understanding of Scotland's national poet as a politically radical writer of republican sympathies, one schooled by knowledge of the American as well as the French Revolution. One of the world's most mercurially alluring writers, Burns is the first modern poet to be acclaimed a national bard.

His erotic verse, like his own life, ranges from the lyrically delicate to the scandalous and bawdy. He lived much of what he wrote about, and Burns lived with dramatic intensity. In 1796 he burned out, dying at the age of 37. His depressive temperament (hinted at early on in the poem 'To Ruin'), his struggles with poverty, and his engagement with his own celebrity status make his life and work remarkably forceful. Repeatedly there is an insistent performative impulse. His poetry is bound up with his own life, but his song-making is also splendidly universal so that verses like those of 'Auld Lang Syne' are relished and used in cultures very different from his own. The innate drama of his life and the reach of his poetry transcend the locally Scottish, and appeal to the global community. The modernity of his radicalism did not compromise his artistic gift, and presses the case that contemporary egalitarian societies round the world should recognise him as both ancestral and familiar, should regard him still as 'The Bard'.

From a Scottish as well as an international perspective it is time for a new and wide-ranging selection of Burns's verse aimed both at general readers and at those who know him well. Newly edited from early printed texts and from manuscripts, *The Best Laid Schemes* is the only substantial selection of Burns's work in print which has line-by-line glossing of the Scots words. Burns himself added a concluding general glossary to his book, but many modern readers will prefer simply to run their eye along the line for a gloss, rather than having to ferret around at the back of the volume. As well as containing outstanding examples of Burns's prose, this selection also includes some rediscovered verse, printed from manuscript and available in no other editions. Seamus Heaney has written in praise of Burns's 'art speech'. This book aims to help readers attend sympathetically to a masterfully constructed, remarkable, and freshly accessible poetic voice.

Born into obscurity, Burns became the first poet in the English-speaking world to be treated in his own lifetime as a national celebrity. Though to some extent he courted this, he did not always cope with it – 'The best laid schemes o' *Mice* an' *Men*, / Gang aft agley'. Poetry is a making and remaking, which can be nurtured by experience without being directly autobiographical. Still, Burns's verse is so often related to his life and to the life of his community and country that it is very helpful to have a sense of the man who authored, collected, and recast the poetry that bears his name. Whilst much modern academic criticism has been anti-biographical in nature, the sometimes wayward movements of Burns's life parallel and contribute so much to his verse that a sense of his biography is invaluable. The present introduction is by no means a full biography of Burns, but it follows the course of the poet's life, and relates that life to the selection of work in this book.

Burns's background and boyhood

Born on 25 January 1759 in a roadside cottage in the rural village of Alloway in Ayrshire, in the west of Scotland, Burns spent his infancy in what is now the most visited small house in his nation. Sensitively restored and managed by the National Trust for Scotland, Burns Cottage is today a small, dignified thatched curiosity surrounded by more modern buildings, but Alloway's old church (ruined even in Burns's boyhood) and its ancient stone bridge over the picturesque River Doon still give visitors a sense of the poet's earliest milieu. The Robert Burns Birthplace and Museum possesses the finest collection of the poet's manuscripts; and exhibitions of Burns-related artefacts give a good sense of eighteenth-century Ayrshire life as well as of some of the poet's legacies. Burns was a country boy, his father a gardener and tenant farmer, in an age where culture and agriculture were still closely bonded. His rural upbringing was vital to Burns – 'To plough & sow, to reap & mow, my father bred me early, O' – but he was also part of a west of Scotland that was one of the most rapidly industrialising areas on earth, and whose seaboard was bound up with the lucrative slave economy of the transatlantic tobacco trade as well as the quickening democratic energies that would produce, during Burns's highly impressionable teenage years, the American Revolution.

If we can see from poems like the fragmentary and sometimes arcane 'When Guilford Good' with its mention of 'America', 'Philadelphia', and its wink towards the Boston Tea-party that Burns had a marked interest in such politics, his political imagination later flowered most famously in the bloodthirsty lines of 'Scots, wha hae' where ostensibly royalist nationalism is ignited by the republican energies of the French Revolution. Still, it was sheer delight in the music of language, in storytelling, and in song that made the young Robert Burns into the man renowned as Scotland's bard. Bardic poetry is traditionally an oral poetry which performs the values of a particular society. It praises the community's heroes, and is passed from generation to generation. While today the word 'bard' is laced with irony, it was still a treasured Scottish ideal in Burns's youth. Highland bards were male, but if the Lowlander Burns encountered a bardic tradition first-hand, it was through his mother's family. Agnes Brown, Burns's mother, had a fine knowledge of ballads and songs and came from an extended family in which such lore was valued. In an age when bards were often figured as illiterate, Burns, growing up with the example of the 'bard' Ossian (whose work entranced Burns's era) fresh before him, liked to relate his poetic gift to the less literate, maternal side of his family.

Oral, vernacular culture was strong in his community. A seasoned storyteller, one of his mother's relatives, Betty Davidson, lived with the Burns family. Bonding agriculture to culture, she 'cultivated the latent seeds of Poesy' in the young Robert. Uncontrollably superstitious, Betty entertained the Burns children with 'the largest collection in the county of tales and songs concerning devils, ghosts, fairies, brownies, witches, warlocks, spunkies, kelpies, elf-candles, dead-lights, wraiths, apparitions, cantraips, giants, enchanted towers, dragons and other trumpery'. Stories and songs like these fascinated the boy, who also loved his mother's sometimes openly erotic traditional Scots vernacular ballads and songs. An early Burns love song such as 'Mary Morison', in a line like 'Ye are na Mary Morison', shows not just a sense of vernacular tenderness but also a wonderful ear for the music of language as it plays variations on repeated and transmuted sounds and syllables. While a poet's ear may be innate, it is also shaped by the surrounding linguistic environment. Arguably the most important part of Burns's vernacular Scots imaginative heritage came to him through the women of his family, and a 'feminine' aspect of his imagination is central to his gift, for all his schooling and indulgence in fraternal laddishness.

Burns was also unusually well read. From a young age he read gleefully as well as for education. His early books were all in English. His educated, literate peasant father, William, had access to the recently founded library in the nearby town of Ayr. Scotland's traditions in democratic library culture found their apotheosis in Burns. He was far less an autodidact than a man formed by systems of education too easily overlooked by those who assume that advanced learning circulates only through universities. To realise what libraries meant to Burns, we should think not of the exclusiveness of an elite academic culture, but of community libraries and today's inclusiveness of the internet. Burns learned through networks – of people, books, and traditions; he was only in a limited sense 'self-taught'. At a time when the Scottish universities increasingly inculcated 'propriety' in language, in 'rhetoric and belles lettres', and in ideology, the non-university networks of Burns's education nourished far less 'proper' radical and vernacular sympathies.

Yet Burns's society, talent, and upbringing let him develop a remarkable social mobility. His parents were friends of local teachers of Latin and of writing; the Kirk minister who baptised Robert in 1759 later became Moderator of the Church of Scotland. Burns's origins in provincial obscurity have often been exaggerated – by himself and others. His location made him aware of international trading ambitions, while his era was one in which economic and political concerns were increasingly not just international but intercontinental. Thanks to his father's efforts the young Robert was tutored for a time by another local teacher, John Murdoch, who taught his pupils to comprehend and to commit to memory passages of English. Sometimes, as in the line 'All hail! inexorable lord!' (in 'To Ruin'), Burns's English can sound grandiose. As is the case with most English speakers across the world today, English was a language he learned and on whose periphery he lived; he is not a 'bard' like Shakespeare for whom the language was his birthright, but a poet who might migrate from his own home, vernacular language to classroom English and back again. Though it made him something of a curiosity to the polite classes of an age obsessed with 'talking proper', this makes him more, not less, modern, and confirms him as a democratically universal, not a merely local and Scottish, bard.

Whether mocking the saved Christian 'elect' of Calvinist predestination in 'Holy Willie's Prayer', voicing extreme libertarian sentiments in his cantata 'The Jolly Beggars', or frolicking in 'Tam o' Shanter', Burns's poetry can be very funny, often in anarchic, taboo-breaking ways. On occasion the young Robert was disciplined by Murdoch for pranks, but he and his younger brother Gilbert were distinguished among Murdoch's pupils. Their teacher taught boys 'to turn verse into its natural prose order; and sometimes to substitute synonimous expressions for poetical words'. Burns grew intimately familiar with the Authorised Version of the Bible and with Arthur Masson's *Collection of Prose and Verse, from the Best English Authors*. The presence of the word 'English' in that title is again a hint that Burns learned in a milieu where there was an emphasis not just on 'the best authors' but on 'the best English'. Burns could certainly engage with this emphasis; he could also, like his admired Scottish poetic precursor Robert Fergusson, react against it with principled vivacity.

As a poet, Burns would call his first book *Poems, Chiefly in the Scottish Dialect*, implying in that subtitle (which he was the first of many poets to adopt) a cultural questioning of the assumed superiority of the King's imperial language. Rather than marking him out as a hick, Burns's sense of loving clearly 'provincial' language is also part of his democratic modernity, and is something he shares with most of today's English-speakers around the world. He loved Alexander Pope's verse, and draws often on high-toned King's English, but most dear to him were the vernacular tones of the people, however much he could sound an orthodox register when it seemed appropriate to do so. As a boy he also read about freedom-fighting rebels – Hannibal, and Sir William Wallace whose narrative 'poured a Scotish [*sic*] prejudice in my veins'.

When Burns was six he moved with his family to the farm of Mount Oliphant, near Alloway, but his father faced financial problems. These were the start of many worries which were to affect the whole family, and contributed to a fear of poverty and failure that would dog Burns even at the height of his success, leading him to pursue at times something of a double life. An incarnation of the Protestant work ethic, William slogged at farmwork during the day, then, after dark, taught his children arithmetic. He spoke to his sons in an instinctive and determinedly egalitarian way as if they were already adults. Encouraged by his father to take an interest in improving, godly books, Robert grew preoccupied with issues of Calvinist theology, much argued over locally, and with questions of democratic church government; he relished too an anthology of 'Letters by the most Eminent Writers' and strove to recreate the English-language eloquence he found there. Unlike his poems, his prose is written almost exclusively in English. Bicultural from boyhood, he enjoyed access to a broad spectrum of language drawn from oral folklore and from books and broadsheets. His diction is nimble and protean.

At the start of his teens Burns was adept with the plough and had picked up some more schooling at the parish school of Dalrymple, a village not far from

Ayr and about six miles inland from the magnificent Culzean Castle near the modern-day golfers' resort of Turnberry. Burns's youthful reading included not just chapbooks and ballads but Samuel Richardson's *Pamela* (a novel about endangered female virtue), some more 'manly' fiction by the Scot Tobias Smollett, and – especially treasured – the poetical works of the brilliantly witty English Catholic poet Alexander Pope. Having taken some lessons in French, before long Burns went on to read Adam Smith's *Theory of Moral Sentiments*, a major work of philosophy first published in the year of the poet's birth. In terms of his literary and linguistic knowledge, Burns was ahead of many of today's university graduates. The range of his learning and the ease with which he incorporates into his poetry modern philosophical and political thinking are still underestimated. They make him a bard not just of his people but of the Enlightenment and post-Enlightenment world in which the ideals of modern democracy were being hotly, often bloodily contested.

One of the early signs of Burns's libertine reaction against the Calvinism which formed him is the eager way he liked to link poetry and sex. In his fifteenth year he was starting to write down songs. In the substantial autobiographical letter included in the present selection Burns writes of how he 'first committed the sin of RHYME' by making a song for a 'bewitching' girl he met when they were both harvesting: ''twas her favorite reel to which I attempted giving an embodied vehicle in rhyme'. Burns had almost no formal musical education, but the way a traditional Scottish tune here undergirds the poet's words (which become an 'embodied vehicle' for it) is important to much of his work. He liked to link poetry with the 'bewitching', the erotic, and with a shifting consciousness of 'sin'. His earliest songs such as 'Mary Morison' draw on his reading as well as on his ear for vernacular music – a combination that would continue to power his best work.

By 1775 Burns was at school again for a time, studying the knowledge of the modern capitalist and commercial world he shared with Adam Smith. He learned the basics of land-surveying in the Ayrshire village of Kirkoswald where he fell in love, talked theology, and read the eighteenth-century English-language poets James Thomson and William Shenstone. The mixture of erotic, theological, and poetic experience gained at this time would fuel his later work, though the young Burns had not yet learned how to bring together in poetry the often clashing elements he relished in his own life.

In 1776 the Burns family moved for economic reasons to the farm of Lochlea near the village of Tarbolton, south of Kilmarnock in Ayrshire. Much of Burns's life was spent at walking pace in this one part of Ayrshire and it is still possible to experience something of the weathered terrain he loved as his native ground and hymned with formal enthusiasm in his manifesto poem, 'The Vision'. In Tarbolton the young poet flirted with local girls and read the older Scottish poetry of Allan Ramsay alongside a collection of English songs. He matured his talent as a poet in the making of songs for local lasses he fancied, and in celebrating '*Nature's* charms' in an Ayrshire where 'Daisies deck the ground / And Blackirds whistle clear' ('Epistle to Davie'). His determination to engage with real people and places, not ideal ones, is part of a wish to value and empower the peasant culture he came from. Yet he also wanted to cut a dash in it, to have a markedly special image. Wild about dancing (on which his father frowned), he assumed a rather dandified appearance. His teenage friend David Sillar (recipient of the epistles 'to Davie') remembered how Burns 'wore the only tied hair in the parish; and in the church, his plaid, which was of a particular colour, I think *fillemot*, he wrapped in a particular manner round his shoulders'. Well versed in theology and (by 1781) in Laurence Sterne's quirky and sometimes scandalous novel *Tristram Shandy*, Burns was well known in the local community where some of his male peers were in awe of his confidence in dealing with members of the opposite sex.

Around this time, like Davie Sillar, he began to play a little on the fiddle. Though Burns had an indifferent singing voice, he spoke magnificently. His own finest productions demand to leave the page and to be performed in front of a living audience, whether the intimate audience of one, or the entire community. His poetry is less about ego than about bonding – bonding with the beloved, the local society, the nation, and (most obviously in republican-inclined poems like 'A Man's a Man for a' That' or 'The Tree of Liberty') the international community. The performativeness of his personality (he liked to act, and to try on voices) enriched his poetry, making it both sociable and social. Yet he also perfected his lyric craft and developed in his verse, so close to the grain of local life, an earthy spirituality which valued the vitality of ordinary people through devoting to them a quality of artistic attention remarkable for its focus and clarity. To this day, some of his best known poems are poems which have a clear social use, whether 'Auld Lang Syne' or 'A Man's a Man'. Just as he often did in his life, so in his performative verse, Burns gathers the community around him.

In addition to his vernacular songs to various sweethearts, the young Burns was turning verses of the Psalms into quatrains. Several of his early English-language poems reflect a concern with dangerous vicissitude; 'To Ruin' is a somewhat oratorical example of this. Among his early works (as in the poems to do with his pet ewe, Mailie), the fearful and the gleeful are often linked, while in his life there begin to be marked indications of a depressive temperament.

Coming of Age

In 1780 Burns helped found the Tarbolton Bachelors' Club, a rural debating society whose all-male fraternity was reminiscent of some aspects of today's American 'frat houses'. Now preserved and open to the public, the substantial upstairs room where the club met is redolent of Burns's milieu, and well worth a visit to Tarbolton. Few other interiors make one feel closer to the spirit that activated the young poet. Each member of the Tarbolton Bachelors' Club had to 'be a professed lover of one or more of the female sex'. Swearing was banned, but social drinking encouraged and haughtiness forbidden: 'the proper person for this society is a cheerful, honest-hearted lad'. For good and ill, and for all his well-read sophistication, laddishness was part of Burns's social performance and make-up, and probably part of his appeal for some of the lasses.

Burns's fascination with what in 'To a Mouse' he called 'Nature's social union' would let him appeal to a later pioneer of ecology and conservation such as John Muir in America, but Burns's farming background meant that his interests lay much more with people and animals than simply with sublime landscape; his sense of what we might now call the 'ecological' was arguably deeper than that of his later, more Romantically egotistical admirer, William Wordsworth. For all that the libertine, plain-speaking, tempestuous Burns was one of the first Romantic poets, he was, too, a child of the Scottish Enlightenment. By 1781 he was also praising the Scot Henry Mackenzie's rather feminine novel of sympathetic sentimentality, *The Man of Feeling* (1771). Soon Burns called this 'a book I prize next to the Bible'. He was a poet who liked physical reactions. He wrote about them with a teasing and sometimes scandalous frankness. He loved laughter in art, but saw nothing wrong with stories, poems and songs that made people cry.

In 1781 in the Ayrshire seaport of Irvine, Burns became a flax-dresser. Flax-dressers removed the seeds and separated the stem from the fibre of the flax plant, which grew well in rainy Ayrshire, before the best of the remaining flax was spun into yarn. Burns's flax-dressing venture failed when the shop in which he worked burned down. He suffered a bout of acute depression in late 1781. Around then he also read the Scots and English poems of Robert Fergusson who had died insane in Edinburgh's madhouse while still in his mid-twenties in 1774. Fergusson's vernacular brio made Burns turn again to poetry, but Fergusson's tragedy would haunt him for the rest of his life, and he often mapped his own experience on to that of the older poet, repeatedly modelling his poems on Fergusson's. 'The Cotter's Saturday Night', for instance, is an arguably inferior version of Fergusson's 'The Farmer's Ingle'.

If Fergusson's poetic dash seemed to come from a kindred spirit, then Burns in Irvine also found a good friend in the sailor Richard Brown with whom he strolled in the countryside. Brown suggested to the still unpublished poet that he should try to publish his poems. Burns was extending his social circle and in 1781 he became a Freemason. Fellow Ayrshire Freemasons whom he would meet, and who became his supporters, included the Scottish Enlightenment philosopher Professor Dugald Stewart of Catrine and the influential Ayrshire landowner Sir John Whitefoord.

William Burnes (who maintained the north-east Scottish 'Burnes' or 'Burness' spelling of the family name) experienced a worsening of his financial problems in the early 1780s and died a broken man in 1784. He is buried in the graveyard at the ruined Kirk Alloway, where his tombstone has recently been restored. Burns loved and admired his father. Its tone may be awkward at times, but 'The Cotter's Saturday Night' shows this in its portrait of noble paternal concern and undaunted domestic virtue. Quoting a line of Oliver Goldsmith, Burns memorialised his father in English verse. Yet, in a characteristically extreme gesture of attempted liberation and backhanded homage, Burns would later set the hellish dancing of 'Tam o' Shanter' among Kirk Alloway's ruins; dancing on his father's grave.

In 1783 Burns had started keeping a Commonplace Book of 'Observations, Hints, Songs, Scraps of Poetry &c.', including his own shrewd critical appraisals of his verse. Some extracts from this manuscript book – taking us as close as we can get to Burns's thoughts in this period – appear in the present volume. Increasingly self-conscious, he was aware of the curious interest that a ploughman's literary concerns might hold for posterity. In addition to recasting humorous song and ballad materials, Burns wrote several poems connected with his father's death; a strange fusion of the comic and elegiac is evident in 'The Death and Dying Words of Poor Mailie, The Author's Only Pet Yowe, An Unco Mournfu' Tale', which carnivalises the anxieties of death and farm struggles, yet maintains a tenderly comic voice. Simultaneously mock-elegy and genuine lament, this poem, like several others by Burns, has a fine, precarious balance. It led to a further work, 'Poor Mailie's Elegy' (composed around 1785), which uses the six-line 'Standard Habbie' verse form inherited from the comic elegy 'The Life and Death of Habbie Simpson, the Piper of Kilbarchan' by the seventeenth-century Scottish poet Robert Sempill of

Beltrees. Burns's poetic craftsmanship led him to give new life to several traditional Scottish verse forms. He deployed the 'Standard Habbie' stanza form in such early masterpieces as his dramatic monologue 'Holy Willie's Prayer' (1785), which mocks Calvinist hypocrisy. Such was Burns's success with this stanza form that some have called it the 'Burns Stanza'. The flicking short lines towards the culmination of every such stanza lend themselves to glancing nods and winks:

> I bless & praise thy matchless might,
> When thousands thou has left in night,
> That I am here before thy sight,
> For gifts & grace,
> A burning & a shining light
> To a' this place.—

Using 'Standard Habbie' in the mid-1780s when he clearly matures as a poet, Burns remade this stanza form and it remade him; each has a conflicted personality. The stanza form transmits metrically an urge to combine the solemn with the lightly risible, the dark and the ridiculously lively, which Burns would inherit, grow, and pass on. By around 1785 most of the facets of his poetic personality had been assembled, including a tendency to see himself as what Robert Fergusson had termed a 'Bardie' – at once resolute aspiring bard of his community and a mocker of any grandiose traits in himself and the people around him.

If Burns knew about Bards from his reading of the 'translated' Gaelic poems of Ossian, his own day-to-day struggles were far removed from the nobly misty realms of that supposed prehistoric bard. After their father's death, Robert and his brother Gilbert leased another wet, exposed Ayrshire farm at Mossgiel in the neighbouring parish of Mauchline, nine miles south of Kilmarnock. Bad drainage and bad weather made the farming especially hard. In 1784, afflicted by 'a kind of slow fever' and 'langor of my spirits', Burns endured another bout of probably psychosomatic illness in this period after his father's death. He also enjoyed a sexual relationship with Elizabeth Paton, an uneducated servant who gave birth to Burns's daughter Elizabeth in May 1785. Burns loved sex, though he could seem callous towards his lovers and his children. His charisma was felt by many men and women. It was partly sexual in nature, but found its most lasting expression in poetic eloquence. Certainly it enhanced his status as the bard of his local, then national society, though it also led to clashes with that society's ruling powers. He corresponded in verse with nearby allies such as fellow farmer-poet John Lapraik who impressed Burns as a contemporary 'Old Scotch Bard'.

Burns also penned flirtatious as well as satirical verse while wooing Jean Armour, a young woman six years his junior who was the literate daughter of a Mauchline stone-mason. His wooing did not stop the poet dallying with other lasses in the area: he had a bright eye for the 'Mauchline belles'. Spurred by the poetic example of Ramsay and Fergusson, he began to develop an aesthetic of the local, aspiring to celebrate his native county in verse. This emphasis on the local should be seen as an act of fidelity, a siding with the particular and vernacular, rather than aspiring to the cultural authority of salon culture, or court life, or other aristocratic pretensions. Yet Burns's 'localness' needs to be understood in the context of the international links enjoyed by many West of Scotland communities in the eighteenth century, including those Burns knew best.

Increasingly aware of himself as a Scottish poet, Burns was being encouraged by Gilbert to publish his poetry. In late 1785 the death of his youngest brother John intensified the poet's sense of the cruelty of fate. This time saw the writing of some of Burns's most significant verse epistles in addition to 'Holy Willie's Prayer' – one of several satires on Ayrshire kirk quarrels and local characters which Burns wrote around the time. Such works include 'The Holy Fair' and 'Death and Dr Hornbook'. Another poem of 1785, 'Address to the Deil', has the devil greeted variously as 'auld Cloots', 'Hornie' and 'Nick'; Burns deploys familiarity of tone while drawing on his wide repertory of folklore. The directness of address is typical of that tone in Burns which we might now recognise as democratic. It is mischievously confident and yoked to an unwavering purposefulness in such different works as 'The Twa Dogs. A Tale' (about social inequality), 'The Vision' (presenting Burns's local Muse in Ossianic 'Duans'), and his superb poems in Standard Habbie. These are not just about obscure Scottish church politics and Ayrshire affairs; they are also examinations of what it means to be fully human. They confront dark places of erotic psychology as well as indulging in glancing wit.

Burns's verse letters were actually sent, and should be seen as intensifying his emphasis on communion with the local. While his poetic outpouring in 1785 manifests resolute confidence, works of the same period such as 'To a Mouse' also show a sense of vulnerability and the need for social sympathy – a sense of the fragility of the best laid schemes of all the creatures of this world. It is such social sympathy that Adam Smith had seen as vital to the functioning of modern societies. Burns, by giving moral sentiments vital articulation in his work (his famous lines in 'To a Louse' about seeing ourselves as others see us are a versification of a passage in Smith's *Theory of Moral Sentiments*), established himself as the poet of emerging democratic communities. It is no accident that his work was so eagerly received in the newly independent United States of America. With his poems reprinted in American newspapers and admired by writers from Thomas Jefferson to Robert Frost and Maya Angelou, for many generations Burns became America's bard. This did nothing to qualify the appeal of his work in Russia or China where he was also seen as a poet of the people.

By the beginning of 1786, as Burns was working on poems like 'The Cotter's Saturday Night', it became apparent that Jean Armour was expecting his child. He procrastinated over marrying her, but evidently assured her he would stand by her. Jean's father detested his daughter's choice of partner and the zealots of the Kirk investigated the 'fornication'. Burns had some notoriety locally for the way he liked (as one of the more earthy lines of 'Brose and Butter' puts it) 'To gully awa wi' his dibble'. If his sexual exploits were getting him into trouble, at least by then he had scheduled the publication (by subscription) of his first collection of verse. A published book, however, was not his only interest. While Jean was off the scene, staying with relatives, Burns found 'another wife'. His new love seems to have fallen ill and died not long afterwards; she was to be remembered by Burns and others as 'Highland Mary'. When Jean came home in early summer 1786 she found Burns maintaining he could not forget his love for his Jean, despite his participation in 'all kinds of dissipation and riot, Mason-meetings, drinking matches, and other mischief'.

Burns now decided he would emigrate, and so escape the wrath of the Kirk and the Armours. His proposed destination was Jamaica, but before he could leave, the Kirk demanded he do penance for his sexual misdemeanours in church by sitting in full view on the stool of repentance. In summer 1786 Burns acquiesced, then bequeathed his share in the Mossgiel farm to his brother Gilbert. Seeking legal redress against the would-be emigrant whom he saw as having wronged his daughter, Jean's father threatened the poet with jail. Fleeing, Burns told friends about his forthcoming *Poems, Chiefly in the Scottish Dialect*, and worked on his Jamaican plans. In the poem 'On a Scotch Bard Gone to the West Indies' he tried to establish the terms in which his departure might be viewed. He had grown up in a county and in a nation where people profited directly or indirectly from the slave trade. His readiness to work in an administrative capacity on a slave plantation has sometimes been airbrushed away.

Burns did not to go to Jamaica, though the most striking modern image of him is a painting by Reinhard Behrens which figures him as a dark-skinned man with dreadlocks, an Ayrshire Bob Marley. Supported by Kilmarnock merchants, and printed by Kilmarnock's John Wilson, Burns's *Poems, Chiefly in the Scottish Dialect* (today often called 'the Kilmarnock edition') was published in late July 1786. The bard's emigration was now to take place in late September, but at the start of that month Jean gave birth to Burns's son Robert and daughter Jean. For the moment thoughts of Jamaica were replaced by paternal emotions, not to mention the hope of a second edition of the *Poems*.

The Bard, the Book, and the City

Published in an edition of 600 copies, the first edition of *Poems, Chiefly in the Scottish Dialect* contains 44 poems, some in English, the majority in Scots, or at least an English with a marked Scots inflection. The book carries a clever preface presenting its poet as a person lacking 'all the advantages of learned art'. Instead, 'Unacquainted with the necessary requisites for commencing Poet by rule', he 'sings the sentiments and manners, he felt and saw in himself and his rustic compeers around him, in his and their native language'. 'The Twa Dogs', 'The Vision' and 'The Cotter's Saturday Night' are among the major set-pieces. The contents and arrangement are revealing, widely varied and veer from elation to despair. They articulate the life of their author.

The Kilmarnock edition was such a success that a second edition was called for in Edinburgh, where Burns's fame began to be established. In the autumn of 1786, visiting Ayrshire friends with Edinburgh connections, Burns lent one of them a two-volume edition of the poems of Ossian and some books of songs and Scottish poetry. Ossian had opened up for later Scottish poets the possibility of being seen as a 'bard', and, pointing to Ossian in his own bookish footnotes, Burns knew that was how he too wished to be regarded. He did all he could to shape that perception, and soon he displaced Ossian in the popular imagination as Scotland's bard. Without Ossian, no Burns. After Burns, every country, even England, was anxious to be seen to have its 'bard'.

Soon Burns was dining with the republican Lord Daer (recently returned from France where he had met leading radicals) and the philosopher Professor Dugald Stewart at the latter's house near Mauchline. Stewart recalled Burns then and later as 'simple, manly, and independent', noting that 'Nothing, perhaps, was more remarkable among his various attainments than the fluency, and precision, and originality of his language, when he spoke in company; more particularly as he aimed at purity in his turn of expression, and avoided, more successfully than most Scotchmen, the peculiarities of Scottish phraseology'. Burns was performing as the gentleman, but also the radical. His *Poems* impressed other local figures too, including Frances Anna Wallace, Mrs Dunlop of Dunlop in Ayrshire, a widowed grandmother who claimed William Wallace as an ancestor and who entered into a long correspondence with the poet. Spurred by his growing band of supporters, who included the Mauchline lawyer Gavin Hamilton and Ayr's influential urban improver the merchant John Ballantine (dedicatee of 'The Brigs of Ayr'), Burns now planned a visit to Scotland's capital, where he hoped to find a publisher for a second edition of his poems. Around this time he wondered if he might seek work as an Excise officer, a scheme he later adopted, though the tensions between the loyalty demanded of a civil servant and Burns's radical sympathies would grow acute.

When Burns arrived in Edinburgh in late November 1786 he was already nationally famous. He took lodgings at the heart of Old Town Edinburgh's stink and bustle. Thanks to help from Masonic allies and others, his welcome was assured. Henry Mackenzie reviewed Burns's *Poems* for the *Lounger* magazine in December 1786, describing their author as a 'Heaven-taught ploughman' whose 'neglected merit' Scotland should recognise. In Edinburgh Burns's fate was always to be patronised, but he turned this to his advantage, and subtly mocked those who looked down their noses at him. He coped with the metropolis, but was never metropolitan; in this aspect, perhaps, he seems furthest away from many English-speakers today, but he and his work are reminders that there is more to human and natural life than the life of the city.

Burns was not short of patrons. The well-off and aristocratic sporting gentlemen of the Caledonian Hunt subscribed en masse to the second edition of his *Poems*, and became its proud dedicatees. The book (today known as 'the Edinburgh edition') was published in April 1787 by the leading Edinburgh bookseller William Creech. Its typesetter was William Smellie, co-founder of the *Encyclopaedia Britannica*. Invited by Smellie, Burns joined an all-male club, the Crochallan Fencibles, then wrote and collected *risqué* and downright obscene songs (such as 'Nine Inch Will Please a Lady') for its members' delectation.

Burns's 416-page Edinburgh edition immediately impressed its audience. While he stressed his 'wild, artless notes', he also footnoted literary references and (as he had done in the shorter Kilmarnock edition) supplied a glossary for readers too polite to confess to understanding Scots words. He had also carefully, even calculatingly augmented his book to take in the vigorous, slyly modulated Scots poems 'Address to the Unco Guid' and 'Death and Dr Hornbook', as well as a less than wholly successful 'Address to Edinburgh'.

Revealingly, when he tries to write about the city (subject of some of the best work of his admired Robert Fergusson) he produces one of his worst lines: 'Edina! *Scotia*'s darling seat!' Edinburgh did impress Burns, but almost always he was at his strongest when he stayed in touch with the language of his native community, however he enriched that by reading and by sheer, nuanced poetic craft. Though in different ways he was an exemplar for Wordsworth, Byron, Clare, and other Romantic poets, Burns was seen as coarse by the Victorian Matthew Arnold. The Scottish poet's concerns were peripheral to those of elite modernists preoccupied with the metropolitan. In our time, though, a strengthened interest in ecological values make Burns the farmer poet, the villager able to find a global audience, seem much more exemplary and culturally important.

In Edinburgh Burns was fêted, gawped at, and sometimes shrewdly observed. Walter Scott, who met him at the house of a friend's father, later wrote a telling portrait of the bard whom all fashionable society wished to meet. For Scott, Burns in his late twenties 'was strong and robust: his manners rustic, not clownish'; he had 'a sort of dignified plainness and simplicity' which made Scott think of 'a very sagacious country farmer of the old Scotch school – *i.e.* none of your modern agriculturists, who keep labourers for their drudgery, but the *douce gudeman* who held his own plough. There was a strong expression of sense and shrewdness in all his lineaments; the eye alone, I think, indicated the poetical character and temperament. It was large, and of a dark cast, and glowed (I say literally *glowed*) when he spoke with feeling or interest'; Scott remembered too Burns discussing his precursor poets Ramsay and Fergusson 'with too much humility as his models'. The bard's 'conversation expressed perfect self-confidence, without the slightest presumption. Among the men who were the most learned of their country, he expressed himself with perfect firmness, but without the least intrusive forwardness; and when he differed in opinion, he did not hesitate to express it firmly, yet at the same time with modesty . . . his dress corresponded with his manner. He was like a farmer dressed in his best to dine with the laird . . . his address to females was extremely deferential, and always with a turn either to the pathetic or humorous, which engaged their attention particularly.' Burns might appear deferential, but he maintained the stance of 'the man of independant mind', even if he had to make occasional concessions or evasions.

Lionised by many among the social elite of Enlightenment Edinburgh, from his new patron the Earl of Glencairn to the blind poet and Kirk minister, Dr Thomas Blacklock, Burns sometimes curbed his verbal exuberance in print.

So, for instance, following the advice of the ageing Rev. Hugh Blair, at that time Edinburgh University's Professor of Rhetoric and Belles Lettres and an arbiter of public taste, the poet excluded 'Love and Liberty' from his Edinburgh edition, and that spirited libertarian poem set in an Ayrshire doss-house was not published until 1799. Its dramatic 'cantata' form allows Burns to express sentiments (which may or may not be his own) through its characters' mouths – most famously in his lines 'COURTS for Cowards were erected, / CHURCHES built to please the Priest.' Burns became used to operating in a climate of censorship, and often exercised self-censorship. Like one of the later East European poets of the Soviet era, he built coded messages into his poetry, so that it carries both sexual innuendo and radical political sub-texts, while appearing on its best behaviour. This, cleverly, served to make him acceptable even to diametrically opposed audiences. Only when the twentieth century was well advanced were there editions which took in the full range of his poetry, from the shockingly bawdy to the polite and even trite.

At a Masonic meeting in Edinburgh Burns heard himself toasted as 'Caledonia's bard, brother Burns'. Such a toast anticipates modern Burns suppers, held round the world each 25th of January, which are themselves an outgrowth of the Enlightenment clubs Burns loved; it also signals how soon Burns established himself as The Bard. In the Scottish capital he mixed with noble patrons as well as with people like the printer Smellie and the Borders law clerk, Robert Ainslie, who became a close companion and confidant. Burns also championed the work of the Scottish poet to whom he felt the greatest affinity. He complained that the remains of Robert Fergusson, 'a man whose talents for ages to come will do honor to our Caledonian name', lay buried in the Canongate Churchyard 'unnoticed and unknown'; here again, these words anticipate the bardolatry that would be Burns's due, as well as hinting at his own fears about celebrity and ruin. Burns's several poems to Fergusson, his 'elder Brother in the muse', show that English – not just the Scots tongue – could be a language for his heart-felt convictions.

If 'his greatest pride' was 'the appellation of, a Scotch Bard', Burns was increasingly celebrated beyond the borders of Scotland. On 5 July 1787 the first London edition of the *Poems* was published by Cadell, soon followed by pirated editions in Belfast, Dublin, Philadelphia, and New York. Within a century Walt Whitman, setting himself up in turn as a nineteenth-century democratic national bard, wrote with both anxiety and perceptiveness about Burns's example.

Assembling a Nation

Part of Burns's establishing himself as Bard was bound up with an urge to be a poet who spoke for the whole of his country, East and West, Highland and Lowland. Arguably, he was the first poet to do this, though he would be emulated in other countries by poets from Whitman to Petőfi. Successful and spurred by poetic and patriotic ambition, Burns began a series of bardic tours in Scotland and northern England in 1787. First, with his friend Robert Ainslie, he headed for the Borders, crossed briefly into England, then progressed eventually to Dumfries, close to which, at beautiful Dalswinton with its wooded lochan, he met his admirer Patrick Miller. Before long Burns was back in Ayrshire and back in the arms of Jean Armour. Soon he was reading *Paradise Lost*, and admiring 'the desperate daring, and noble defiance of hardship, in that great Personage, Satan'. Successive generations of Romantic poets would take this line, but the instinctive (yet sometimes lord-loving) rebel Burns was the first to articulate it.

In the summer of 1787 Burns, the Lowland poet one of whose most famous songs was 'My Heart's in the Highlands', toured the mountainous west of Scotland north of the Clyde, then returned again to his affair with Armour. Further Highland travels ensued, on which Burns was accompanied by his Jacobite friend William Nicol. Highlights of this tour included a visit to Bannockburn, the battlefield associated with 'glorious' King Robert the Bruce who had defeated the English there in 1314. Burns travelled not only to see sights but also to meet people. In Perthshire he hit it off with the 'honest highland' fiddler Niel Gow whose 'kind open-heartedness' appealed to the poet. Another highlight of this tour was the supposed location of Ossian's grave. Visiting not only musicians but also noble families keen to meet the bard, Burns progressed to Loch Ness and Culloden. On his return journey, despite the fact Jean Armour was once more expecting his child, Burns pursued the elusive Margaret Chalmers, who turned him down and married a banker instead. The poet's Scottish travels nurtured and reinforced his fascination with Lowland ballads and songs in addition to Ossianic Highland lore; the tours suggest Burns's desire to assemble a sense of multiple Scotlands and they underpinned his growing endeavours as an anthologist and recaster of songs and popular poetry. Though rooted in the countryside of Ayrshire and south-west Scotland, when he travelled he was also a tourist, a bard, a tourist-bard.

Readers of the present book will see how closely Burns scrutinised his early life in his long autobiographical letter of summer 1787 addressed to the London Scottish novelist Dr John Moore in a 'miserable fog of Ennui'. But this letter does not deal with Burns's experiences in Edinburgh, where he met a man whose 'honest Scotch enthusiasm' quickened in him one of his greatest projects. James Johnson, an Edinburgh engraver, planned to assemble 'all our native Songs' for a large, six-volume anthology with music. Burns collected, rewrote, and wrote work for Johnson's *Scots Musical Museum*, and became for all practical purposes the artistic director of this national anthology, publishing in it more than 150 of his own songs, while re-creating others that he gathered on his travels. In songs such as the male-voiced 'O my Luve's like a red, red rose' or the female-voiced 'John Anderson my Jo' the poet is as much a tradition-bearer as a creator. In songs like these Burns established himself not simply as one of the greatest of love poets, but as a bard of friendship too. He intensified the emotional charge of the work he collected and remade, but he did this through craftsmanship rather than through direct self-revelation. To be a bard was not just a pose, it required artistic finesse. The quality of 'I Love my Jean' or 'My Love She's but a Lassie Yet' lies most of all in the song's fluid lightness.

At a polite Edinburgh gathering in late 1787 Burns met Mrs Agnes McLehose, a striking woman a year his junior who was at that time separated from her abusive husband. As 'Sylvander' and 'Clarinda', Robert and Agnes developed a remarkable, intense and mannered epistolary affair, one made all the more heated by the circumstance that for part of the time Burns was confined to his apartment as a result of a knee injury and endured depressive episodes. Playing 'Sylvander' appealed to Burns, though this time he acted the role in English prose rather than in vernacular verse. As they exchanged titillating letters, Mrs McLehose worried about her reputation, and Burns applied for a job as an Excise officer. Back in Ayrshire Gilbert's Mossgiel farm was failing, and Jean Armour's parents had cast out their pregnant daughter. Returning from Edinburgh to the west, Burns met Jean and arranged to lease from Patrick Miller Ellisland farm, near Dumfries. Having failed to bed Clarinda in Edinburgh, he had sex with her maidservant, Jenny Clow, who gave birth to a son in November 1788. Early 1788 saw Burns not only wooing Clarinda but also making 'thundering' love to Jean Armour, who was already heavily pregnant. Early the next year she gave birth to twins, who soon died. Burns's letter to Robert Ainslie of 3 March 1788 about having sex with the pregnant Jean is a *tour de force* of eroticised verbal energy; a fascinating, but also a disturbing document. Sexual performance for Burns could be bound up with a Calvinist's determination to be libertine.

The Devil and the Civil Servant

As Burns grew devilishly wilder, sexually, politically, and in his writing, he also became a civil servant. In early 1788 he was inducted into the Excise. Around that point he started calling Jean Armour his wife. In August 1788, by which time Burns had made a start at Ellisland, he and Jean were formally admonished by the Kirk elders at Mauchline for irregular conduct, and 'solemnly bound to adhere to one another as Husband & Wife all the days of their life'.

Far from Enlightenment Edinburgh, at the beautiful but insufficiently remunerative farm of Ellisland by the River Nith, Burns sometimes felt isolated. He once complained the locals had 'as much idea of a Rhinoceros as a Poet'. The remark is revealing, for it signals Burns's full awareness of his giftedness, and ways in which, for all his bardic vocation, he felt set apart by it. Still gathering songs, he was able to befriend neighbours like the gentleman-amateur musician Robert Riddell of Glenriddell for whom the bard put together a two-volume collection of his unpublished poems and letters (today known as the Glenriddell Manuscripts). For Riddell Burns also annotated an interleaved copy of *The Scots Musical Museum.*

By the autumn of 1789, just after the French Revolution (which was widely reported in the local and national press), Jean gave birth to Burns's son Francis Wallace, and Burns began work as a Dumfries Exciseman. His work meant that frequently he had to ride 30 or 40 miles a day, hunting out contraband materials; trying to run his Excise career alongside Ellisland farm tired Burns, even though Jean helped manage domestic and agricultural matters. Remarkable for her loyalty and tenacity, she also sang, and reacted to Burns's poetry with close attention, as well as bearing, nursing, and bringing up the children. At home the poet experienced further headaches and depression. Events seemed to take a turn for the better in 1790 when Burns was promoted to an Excise post in the town of Dumfries. At the Globe inn there he had a passionate affair with a barmaid, Ann Park. She gave birth to his daughter, Elizabeth, in March 1791, just days before Burns's wife bore him William Nicol Burns. While he conducted his affair with Park in the pub, Burns rode back and forwards regularly between Dumfries and Ellisland, sometimes at night; it was during this period he composed 'Tam o' Shanter', that poem which relishes extra-marital sexual excitement, and celebrates how 'heroic Tam' only just gets away with it.

Burns wrote a good deal of poetry at Ellisland, where the farmhouse he lived in still stands in its idyllic setting and is now an attractive small museum. The poems he composed there include the erotic lyrics 'I Love my Jean' and 'O, Were I on Parnassus Hill'. Gathering songs and ballads, he refashioned numerous traditional lyrics, including 'My Heart's in the Highlands' and 'Auld Lang Syne'.

For his 'kind funny friend', the rotund English antiquary, Captain Francis Grose, then researching his *Antiquities of Scotland*, Burns wrote 'Tam o' Shanter. A Tale'. This rollicking mock-heroic work opens with Tam unencumbered by his wife but surrounded by male 'drouthy cronies' in the pub. Soon, the worse for drink, Tam rides home through a stormy night, passing Kirk Alloway where he spies 'Warlocks and witches in a dance'; aroused by the sight of a young witch in a short shirt, Tam shouts aloud and is pursued by the 'hellish legion'. Fortunately for him his 'grey mare, Meg' rescues Tam, but (in a sort of mock castration) loses her tail when the witch snatches it off. 'Tam o' Shanter. A Tale' ends abruptly (as if its own tail has been snatched off) with a solemn mock-moral: 'Remember Tam o' Shanter's mare'. In a country whose Calvinist tradition had deprived it of a strong theatrical heritage, the hudibrastic couplets of 'Tam o' Shanter' offer verse drama in the form of accelerating, sometimes supercharged storytelling. Superb in its changes of pace, balancing Gothic horror with nimble glee, it is a poem which magnetically attracts an audience. Like much of Burns's best poetry it calls together a community. Yet it is also a social poem about isolation, and the triumph of a performer.

In late summer 1791 Burns left farming at Ellisland, and transplanted his family to a tenement in Dumfries. Though he loved aspects of Dumfries (not least its new theatre where he enjoyed attending performances as well as scripting monologues such as 'The Rights of Woman', written for the actress Louisa Fontenelle), his life was again in erotic turmoil. He made a sudden visit to Edinburgh where Jenny Clow was fatally ill. In the Scottish capital Burns and Agnes McLehose exchanged locks of hair: 'Ae fond kiss, and then we sever; / Ae farewell and then for ever!' Though he and Agnes continued to correspond, in January 1792 she set sail for her husband in Jamaica.

Back in Dumfries, Exciseman Burns was involved in early 1792 in the capture of a smuggling schooner in the Solway Firth, and received news he had been made an honorary member of the monarch's ceremonial bodyguard. Still, in poems like 'Here's a Health to them that's awa' and in private letters Burns sometimes inclined towards political radicalism, and even (as, most obviously, in 'The Tree of Liberty', a poem not publicly attributed to Burns in his lifetime) towards the republican cause in France. Britain, however, was soon at war with that newly republican nation. The bard's employer, the Board of Excise, began to question their employee's political allegiance. Despite protestations of orthodoxy, Burns's politics, as set out in his writings, are more complicated. If he wrote verse for local election contests – asking 'To paughty Lordlings shall we jouk [bow]'? – he was aware too of bigger issues. Certainly in 1795–6 he wrote the loyal sentiments of 'Does haughty Gaul invasion threat', but more memorably in 1793 he had written approvingly of revolt against 'Chains and slaverie' in 'Bruce to his Troops on the Eve of the Battle of Bannock-burn'. Before that he had cursed too the loss of Scottish political independence in 'Such a Parcel of Rogues in a Nation'; in 1795 there appeared in the *Glasgow Magazine* Burns's song 'For a' that', a paean to universal fraternity which ends with a stanza that Marilyn Butler in the 1997 essay collection *Robert Burns and Cultural Authority* calls 'probably the closest rendering in English of the letter and spirit of the notorious Jacobin "Ça ira" ':

Then let us pray, that come it may,
  As come it will for a' that,
That Sense & Worth, o'er a' the earth,
  May bear the gree & a' that.—
For a' that, & a' that,
  Its comin yet for a' that,
That Man to Man, the warld o'er,
  Shall brothers be for a' that.—

Recent research has stressed the full depth and danger of Burns's republican commitment. His strength as a political poet lies not just in a democratic tone but also in an inflection which can be republican and Scottish nationalist. This makes him continuously dangerous to the British establishment which has constantly tried to tame him.

The extent of Burns's anthologising of songs became apparent with the publication in 1792 of volume four of *The Scots Musical Museum*; Burns wrote or at least reworked some sixty of the book's hundred songs. Beyond that, he agreed to send songs to the *Select Collection of Original Scotish Airs* announced by Edinburgh amateur musician George Thomson. Burns asked for no financial reward and wished his contributions to involve 'at least a sprinkling of our native tongue'. He gave more than 100 songs to the *Select Collection*, which was published in six volumes between 1793 and 1841. Haydn, Beethoven, Weber and Hummel were among those who composed settings for this anthology. Burns's work has been creatively misinterpreted by generations of great composers, including, in our own day, Arvo Pärt, who loves 'My Heart's in the

Highlands' and has turned it into a wistful, celestial song of transcendental longing.

By 1793 when the Burns family moved to a larger, red-sandstone house (now the Burns House museum) in Dumfries, the poet devoted much of his energy to song. Stimulated by hearing a friend play the air 'Hey tutti taitie' on the oboe, the bard, familiar with the tradition that this tune had been King Robert the Bruce's march at the Battle of Bannockburn, worked himself up 'to a pitch of enthusiasm on the theme of Liberty & Independance' and created one of his best-known songs:

> Scots, wha hae wi' WALLACE bled,
> Scots, wham BRUCE has aften led;
> Welcome to your gory bed,
> Or to victorie.

Burns confessed that in his mind this 'glorious struggle for Freedom' brought to mind other struggles '*not quite so ancient*' – he surely meant the democratic revolution in France which had got rid of the monarchy. Burns's dangerous volatility in politics and in sexual relationships makes his biography continually dramatic, and undeniably fuels his poetry. Though he went on making and remaking Scottish songs, in 1794 Burns once again endured 'low spirits & blue devils'. Travelling in south-west Scotland that summer, he also praised the American General Washington in a rather grandiose 'Ode' written for Washington's birthday and hymning 'sons of Liberty' as well as 'The Royalty of Man' – surely another celebration of a rebel struggle for liberty in America, in England, and in Scotland. Jean Armour gave birth to another child that August, but Burns had not given up all thoughts of Agnes McLehose (his affair with her underlies the formal yet feverish 'My Steps Fate on a Mad Conjuncture Thrust'), while he went on addressing songs to a further beauty, Jean Lorimer. The poet's final eighteen months were marred by illness, family bereavement and a falling out with one of his oldest admirers. 1795 brought blizzards and high snowdrifts. Promoted again in the Excise service, Burns was once more riding long distances, and, though he was only 36, he grew exhausted and complained about 'stiffening joints of Old Age coming fast o'er my frame'. That January Mrs Dunlop was horrified by his description of France's King Louis XVI and Marie Antoinette as 'a perjured Blockhead & an unprincipled Prostitute'. No radical, she put an end to her correspondence with the poet, who was becoming increasingly tired out. Continuing his long interest in local politics, in 1795 he wrote a series of poems in support of the successful Whig candidate for a nearby by-election, Patrick Heron. For all his radical inclinations, and his friendly association with his doctor, the notorious Jacobin William Maxwell, Burns played an active part in a local loyal militia, the Dumfries Volunteers. A late poem such as 'To the Tooth-Ach' clearly signals worsening health, but does so with resolute wit in Standard Habbie. After the death of his infant daughter Elizabeth Riddell in September 1795 Burns experienced a severe illness which apparently lasted much of the winter, and was partly depressive in nature.

Though the poet returned to his Excise work for a time in 1796, and went on sending Thomson songs he had collected, a recurrence of 'PAIN! Rheumatism, Cold & Fever' coincided with financial worries. His doctors advised him his 'last & only chance' was 'bathing & country quarters & riding'. So, following this counsel, the gravely ill Burns underwent regular sea-bathing in the cold spring tides of the Solway Firth, then returned to Dumfries, at death's door. For a young neighbour, Jessie Lewars, who helped nurse him, he wrote his last song:

Oh wert thou in the cauld blast,
  On yonder lea, on yonder lea;
My plaidie to the angry airt,
  I'd shelter thee, I'd shelter thee:
Or did misfortune's bitter storms
  Around thee blaw, around thee blaw,
Thy bield should be my bosom,
  To share it a', to share it a'.

Too weak to help Jean, who was again pregnant, Burns died at home in Dumfries on 21 July 1796, most likely of rheumatic heart disease complicated by bacterial endocarditis. He was buried (and later reburied with an inappropriately elaborate memorial) in St Michael's churchyard, Dumfries.

He had hoped his Excise career would let him find financial security and, eventually, leisure time in which to write much more poetry. Ironically, though, his plans and his early death provide a stark example of the way 'The best laid schemes o' *Mice* an' *Men*, /Gang aft agley'. The selection of poetry and prose in this book shows how, 250 years after Robert Burns's birth, his work, emanating from a life of sexual, political, and financial drama, and from a sense of the democratic strength of a whole, if conflicted community, allowed him not only to articulate intimate longing, biting humour, and deft virtuosity, but also, through a perfected tone of address, to sound for the first time in great poetry the egalitarian ideals of modern democracy memorably, surely, and with an insistent kick of life.

Further Reading

Biography:

Robert Crawford, *The Bard* (Jonathan Cape and Princeton University Press, 2009).

Criticism:

Robert Crawford, ed., *Robert Burns and Cultural Authority* (Edinburgh University Press and Iowa University Press, 1997).

Thomas Crawford, *Burns: A Study of the Poems and Songs*, Second Edition with a new introduction (James Thin, 1978).

David Daiches, *Robert Burns: The Poet* (Saltire Society, 1994).

Carol McGuirk, *Robert Burns and the Sentimental Era* (University of Georgia Press, 1985).

Carol McGuirk, ed., *Critical Essays on Robert Burns* (G. K. Hall, 1998).

Liam McIlvanney, *Burns the Radical: Poetry and Politics in Late Eighteenth-Century Scotland* (Tuckwell Press, 2002).

Kenneth Simpson, ed., *Love and Liberty: Robert Burns, A Bicentenary Celebration* (Tuckwell Press, 1997).

Burns's Scottish Precursors:

Robert Crawford, ed., *Heaven-Taught Fergusson: Robert Burns's Favourite Scottish Poet* (Tuckwell Press, 2003).

Christopher MacLachlan, ed., *Before Burns: Eighteenth-Century Scottish Poetry* (Canongate, 2002).

Complete Editions of Burns:

James Kinsley, ed., *The Poems and Songs of Robert Burns,* 3 vols (Clarendon Press, Oxford, 1968).

J. De Lancey Ferguson, ed., *The Letters of Robert Burns*, Second Edition edited by G. Ross Roy, 2 vols. (Clarendon Press, Oxford, 1985).

History of Scottish Literature:

Robert Crawford, *Scotland's Books* (Penguin, 2007; Oxford University Press, New York, 2009).

Poems

My Father was a Farmer

My father was a farmer upon the Carrick border O
And carefully he bred me, in decency & order O
He bade me act a manly part, though I had ne'er a farthing O
For without an honest manly heart, no man was worth regarding O
Chorus Row de dow &c.

Then out into the world my course I did determine. O
Tho' to be rich was not my wish, yet to be great was charming. O
My talents they were not the worst, nor yet my education: O
Resolv'd was I, at least to try, to mend my situation. O

In many a way, & vain essay, I courted fortune's favor; O
Some cause unseen, still stept between, & frustrate each endeavor; O
Some times by foes I was o'erpower'd, sometimes by friends forsaken; O
And when my hope was at the top, I still was worst mistaken. O

Then sore harass'd, & tir'd at last, with fortune's vain delusion; O
I dropt my schemes, like idle dreams and came to this conclusion; O
The past wast bad, & the future hid; its good or ill untryed; O
But the present hour was in my pow'r, & so I would enjoy it, O

No help, nor hope, nor view had I; nor person to befriend me; O
So I must toil, & sweat & moil, & labor to sustain me, O
To plough & sow, to reap & mow, my father bred me early, O
For one, he said, to labor bred, was a match for fortune fairly, O

Thus all obscure, unknown, & poor, thro' life I'm doom'd to wander, O
Till down my weary bones I lay in everlasting slumber: O
No view nor care, but shun whate'er might breed me pain or sorrow; O
I live today as well's I may, regardless of tomorrow, O

But chearful still, I am as well as a Monarch in a palace; O
Tho' fortune's frown still hunts me down with all her wonted malice: O
I make indeed, my daily bread, but ne'er can make it farther; O
But as daily bread is all I heed, I do not much regard her. O

When sometimes by my labor I earn a little money, O
Some unforseen misfortune comes generally upon me; O
Mischance, mistake, or by neglect, or my good natur'd folly; O
But come what will I've sworn it still, I'll ne'er be melancholy, O

All you who follow wealth & power with unremitting ardor, O
The more in this you look for bliss, you leave your view the farther; O
Had you the wealth Potosi boasts, or nations to adore you, O
A chearful honest-hearted clown I will prefer before you. O

To Ruin.

All hail! inexorable lord!
At whose destruction-breathing word,
  The mightiest empires fall!
Thy cruel, woe-delighted train,
The ministers of Grief and Pain,
  A sullen welcome, all!
With stern-resolv'd, despairing eye,
  I see each aimed dart;
For one has cut my *dearest tye*,
  And quivers in my heart.
    Then low'ring, and pouring,
      The *Storm* no more I dread;
    Tho' thick'ning, and black'ning,
      Round my devoted head.

And thou grim Pow'r, by Life abhorr'd,
While Life a *pleasure* can afford,
  Oh! hear a wretch's pray'r!
No more I shrink appall'd, afraid;
I court, I beg thy friendly aid,
  To close this scene of care!
When shall my soul, in silent peace,
  Resign Life's *joyless* day?
My weary heart it's throbbings cease,
  Cold-mould'ring in the clay?
    No fear more, no tear more,
      To stain my lifeless face,
    Enclasped, and grasped,
      Within thy cold embrace!

The Death and Dying Words of Poor Mailie,
The Author's Only Pet Yowe, *ewe*
An Unco Mournfu' Tale *extraordinarily*

As Mailie, an' her lambs thegither, *and; together*
Was ae day nibbling on the tether, *one*
Upon her cloot she coost a hitch, *hoof; cast*
An' owre she warsl'd in the ditch: *over; wriggled*
There, groaning, dying, she did ly, *lie*
When *Hughoc*[1] he cam doytan by. *came stumbling*

Wi' glowrin een, an' lifted han's *with glowering eyes; hands*
Poor *Hughoc* like a statue stan's; *stands*
He saw her days were near hand ended,
But, waes my heart! he could na mend it! *woe is; not*
He gaped wide, but naething spak, *nothing spoke*
At length poor *Mailie* silence brak. *broke*

'O thou, whase lamentable face *whose*
Appears to mourn my woefu' case! *woeful*
My *dying words* attentive hear,
An' bear them to my *Master* dear. *and*

Tell him, if e'er again he keep
As muckle gear as buy a *sheep*, *much wealth*
O, bid him never tye them mair, *tie; more*
Wi' wicked strings o' hemp or hair! *with; of*
But ca them out to park or hill, *drive*
An' let them wander at their will: *and*
So, may his flock increase an' grow
To *scores* o' lambs, an' *packs* of woo'! *wool*

Tell him, he was a Master kin', *kind*
An' ay was guid to me an' mine; *and always; good*

1 A neibor herd-callan [Burns's note]. *neighbour herd-lad*

An' now my *dying* charge I gie him,	*give*
My helpless *lambs*, I trust them wi' him.	*with*
O, bid him save their harmless lives,	
Frae dogs an' tods, an' butchers' knives!	*from; foxes*
But gie them guid *cow-milk* their fill,	*give; good*
Till they be fit to fend themsel;	*themselves*
An' tent them duely, e'en an' morn,	*tend; duly; evening*
Wi' taets o' *hay* an' ripps o' *corn.*	*tufts of; handfuls of*
An' may they never learn the gaets,	*ways*
Of ither vile, wanrestfu' *Pets!*	*other; restless*
To slink thro' slaps, an' reave an' steal,	*through gaps; rob*
At stacks o' pease, or stocks o' kail.	*cole, cabbage*
So may they, like their great *forbears*,	
For monie a year come thro' the sheers:	*many; shears*
So *wives* will gie them bits o' bread,	*give*
An' *bairns* greet for them when they're dead.	*children weep*
My poor *toop-lamb*, my son an' heir,	*ram-*
O, bid him breed him up wi' care!	*with*
An' if he live to be a beast,	*and*
To pit some havins in his breast!	*put; manners*
An' warn him ay at ridin time,	*always; breeding*
To stay content wi' *yowes* at hame;	*with ewes; home*
An' no to rin an' wear his cloots,	*not; run; hooves*
Like ither menseless, graceless brutes.	*other ill-bred*
An' niest my *yowie*, silly thing,	*next; ewe-lamb*
Gude keep thee frae a *tether string!*	*go[o]d; from*
O, may thou ne'er forgather up,	*never meet*
Wi' onie blastet, moorlan *toop;*	*any cursed moorland ram*
But aye keep mind to moop an' mell,	*always; munch and mingle*
Wi' sheep o' credit like thysel!	*yourself*
And now, *my bairns*, wi' my last breath,	*children*
I lea'e my blessin wi' you baith:	*leave; both*
An' when ye think upo' your Mither,	*upon; mother*
Mind to be kind to ane anither.	*remember; one another*

Now, honest Hughoc, dinna fail, *do not*
To tell my Master a' my tale; *all*
An' bid him burn this cursed *tether*,
An' for thy pains thou'se get my blather. *you will; bladder*

This said, poor *Mailie* turn'd her head,
An' clos'd her een amang the dead! *eyes; among*

Poor Mailie's Elegy.

Lament in rhyme, lament in prose,
Wi' saut tears trickling down your nose; *with salt*
Our *Bardie's* fate is at a close, *[minor] poet's*
        Past a' remead! *all remedy*
The last, sad cape-stane of his woes; *cope-stone*
        Poor Mailie's dead!

It's no the loss o' warl's gear, *not; of worldly wealth*
That could sae bitter draw the tear, *so*
Or make our *Bardie*, dowie, wear *dismal*
        The mourning weed: *garment*
He's lost a friend and neebor dear, *neighbour*
        In *Mailie* dead.

Thro' a' the town she trotted by him; *through all*
A lang half-mile she could descry him; *long; spot*
Wi' kindly bleat, when she did spy him, *with*
        She ran wi' speed:
A friend mair faithfu' ne'er came nigh him, *more faithful never*
        Than *Mailie* dead.

I wat she was a *sheep* o' sense, *know*
An' could behave hersel wi' mense: *with decorum*
I'll say't, she never brak a fence, *broke*
        Thro' thievish greed.
Our *Bardie*, lanely, keeps the spence *lonely, sits in the best room*
        Sin' *Mailie's* dead. *since*

Or, if he wanders up the howe, *valley*
Her living image in *her yowe*, *ewe*
Comes bleating till him, owre the knowe, *to; over the knoll*
        For bits o' bread;
An' down the briny pearls rowe *roll*
        For *Mailie* dead.

She was nae get o' moorlan tips, *no offspring; rams*
Wi' tauted ket, an' hairy hips; *tangled fleece*
For her forbears were brought in ships,
        Frae 'yont the TWEED. *from beyond*
A bonier *fleesh* ne'er cross'd the clips *prettier fleece never; clippers*
        Than *Mailie's* dead.

Wae worth that man wha first did shape *woe; who*
That vile, wanchancie thing—*a raep!* *unlucky; rope*
It maks guid fellows girn an' gape, *makes good; grimace*
        Wi' chokin dread; *choking*
An' *Robin's* bonnet wave wi' crape *black mourning ribbons*
        For *Mailie* dead.

O, a' ye *Bards* on bonie DOON! *all*
An' wha on AIRE your chanters tune! *who; pipes*
Come, join the melancholious croon *moan*
        O' *Robin's* reed! *reed-pipe*
His heart will never get aboon! *recover, get over it*
        His *Mailie's* dead!

Mary Morison

O Mary at thy window be,
   It is the wish'd the trysted hour, *appointed*
Those smiles & glances let me see,
   That make the miser's treasure poor.
How blythely wad I bide the stoure, *would; endure the struggle*
   A weary slave frae sun to sun, *from*
Could I the rich reward secure,
   The lovely Mary Morison!

Yestreen when to the trembling string *yesterday evening*
   The dance gaed through the lighted ha', *went; hall*
To thee my fancy took its wing,
   I sat, but neither heard, nor saw:
Though this was fair, & that was braw, *fine*
   And yon the toast of a' the town, *that one; all*
I sigh'd, & said amang them a', *among*
   'Ye are na Mary Morison.' *not*

O Mary canst thou wreck his peace
   Wha for thy sake wad gladly die. *who: would*
Or canst thou break that heart of his,
   Whase only faute is loving thee! *whose; fault*
If love for love thou wilt na gie, *not give*
   At least be pity to me shown,
A thought ungentle canna be *cannot*
   The thought o' Mary Morison.—

On a Noisy Polemic.

Below thir stanes lie Jamie's banes; *these stones; bones*
O Death, it's my opinion,
Thou ne'er took such a bleth'ran b[i]tch, *talkative nuisance*
Into thy dark dominion!

For the Author's Father.

O ye whose cheek the tear of pity stains,
Draw near with pious rev'rence and attend!
Here lie the loving Husband's dear remains,
The tender Father, and the gen'rous Friend.
The pitying Heart that felt for human Woe;
The dauntless heart that fear'd no human Pride;
The Friend of Man, to vice alone a foe;
'For ev'n his failings lean'd to Virtue's side.'[1]

1 Goldsmith [Burns's footnote, referring to Oliver Goldsmith's 'The Deserted Village' (1770), line 164].

A Fragment. [When Guilford Good our Pilot Stood]

When *Guilford* good our Pilot stood,
  An' did our hellim thraw, man, *and; helm turn*
Ae night, at tea, began a plea, *one*
  Within *America*, man:
Then up they gat the maskin-pat, *got; tea-pot*
  And in the sea did jaw, man; *pour*
An' did nae less, in full Congress, *no*
  Than quite refuse our law, man.

Then thro' the lakes *Montgomery* takes, *through*
  I wat he was na slaw, man; *know; not slow*
Down *Lowrie's burn* he took a turn, *St Lawrence river*
  And *C[a]rl[e]t[o]n* did ca', man: *drive*
But yet, whatreck, he, at *Quebec*, *nevertheless*
  Montgomery-like did fa', man, *fall*
Wi' sword in hand, before his band, *with*
  Amang his en'mies a', man. *among; all*

Poor *Tammy G[a]ge* within a cage
  Was kept at *Boston-ha'*, man; *-hall*
Till *Willie H[ow]e* took o'er the knowe *went over; hill*
  For *Philadelphia*, man:
Wi' sword an' gun he thought a sin
  Guid Christian bluid to draw, man; *good; blood*
But at *New-York*, wi' knife an' fork,
  Sir Loin he hacked sma', man. *beef; small*

B[u]rg[oy]ne gaed up, like spur an' whip, *went*
  Till *Fraser* brave did fa', man; *fall*
Then lost his way, ae misty day, *one*
  In *Saratoga* shaw, man. *thicket, wood*
C[o]rnw[a]ll[i]s fought as lang's he dought, *long as he could*
  An' did the Buckskins claw, man; *Americans strike*
But *Cl[i]nt[o]n's* glaive frae rust to save *sword from*
  He hung it to the wa', man. *wall*

Then *M[o]nt[a]gue*, an' *Guilford* too,
Began to fear a fa', man; *fall*
And *S[a]ckv[i]lle* doure, wha stood the stoure, *stern; who; strife*
The German Chief to thraw, man: *thwart*
For Paddy *B[u]rke*, like ony Turk, *any*
Nae mercy had at a', man; *no; all*
An' *Charlie F[o]x* threw by the box, *dice-cup*
An' lows'd his tinkler jaw man. *released his uncouth tongue*

Then *R[o]ck[i]ngh[a]m* took up the game;
Till Death did on him ca', man; *call*
When *Sh[e]lb[u]rne* meek held up his cheek,
Conform to Gospel law, man:
Saint Stephen's boys, wi' jarring noise,
They did his measures thraw, man, *oppose*
For *N[o]rth* an' *F[o]x* united stocks,
An' bore him to the wa', man. *wall*

Then Clubs an' Hearts were *Charlie's* cartes, *playing-cards*
He swept the stakes awa', man, *away*
Till the Diamond's Ace, of *Indian* race,
Led him a sair *faux pas*, man: *sore false step*
The Saxon lads, wi' loud placads, *placards, proclamations*
On *Chatham's Boy* did ca', man; *call*
An' Scotland drew her pipe an' blew,
'Up, Willie, waur them a', man!' *get the better of; all*

Behind the throne then *Gr[e]nv[i]lle's* gone,
A secret word or twa, man; *two*
While slee *D[u]nd[a]s* arous'd the class *sly*
Be-north the Roman wa', man: *Hadrian's Wall, the Scottish border*
An' *Chatham's* wraith, in heav'nly graith, *attire*
(Inspired Bardies saw, man) *minor poets*
Wi' kindling eyes cry'd, '*Willie*, rise!
Would I hae fear'd them a', man!' *have; all*

But, word an' blow, *N[o]rth*, *F[o]x*, *and Co.*
  Gowff'd *Willie* like a ba', man, *golfed, struck; ball*
Till *Suthron* raise, an' coost their claise *Englishmen rose; threw off; clothes*
  Behind him in a raw, man: *row*
An' *Caledon* threw by the drone, *Scotland; bagpipe*
  An' did her whittle draw, man; *knife*
An' swoor fu' rude, thro' dirt an' blood, *swore full or very*
  To mak it guid in law, man. *make; good*

* * *

Address to the Unco Guid, or the Rigidly Righteous.

[*extraordinarily good*

My Son, these maxims make a rule,
And lump them ay thegither; — *always together*
The Rigid Righteous *is a fool,*
The Rigid Wise *anither:* — *another*
The cleanest corn that e'er was dight — *winnowed*
May hae some pyles o' caff in; — *have small quantities of chaff*
So ne'er a fellow-creature slight
For random fits o' daffin. — *folly*

Solomon – Eccles. ch. vii. vers. 16.

O ye wha are sae guid yoursel, — *you who; so good yourselves*
Sae pious and sae holy, — *so*
Ye've nought to do but mark and tell
Your Neebours' fauts and folly! — *neighbours' faults*
Whase life is like a weel-gaun mill, — *whose; well-running*
Supply'd wi' store o' water, — *with; of*
The heaped happer's ebbing still, — *hopper*
And still the clap plays clatter. — *clapper*

Hear me, ye venerable Core, — *company*
As counsel for poor mortals, — *advocate*
That frequent pass douce Wisdom's door — *prudent*
For glaikit Folly's portals; — *senseless*
I, for their thoughtless, careless sakes
Would here propone defences, — *plead (Scots legal term)*
Their donsie tricks, their black mistakes, — *stupid*
Their failings and mischances.

Ye see your state wi' theirs compar'd,
And shudder at the niffer, — *(implied) exchange*
But cast a moment's fair regard
What maks the mighty differ; — *makes*

Discount what scant occasion gave,
That purity ye pride in,
And (what's aft mair than a' the lave) *often more than all the rest*
Your better art o' hiding.

Think, when your castigated pulse
Gies now and then a wallop, *gives; flutter*
What ragings must his veins convulse,
That still eternal gallop:
Wi' wind and tide fair i' your tail, *in*
Right on ye scud your sea-way; *sail quickly*
But, in the teeth o' baith to sail, *both*
It maks an unco leeway. *makes; extraordinary*

See Social-life and Glee sit down,
All joyous and unthinking,
Till, quite transmugrify'd, they're grown *transmogrified*
Debauchery and Drinking:
O would they stay to calculate
Th'eternal consequences;
Or your more dreaded h[e]ll to state,
D[a]mnation of expenses!

Ye high, exalted, virtuous Dames,
Ty'd up in godly laces, *tied*
Before ye gie poor *Frailty* names, *give*
Suppose a change o' cases;
A dear-lov'd lad, convenience snug,
A treacherous inclination—
But, let me whisper i' your lug, *in your ear*
Ye're aiblins nae temptation. *possibly no*

Then gently scan your brother Man,
Still gentler sister Woman;
Tho' they may gang a kennin wrang, *go a trifle wrong*
To step aside is human:
One point must still be greatly dark,
The moving *Why* they do it;
And just as lamely can ye mark,
How far perhaps they rue it.

Who made the heart, 'tis *He* alone
  Decidedly can try us,
He knows each chord its various tone,
  Each spring its various bias:
Then at the balance let's be mute,
  We never can adjust it;
What's *done* we partly may compute,
  But know not what's *resisted*.

O Leave Novels

O leave novels, ye Mauchline belles,
Ye're safer at your spinning wheel;
Such witching books, are baited hooks
For rakish rooks like Rob Mossgiel.
Your fine Tom Jones And Grandisons
They make your youthful fancies reel
They heat your brains, and fire your veins
And then you're prey for Rob Mossgiel.

Beware a tongue that's smoothly hung;
A heart that warmly seems to feel;
That feelin heart but acks a part, *feeling; acts*
'Tis rakish art in Rob Mossgiel.
The frank address, the soft caress,
Are worse than poisoned darts of steel,
The frank address, and politesse,
Are all finesse in Rob Mossgiel. *artfulness*

Green Grow the Rashes. A Fragment.

CHORUS.
Green grow the rashes, O; *rushes*
Green grow the rashes, O;
The sweetest hours that e'er I spend,
Are spent amang the lasses, O. *among*

There's nought but care on ev'ry han', *hand*
In ev'ry hour that passes, O:
What signifies the life o' man,
An' 'twere na for the lasses, O. *if it were not*
Green grow, &c.

The warly race may riches chase, *worldly*
An' riches still may fly them, O; *and*
An' tho' at last they catch them fast,
Their hearts can ne'er enjoy them, O.
Green grow, &c.

But gie me a canny hour at e'en, *give; favourable; evening*
My arms about my Dearie, O;
An' warly cares, an' warly men, *worldly*
May a' gae tapsalteerie, O! *all go topsy-turvy*
Green grow, &c.

For you sae douse, ye sneer at this, *so prim*
Ye're nought but senseless asses, O:
The wisest Man the warl' saw, *world*
He dearly lov'd the lasses, O.
Green grow, &c..

Auld Nature swears, the lovely Dears *old*
Her noblest work she classes, O:
Her prentice han' she try'd on man, *hand*
An' then she made the lasses, O.
Green grow, &c.

* * *

Epistle to Davie, A Brother Poet.

January [*1785*]

While winds frae off BEN-LOMOND blaw, *from; blow*
And bar the doors wi' driving snaw, *with; snow*
  And hing us owre the ingle, *hang; over; fireside*
I set me down, to pass the time,
And spin a verse or twa o' rhyme, *two of*
  In hamely, *westlin* jingle. *homely, west country*
While frosty winds blaw in the drift, *blow*
  Ben to the chimla lug, *in; chimney side*
I grudge a wee the *Great-folk's* gift, *little*
  That live sae bien an' snug: *so comfortably and*
    I tent less, and want less *heed*
      Their roomy fire-side;
    But hanker, and canker, *obsess about; get irritated*
      To see their cursed pride.

It's hardly in a body's pow'r,
To keep, at times, frae being sour, *from*
  To see how things are shar'd;
How *best o' chiels* are whyles in want, *fellows; at times*
While *Coofs* on countless thousands rant, *fools; make merry*
  And ken na how to wair't: *know not; spend it*
But DAVIE lad, ne'er fash your head, *never trouble*
  Tho' we hae little gear, *have; property*
We're fit to win our daily bread,
  As lang's we're hale and fier: *long as; healthy*
    'Mair spier na, nor fear na,'[1] *more ask not*
      Auld age ne'er mind a feg; *old; fig*
    The last o't, the warst o't, *of it; worst*
      Is only but to beg.

1 Ramsay [Burns's footnote, referring to line 53 of 'The Poet's Wish: An Ode' by Allan Ramsay (1685–1758)].

To lye in kilns and barns at e'en, *even[ing]*
When banes are craz'd, and bluid is thin, *bones; blood*
Is, doubtless, great distress!
Yet then *content* could make us blest;
Ev'n then, sometimes we'd snatch a taste *even*
Of truest happiness.
The honest heart that's free frae a' *from all*
Intended fraud or guile,
However Fortune kick the ba', *ball*
Has ay some cause to smile: *always*
And mind still, you'll find still, *remember*
A comfort this nae sma'; *not small*
Nae mair then, we'll care then, *no more*
Nae *farther* we can *fa'*. *no; fall*

What tho', like Commoners of air,
We wander out, we know not where,
But either house or hal'? *without; home*
Yet *Nature's* charms, the hills and woods,
The sweeping vales, and foaming floods,
Are free alike to all.
In days when Daisies deck the ground,
And Blackbirds whistle clear,
With honest joy, our hearts will bound,
To see the *coming* year:
On braes when we please then, *hillsides*
We'll sit and *sowth* a tune; *hum*
Syne *rhyme* till't, well time till't, *then; to it*
And sing't when we hae done. *sing it; have*

It's no in titles nor in rank; *not*
It's no in wealth like *Lon'on Bank*, *London*
To purchase peace and rest;
It's no in makin muckle, *mair:* *making much [into] more*
It's no in books; it's no in Lear, *learning*
To make us truly blest:
If Happiness hae not her seat *have*

And center in the breast, *centre*
We may be *wise*, or *rich*, or *great*,
But never can be *blest:*
Nae treasures, nor pleasures *no*
Could make us happy lang; *long*
The *heart* ay's the part ay, *always is; always*
That makes us right or wrang. *wrong*

Think ye, that sic as *you* and *I*, *such*
Wha drudge and drive thro' wet and dry, *who*
Wi' never-ceasing toil; *with*
Think ye, are we less blest than they,
Wha scarcely tent us in their way, *who; heed*
As hardly worth their while?
Alas! how aft, in haughty mood, *oft[en]*
GOD's creatures they oppress!
Or else, neglecting a' that's guid, *all; good*
They riot in excess!
Baith careless, and fearless, *both*
Of either Heaven or Hell;
Esteeming, and deeming,
It a' an idle tale! *all*

Then let us chearfu' acquiesce; *cheerful[ly]*
Nor make our scanty Pleasures less,
By pining at our state:
And, ev'n should Misfortunes come,
I, here wha sit, hae met wi' some, *who; have; with*
An's thankfu' for them yet. *and am thankful*
They gie the wit of *Age* to *Youth;* *give*
They let us ken oursel; *know ourselves*
They make us see the naked truth,
The *real* guid and ill. *good*
Tho' losses, and crosses,
Be lessons right severe,
There's *wit* there, ye'll get there,
Ye'll find nae other where. *no*

But tent me, DAVIE, *Ace o' Hearts!* *attend to; of*
(To say aught less wad wrang the *cartes*, *anything; would wrong; cards*
And flatt'ry I detest)
This life has joys for you and I;
And joys that riches ne'er could buy;
And joys the very best.
There's a' the *Pleasures o' the Heart*, *all; of*
The *Lover* and the *Frien';* *friend*
Ye hae your MEG, your dearest part, *have*
And I my darling JEAN!
It warms me, it charms me,
To mention but her *name:*
It heats me, it beets me, *kindles*
And sets me a' on flame! *all*

O, all ye *Pow'rs* who rule above!
O THOU, whose very self art *love*!
THOU know'st my words sincere!
The *life blood* streaming thro' my heart,
Or my more dear *Immortal part*,
Is not more fondly dear!
When heart-corroding care and grief
Deprive my soul of rest,
Her dear idea brings relief,
And solace to my breast.
Thou BEING, Allseeing,
O hear my fervent pray'r!
Still take her, and make her,
THY most peculiar care! *particular*

All hail! ye tender feelings dear!
The smile of love, the friendly tear,
The sympathetic glow!
Long since, this world's thorny ways
Had number'd out my weary days,
Had it not been for you!
Fate still has blest me with a friend,
In ev'ry care and ill;

And oft a more *endearing* band,
A *tye* more tender still. — *tie*
It lightens, it brightens,
The tenebrific scene, — *gloomy*
To meet with, and greet with,
My DAVIE or my JEAN!

O, how that *name* inspires my style!
The words come skelpan, rank and file, — *galloping*
Amaist before I ken! — *almost; know*
The ready measure rins as fine, — *runs*
As *Phœbus* and the famous *Nine*
Were glowran owre my pen. — *staring over*
My spavet *Pegasus* will limp, — *spavined*
Till ance he's fairly het; — *once; thoroughly hot*
And then he'll hilch, and stilt, and jimp, — *hobble; halt; jump*
And rin an unco fit: — *run; uncommon pace*
But least then, the beast then, — *lest*
Should rue this hasty ride,
I'll light now, and dight now, — *rub down*
His sweaty, wizen'd hide.

Holy Willie's Prayer

And send the Godly in a pet to pray—
POPE [*The Rape of the Lock*, IV, 64]

ARGUMENT

Holy Willie was a rather oldish batchelor Elder in the parish of Mauchline, & much & justly famed for that polemical chattering which ends in tippling Orthodoxy, & for that Spiritualized Bawdry which refines to Liquorish Devotion.— In a Sessional process with a gentleman in Mauchline, a Mr. Gavin Hamilton, Holy Willie, & his priest, father Auld, after full hearing in the Presbytery of Ayr, came off but second best; owing partly to the oratorical powers of Mr Robt. Aiken, Mr Hamilton's Counsel; but chiefly to Mr. Hamilton's being one of the most irreproachable & truly respectable characters in the country.— On losing his Process, the Muse overheard him at his devotions as follows—

O thou that in the heavens does dwell!
Wha, as it pleases best thysel, — *who; thyself*
Sends ane to heaven & ten to h[e]ll, — *one*
        A' for thy glory! — *all*
And no for ony gude or ill — *not; any good*
        They've done before thee.—

I bless & praise thy matchless might,
When thousands thou has left in night,
That I am here before thy sight,
        For gifts & grace,
A burning & a shining light
        To a' this place.— — *all*

What was I, or my generation,
That I should get such exaltation?
I, wha deserv'd most just damnation, — *who*
        For broken laws
Sax thousand years ere my creation, — *six*
        Thro' Adam's cause.

When from my mother's womb I fell,
Thou might hae plunged me deep in hell, *have*
To gnash my gooms, & weep, & wail, *gums*
In burning lakes,
Where damned devils roar & yell
Chain'd to their stakes.—

Yet I am here, a chosen sample,
To shew thy grace is great & ample: *show*
I'm here, a pillar o' thy temple *of*
Strong as a rock,
A guide, a ruler & example
To a' thy flock.— *all*

But yet—O L[or]d—confess I must—
At times I'm fash'd wi' fleshly lust; *afflicted with*
And sometimes too, in warldly trust *worldly*
Vile Self gets in;
But thou remembers we are dust,
Defil'd wi' sin.—

O L[or]d—yestreen—thou kens—wi' Meg— *last night; knows; with*
Thy pardon I sincerely beg!
O may't ne'er be a living plague,
To my dishonor!
And I'll ne'er lift a lawless leg
Again upon her.—

Besides, I farther maun avow, *must*
Wi' Leezie's lass, three times—I trow— *think*
But L[or]d, that friday I was fou *drunk*
When I cam near her; *came*
Or else, thou kens, thy servant true *know*
Wad never steer her.— *would; touch*

Maybe thou lets this fleshly thorn
Buffet thy servant e'en & morn, *evening*
Lest he o'er proud & high should turn, *over*
That he's sae gifted; *so*

If sae, thy hand maun e'en be borne *must even*
Untill thou lift it.—

L[or]d bless thy Chosen in this place,
For here thou has a chosen race:
But G[o]d, confound their stubborn face,
And blast their name,
Wha bring thy rulers to disgrace *who*
And open shame.—

L[or]d mind Gaun Hamilton's deserts! *remember Gavin*
He drinks, & swears, & plays at cartes, *cards*
Yet has sae mony taking arts *so many*
Wi' Great & Sma', *small*
Frae G[o]d's ain priest the people's hearts *from; own*
He steals awa.— *away*

And when we chasten'd him therefore,
Thou kens how he bred sic a splore, *knows; such a fuss*
And set the warld in a roar *world*
O' laughin at us: *of laughing*
Curse thou his basket and his store,
Kail & potatoes.— *cabbage*

L[or]d hear my earnest cry and prayer
Against that Presbytry of Ayr!
Thy strong right hand, L[or]d, make it bare
Upon their heads!
L[or]d visit them, & dinna spare, *do not*
For their misdeeds!

O L[or]d my G[o]d, that glib-tongu'd Aiken!
My very heart & flesh are quaking
To think how I sat, sweating, shaking,
And p[i]ss'd wi' dread,
While Auld wi' hingin lip gaed sneaking, *hanging; went*
And hid his head!

L[or]d, in thy day o' vengeance try him!
L[or]d visit him that did employ him!
And pass not in thy mercy by them;
    Nor hear their prayer;
But for thy people's sake destroy them,
    And dinna spare! *do not*

But L[or]d, remember me & mine
Wi' mercies temporal & divine! *with*
That I for grace & gear may shine, *possessions*
    Excell'd by nane! *none*
And a' the glory shall be thine! *all*
    Amen! Amen!

Death and Doctor Hornbook.
A True Story.

Some books are lies frae end to end, *from*
And some great lies were never penn'd:
Ev'n Ministers they hae been kenn'd, *even; have; known*
    In holy rapture,
Great lies and nonsense baith to vend, *both; sell, utter*
    And nail't wi' Scripture. *nail it, confirm it; with*

But this that I am gaun to tell, *going*
Which lately on a night befel, *befell*
Is just as true's the Deil's in h[e]ll, *true as; Devil is*
    Or Dublin city:
That e'er he nearer comes oursel *ever; ourselves*
    'S a muckle pity. *is a great*

The Clachan yill had made me canty, *village ale; cheerful*
I was na fou, but just had plenty; *not full or drunk*
I stacher'd whyles, but yet took tent ay *staggered sometimes; care always*
    To free the ditches; *jump over*
An' hillocks, stanes, an' bushes kenn'd ay *and; stones; knew always*
    Frae ghaists an' witches. *from ghosts and*

The rising Moon began to glowr *look*
The distant *Cumnock* hills out-owre; *-over*
To count her horns, wi' a' my pow'r, *with all my power*
    I set mysel, *myself*
But whether she had three or four,
    I cou'd na tell. *could not*

I was come round about the hill,
And todlin down on *Willie's mill*, *walking unsteadily*
Setting my staff wi' a' my skill, *with all*
    To keep me sicker; *sure, steady*
Tho' leeward whyles, against my will, *sometimes*
    I took a bicker. *stumble*

I there wi' *Something* does forgather, *with; meet*
That pat me in an eerie swither; *put; fearful panic*
An awfu' scythe, out-owre ae shouther, *awful; over one shoulder*
        Clear-dangling, hang; *hung*
A three-tae'd leister on the ither *three-pronged fish-spear; other*
        Lay, large an' lang. *and long*

Its stature seem'd lang Scotch ells twa, *long; two yards*
The queerest shape that e'er I saw,
For fient a wame it had ava, *never a belly; at all*
        And then its shanks, *legs*
They were as thin, as sharp an' sma' *and small*
        As cheeks o' branks. *side-pieces of a halter*

'Guid-een,' quo' I; 'Friend! hae ye been mawin, *good evening; mowing*
When ither folk are busy sawin?'[1] *other; sowing*
It seem'd to mak a kind o' stan', *make; of stand*
        But naething spak; *nothing spoke*
At length, says I, 'Friend! whare ye gaun, *where are you going*
        Will ye go back?'

It spak right howe—'My name is *Death*, *spoke; hollow*
But be na' fley'd.'—Quoth I, 'Guid faith, *not frightened; good*
Ye're maybe come to stap my breath; *stop*
        But tent me, billie; *heed; friend*
I red ye weel, tak care o' skaith, *advise; well; take; injury*
        See, there's a gully!' *knife*

'Gudeman,' quo' he, 'put up your whittle, *goodman; said; knife*
I'm no design'd to try its mettle; *not intending*
But if I did, I wad be kittle *would; likely*
        To be mislear'd, *unskilled*
I wad na' mind it, no that spittle *would not; not*
        Out-owre my beard.' *out over*

'Weel, weel!' says I, 'a bargain be't; *well; be it*
Come, gie's your hand, an' sae we're gree't; *give us; and so; agreed*

1 This rencounter [meeting] happened in seed-time 1785 [Burns's note].

We'll ease our shanks an' tak a seat, *and take*
    Come, gie's your news! *give us*
This while[2] ye hae been mony a gate, *have; many a way*
    At mony a house.' *many*

'Ay, ay!' quo' he, an' shook his head, *yes*
'It's e'en a lang, lang time indeed *even; long*
Sin I began to nick the thread, *since; cut*
    An' choke the breath: *and*
Folk maun do something for their bread, *must*
    An' sae maun *Death*. *and so must*

Sax thousand years are near hand fled *six; almost*
Sin' I was to the butching bred, *since; butchering*
And mony a scheme in vain's been laid, *many*
    To stap or scar me; *stop; scare*
Till ane Hornbook's[3] ta'en up the trade, *one; taken*
    And faith, he'll waur me. *worst, outdo*

Ye ken *Jock Hornbook* i' the Clachan, *know; in; village*
Deil mak his king's-hood in a spleuchan! *devil make: stomach; pouch*
He's grown sae weel acquaint wi' *Buchan*,[4] *so well*
    And ither chaps, *other*
The weans haud out their fingers laughin, *children hold; laughing*
    And pouk my hips. *pluck*

See, here's a scythe, and there's dart,
They hae pierc'd mony a gallant heart; *have; many*
But Doctor *Hornbook*, wi' his art *with*
    And cursed skill,
Has made them baith no worth a f[ar]t, *both not*
    D[am]n'd haet they'll kill! *not a thing*

2 An epidemical fever was then raging in that country [Burns's note].

3 This gentleman, Dr. Hornbook, is, professionally, a brother of the sovereign Order of the Ferula; but, by intuition and inspiration, is at once an Apothecary, Surgeon, and Physician [Burns's note: *ferula* is Latin for a rod or cane, such as was used by a schoolmaster; a hornbook was a common lesson aid, a simple list of numbers and letters. Dr Hornbook's real name was John Wilson (*c.*1751–1837)].

4 Buchan's Domestic Medicine [Burns's note, referring to the popular 1769 book *Domestic Medicine* by William Buchan (1729–1805)].

'Twas but yestreen, nae farther gaen, — *yesterday evening; no; gone*
I threw a noble throw at ane; — *one*
Wi' less, I'm sure, I've hundreds slain; — *with*
　　But deil-ma-care! — *devil take it*
It just play'd dirl on the bane, — *clatter; bone*
　　But did nae mair. — *no more*

Hornbook was by, wi' ready art, — *with*
And had sae fortify'd the part, — *so*
That when I looked to my dart,
　　It was sae blunt, — *so*
Fient haet o't wad hae pierc'd the heart — *nothing of it would have*
　　Of a kail-runt. — *cabbage-stump*

I drew my scythe in sic a fury, — *such*
I nearhand cowpit wi' my hurry, — *almost fell over with*
But yet the bauld *Apothecary* — *bold*
　　Withstood the shock;
I might as weel hae try'd a quarry — *well have tried*
　　O' hard whin-rock. — *of; flint*

E'en them he canna get attended, — *even; cannot*
Altho' their face he ne'er had kend it, — *never; known*
Just sh[ite] in a kail-blade and send it, — *cabbage-leaf*
　　As soon's he smells't, — *soon as; smells it*
Baith their disease, and what will mend it, — *both*
　　At once he tells't. — *recognises it*

And then a' doctor's saws an' whittles, — *all; knives*
Of a' dimensions, shapes, an' mettles, — *and qualities*
A' kind o' boxes, mugs, an' bottles, — *all; of*
　　He's sure to hae; — *have*
Their Latin names as fast he rattles
　　As A B C.

Calces o' fossils, earths, and trees; — *powders*
True Sal-marinum o' the seas; — *salt*
The Farina of beans and pease, — *meal*
　　He has't in plenty; — *has it*
Aqua-fontis, what you please, — *spring water*
　　He can content ye.

Forbye some new, uncommon weapons, *besides*
Urinus Spiritus of capons; *urine*
Or Mite-horn shavings, filings, scrapings,
Distill'd *per se;* *by themselves*
Sal-alkali o' Midge-tail clippings, *soda of*
And mony mae.' *many more*

'Waes me for *Johnny Ged's Hole*[5] now,' *woe is*
Quoth I, 'if that thae news be true! *those*
His braw calf-ward whare gowans grew, *fine; enclosure; where daisies*
Sae white an' bonie, *so; and pretty*
Nae doubt they'll rive it wi' the plew; *no; tear; with; plough*
They'll ruin *Johnie!*'

The creature grain'd an eldritch laugh, *growled; unearthly*
And says, 'Ye needna yoke the pleugh, *need not; plough*
Kirk-yards will soon be till'd eneugh, *church-yards; tilled enough*
Tak ye nae fear: *take; no*
They'll a' be trench'd wi' mony a sheugh, *all; with many a ditch*
In twa-three year. *two or three*

Whare I kill'd ane, a fair strae-death, *where; one; natural death*
By loss o' blood, or want o' breath, *of*
This night I'm free to tak my aith, *take my oath*
That *Hornbook*'s skill
Has clad a score i' their last claith, *in; cloth*
By drap and pill. *drop, medicine*

An honest Wabster to his trade, *weaver*
Whase wife's twa nieves were scarce weel-bred, *whose; two fists; well-*
Gat tippence-worth to mend her head, *got two-pence-worth*
When it was sair; *sore*
The wife slade cannie to her bed, *slid; carefully*
But ne'er spak mair. *never spoke more*

A countra Laird had ta'en the batts, *country landowner; taken; colic*
Or some curmurring in his guts, *flatulence*
His only son for *Hornbook* sets,
And pays him well,

5 The grave-digger [Burns's note].

The lad, for twa guid gimmer-pets, *two good pet ewes*
Was Laird himsel. *landowner*

A bonie lass, ye kend her name, *pretty; knew*
Some ill-brewn drink had hov'd her wame, *badly-brewed; swollen; stomach*
She trusts hersel, to hide the shame, *herself*
In *Hornbook*'s care;
Horn sent her aff to her lang hame, *off; long home, grave*
To hide it there.

That's just a swatch o' *Hornbook*'s way, *sample of*
Thus goes he on from day to day,
Thus does he poison, kill, an' slay,
An's weel pay'd for't; *and is well paid for it*
Yet stops me o' my lawfu' prey, *deprives; of; lawful*
Wi' his d[a]mn'd dirt! *with*

But hark! I'll tell you of a plot,
Tho' dinna ye be speakin o't; *do not; of it*
I'll nail the self-conceited Sot,
As dead's a herrin: *herring*
Niest time we meet, I'll wad a groat, *next; bet; small coin*
He gets his fairin!' *reward*

But just as he began to tell,
The auld kirk-hammer strak the bell *old church-; struck*
Some wee, short hour ayont the *twal*, *small; beyond; twelve*
Which rais'd us baith: *both*
I took the way that pleas'd mysel, *myself*
And sae did *Death*. *so*

Epistle to J. L[aprai]k, An Old Scotch Bard.

April 1st, 1785.

While briers an' woodbines budding green, *and*
An' Paitricks scraichan loud at e'en, *partridges screeching; evening*
And morning Poossie whiddan seen, *hare running*
    Inspire my Muse,
This freedom, in an *unknown* frien', *friend*
    I pray excuse.

On Fasteneen we had a rockin, *Shrove Tuesday; spinning session*
To ca' the crack and weave our stockin; *spread the gossip; stocking*
And there was muckle fun and jokin, *much; joking*
    Ye need na doubt; *not*
At length we had a hearty yokin, *session*
    At *sang about.* *exchanging songs*

There was ae *sang*, amang the rest, *one song among*
Aboon them a' it pleas'd me best, *above; all*
That some kind husband had addrest,
    To some sweet wife:
It thirl'd the heart-strings thro' the breast, *pierced*
    A' to the life. *all*

I've scarce heard ought describ'd sae weel, *so well*
What gen'rous, manly bosoms feel;
Thought I, 'Can this be *Pope*, or *Steele*,
    Or *Beattie's* wark;' *work*
They tald me 'twas an odd kind chiel *told; fellow*
    About *Muirkirk*. *from near*

It pat me fidgean-fain to hear't, *put; restless; hear it*
An' sae about him there I spier't; *and so; enquired*
Then a' that kent him round declar'd, *all; knew*
    He had *ingine.* *ability, genius*
That nane excell'd it, few cam near't, *none; came*
    It was sae fine: *so*

That set him to a pint of ale,
An' either douse or merry tale, *and; sweet, pleasant*
Or rhymes an' sangs he'd made himsel, *songs; himself*
Or witty catches, *songs*
'Tween Inverness and Tiviotdale, *between*
He had few matches.

Then up I gat, an' swoor an aith, *got; swore; oath*
Tho' I should pawn my pleugh an' graith, *plough; equipment*
Or die a cadger pownie's death, *travelling dealer's pony's*
At some dyke-back, *wall-*
A *pint* an' *gill* I'd gie them *baith*, *give; both*
To hear your crack. *talk*

But first an' foremost, I should tell,
Amaist as soon as I could spell, *almost*
I to the *crambo-jingle* fell, *rhyming*
Tho' rude an' rough,
Yet crooning to a body's sel, *self*
Does weel eneugh. *well enough*

I am nae *Poet*, in a sense, *no*
But just a *Rhymer* like by chance,
An' hae to Learning nae pretence, *have; no*
Yet, what the matter?
Whene'er my Muse does on me glance,
I jingle at her.

Your Critic-folk may cock their nose,
And say, 'How can you e'er propose,
You wha ken hardly *verse* frae *prose*, *who know; from*
To mak a *sang*?' *song*
But by your leaves, my learned foes,
Ye're maybe wrang. *wrong*

What's a' your jargon o' your Schools, *all; of*
Your Latin names for horns an' stools; *and*
If honest Nature made you *fools*,
What sairs your Grammars? *serves*

Ye'd better taen up *spades* and *shools*, *taken; shovels*
Or *knappin-hammers.* *knapping-*

A set o' dull, conceited Hashes, *bunglers*
Confuse their brains in *Colledge-classes!* *college-*
They *gang in* Stirks, and *come out* Asses, *go; bullocks*
Plain truth to speak;
An' syne they think to climb Parnassus *then*
By dint o' Greek! *means*

Gie me ae spark o' Nature's fire, *give; one*
That's a' the learning I desire; *all*
Then tho' I drudge thro' dub an' mire *puddle*
At pleugh or cart, *plough*
My Muse, tho' hamely in attire, *homely*
May touch the heart.

O for a spunk o' ALLAN'S glee, *spark*
Or FERGUSON'S, the bauld an' slee, *bold and sly*
Or bright L[APRAI]K'S, my friend to be,
If I can hit it!
That would be *lear* eneugh for me, *learning enough*
If I could get it.

Now, Sir, if ye hae friends enow, *have; enough*
Tho' *real friends* I b'lieve are few,
Yet, if your catalogue be fow, *full*
I'se no insist; *I shall not*
But gif ye want ae friend that's true, *if; one*
I'm on your list.

I winna blaw about *mysel*, *will not boast; myself*
As ill I like my fauts to tell; *faults*
But friends an' folk that wish me well,
They sometimes roose me; *praise*
Tho' I maun own, as mony still, *must admit; many*
As far abuse me.

There's ae *wee faut* they whiles lay to me, *one small fault; sometimes*
I like the lasses—Gude forgie me! *Go[o]d forgive*

For monie a Plack they wheedle frae me, *many; coin; from*
At dance or fair:
Maybe some *ither thing* they gie me *other; give*
They weel can spare. *well*

But MAUCHLINE Race or MAUCHLINE Fair,
I should be proud to meet you there;
We'se gie ae night's discharge to *care*, *we shall give one*
If we forgather, *meet together*
An' hae a swap o' *rhymin-ware,* *have*
Wi' ane anither. *with one another*

The *four-gill chap*, we'se gar him clatter, *drinking-vessel; we'll make*
An' kirs'n him wi' reekin water; *christen; steaming*
Syne we'll sit down an' tak our whitter, *then; take; chatter*
To cheer our heart;
An' faith, we'se be *acquainted* better *we'll*
Before we part.

Awa ye selfish, warly race, *away; worldly*
Wha think that havins, sense an' grace, *who; possessions*
Ev'n love an' friendship should give place
To *catch-the-plack!* *money-making*
I dinna like to see your face, *don't*
Nor hear your crack. *talk*

But ye whom social pleasure charms,
Whose hearts the *tide of kindness* warms,
Who hold your *being* on the terms,
'Each aid the others,'
Come to my bowl, come to my arms, *punch-bowl*
My friends, my brothers!

But to conclude my lang epistle, *long*
As my auld pen's worn to the grissle; *old; gristle*
Twa lines frae you wad gar me fissle, *two; from; would make; excited*
Who am, most fervent,
While I can either sing, or whissle, *whistle*
Your friend and servant.

The Vision.

DUAN FIRST.[1]

The sun had clos'd the *winter-day*,
The Curlers quat their roaring play, *quit*
And hunger'd Maukin taen her way *hare had taken*
    To kail-yards green, *cabbage-patches*
While faithless snaws ilk step betray *snows each*
    Whare she has been. *where*

The Thresher's weary *flingin-tree*, *part of a flail*
The lee-lang day had tir'd me; *live-long*
And when the Day had clos'd his e'e, *eye*
    Far i' the West, *in*
Ben i' the *Spence*, right pensivelie, *inside the parlour*
    I gaed to rest. *went*

There, lanely, by the ingle-cheek, *lonely; chimney-breast*
I sat and ey'd the spewing reek, *smoke*
That fill'd, wi' hoast-provoking smeek, *cough-inducing smoke*
    The auld, clay biggin; *old; building*
And heard the restless rattons squeak *rats*
    About the riggin. *roofing, thatch*

All in this mottie, misty clime, *smutty*
I backward mus'd on wasted time,
How I had spent my *youthfu' prime*, *youthful*
    An' done nae-thing, *and; nothing*
But stringing blethers up in rhyme *idle talk*
    For fools to sing.

1 Duan, a term of Ossian's for the different divisions of a digressive Poem. See his Cath-Loda, Vol. 2. of M'Pherson's Translation [Burns's note, referring to 'Cath-loda', one of the prose-poems published in 1765 by James Macpherson (1736-96) as what he claimed were translations from Scottish Gaelic into English].

Had I to guid advice but harket, *good; hearkened, heeded*
I might, by this, hae led a market, *have*
Or strutted in a Bank and clarket *registered*
My *Cash-Account;*
While here, half-mad, half-fed, half-sarket, *half-dressed*
Is a' th' amount. *all*

I started, mutt'ring blockhead! coof! *fool*
And heav'd on high my wauket loof, *calloused palm*
To swear by a' yon starry roof, *all yonder*
Or some rash aith, *oath*
That I, henceforth, wad be *rhyme-proof* *would*
Till my last breath—

When click! the *string* the *snick* did draw; *latch*
And jee! the door gaed to the wa'; *swing; went; wall*
And by my ingle-lowe I saw, *fire-light*
Now bleezan bright, *blazing*
A tight, outlandish *Hizzie*, braw, *foreign woman; fine*
Come full in sight.

Ye need na doubt, I held my whisht; *not; kept quiet*
The infant aith, half-form'd, was crusht; *oath; crushed*
I glowr'd as eerie's I'd been dusht, *stared; dumbstruck as; rammed*
In some wild glen; *valley*
When sweet, like *modest Worth*, she blusht,
And stepped ben. *inside*

Green, slender, leaf-clad *Holly-boughs*
Were twisted, gracefu', round her brows, *graceful[ly]*
I took her for some SCOTTISH MUSE,
By that same token;
And come to stop those reckless vows,
Would soon been broken.

A 'hair-brain'd, sentimental trace'
Was strongly marked in her face;
A wildly-witty, rustic grace
Shone full upon her;
Her *eye*, ev'n turn'd on empty space,
Beam'd keen with *Honor*.

Down flow'd her robe, a *tartan* sheen,
Till half a leg was scrimply seen; *barely*
And such a *leg!* my BESS, I ween, *think*
Could only peer it; *equal*
Sae straught, sae taper, tight and clean, *so straight*
Nane else came near it. *none*

Her *Mantle* large, of greenish hue,
My gazing wonder chiefly drew;
Deep *lights* and *shades*, bold-mingling, threw
A lustre grand;
And seem'd, to my astonish'd view,
A *well-known* Land.

Here, rivers in the sea were lost;
There, mountains to the skies were tost: *tossed, raised*
Here, tumbling billows mark'd the coast,
With surging foam;
There, distant shone, *Art's* lofty boast,
The lordly dome.

Here, DOON pour'd down his far-fetch'd floods; *the river Doon*
There, well-fed IRWINE stately thuds: *the river Irvine*
Auld, hermit AIRE staw thro' his woods, *old; the river Ayr stole*
On to the shore;
And many a lesser torrent scuds,
With seeming roar.

Low, in a sandy valley spread,
An ancient BOROUGH rear'd her head; *Ayr*
Still, as in *Scottish Story* read,
She boasts a *Race*,
To ev'ry nobler virtue bred,
And polish'd grace.

Duan Second.

With musing-deep, astonish'd stare,
I view'd the heavenly-seeming *Fair;*
A whisp'ring *throb* did witness bear
Of kindred sweet,
When with an elder Sister's air
She did me greet.

'All hail! *my own* inspired Bard!
In me thy native Muse regard!
Nor longer mourn thy fate is hard,
Thus poorly low!
I come to give thee such *reward*,
As *we* bestow.

Know, the great *Genius* of this Land,
Has many a light, aerial band,
Who, all beneath his high command,
Harmoniously,
As *Arts* or *Arms* they understand,
Their labors ply.

They SCOTIA'S Race among them share; *Scotland's*
Some fire the *Sodger* on to dare; *soldier*
Some rouse the *Patriot* up to bare
Corruption's heart:
Some teach the *Bard*, a darling care,
The tuneful Art.

'Mong swelling floods of reeking gore,
They ardent, kindling spirits pour;
Or, mid the venal Senate's roar, *amid*
They, sightless, stand,
To mend the honest *Patriot-lore*,
And grace the hand.

Hence, FULLARTON, the brave and young;
Hence, DEMPSTER'S truth-prevailing tongue;

Hence, sweet harmonious BEATTIE sung
    His 'Minstrel lays;'
Or tore, with noble ardour stung,
    The *Sceptic's* bays.

To lower Orders are assign'd,
The humbler ranks of Human-kind,
The rustic Bard, the lab'ring Hind, *farm-worker*
    The Artisan;
All chuse, as, various they're inclin'd, *choose*
    The various man.

When yellow waves the heavy grain,
The threat'ning *Storm*, some, strongly, rein;
Some teach to meliorate the plain,
    With *tillage-skill*;
And some instruct the Shepherd-train,
    Blythe o'er the hill.

Some hint the Lover's harmless wile;
Some grace the Maiden's artless smile;
Some soothe the Lab'rer's weary toil,
    For humble gains,
And make his *cottage-scenes* beguile
    His cares and pains.

Some, bounded to a district-space,
Explore at large Man's *infant race*,
To mark the embryotic trace, *embryonic*
    Of *rustic Bard*;
And careful note each op'ning grace,
    A guide and guard.

Of these am I—COILA my name;
And this district as mine I claim,
Where once the *Campbell's*, chiefs of fame, *a Scottish Highland clan*
    Held ruling pow'r:
I mark'd thy embryo-tuneful flame,
    Thy natal hour.

With future hope, I oft would gaze,
Fond, on thy little, early ways,
Thy rudely-caroll'd, chiming phrase,
          In uncouth rhymes,
Fir'd at the simple, artless lays
          Of other times.

I saw thee seek the sounding shore,
Delighted with the dashing roar;
Or when the *North* his fleecy store
          Drove thro' the sky,
I saw grim Nature's visage hoar,
          Struck thy young eye.

Or when the deep-green-mantl'd Earth,
Warm-cherish'd ev'ry floweret's birth,
And joy and music pouring forth,
          In ev'ry grove,
I saw thee eye the gen'ral mirth
          With boundless love.

When ripen'd fields, and azure skies,
Call'd forth the *Reaper's* rustling noise,
I saw thee leave their ev'ning joys,
          And lonely stalk,
To vent thy bosom's swelling rise,
          In pensive walk.

When *youthful Love*, warm-blushing, strong,
Keen-shivering shot thy nerves along,
Those accents, grateful to thy tongue,
          Th'adored *Name*,
I taught thee how to pour in song,
          To soothe thy flame.

I saw thy pulse's maddening play,
Wild-send thee Pleasure's devious way,
Misled by Fancy's *meteor-ray*,
          By Passion driven;
But yet the *light* that led astray,
          Was *light* from Heaven.

I taught thy manners-painting strains,
The *loves*, the *ways* of simple swains,
Till now, o'er all my wide domains,
Thy fame extends;
And some, the pride of *Coila's* plains,
Become thy friends.

Thou canst not learn, nor I can show,
To paint with *Thomson's* landscape-glow;
Or wake the bosom-melting throe,
With *Shenstone's* art;
Or pour, with *Gray*, the moving flow,
Warm on the heart.

Yet all beneath th' unrivall'd Rose,
The lowly Daisy sweetly blows;
Tho' large the forest's Monarch throws
His army shade, *many-armed*
Yet green the juicy Hawthorn grows,
Adown the glade.

Then never murmur nor repine;
Strive in thy *humble sphere* to shine;
And trust me, not *Potosi's mine*,
Nor *King's regard*,
Can give a bliss o'ermatching thine,
A *rustic Bard*.

To give my counsels all in one,
Thy *tuneful flame* still careful fan;
Preserve *the dignity of Man*,
With Soul erect;
And trust, the UNIVERSAL PLAN
Will all protect.

And wear thou this'—She solemn said,
And bound the *Holly* round my head:
The polish'd leaves, and berries red,
Did rustling play;
And, like a passing thought, she fled,
In light away.

To a Mouse

On turning her up in her Nest, with the Plough, November, 1785.

Wee, sleeket, cowran, tim'rous *beastie*,	*little, sleek, cowering*
O, what a panic's in thy breastie!	
Thou need na start awa sae hasty,	*not; away so*
Wi' bickering brattle!	*with quarrelsome chatter*
I wad be laith to rin an' chase thee,	*would; loath; run and*
Wi' murd'ring *pattle!*	*with; plough-staff*
I'm truly sorry Man's dominion	
Has broken Nature's social union,	
An' justifies that ill opinion,	*and*
Which makes thee startle,	
At me, thy poor, earth-born companion,	
An' *fellow-mortal!*	
I doubt na, whyles, but thou may *thieve;*	*not; sometimes*
What then? poor beastie, thou maun live!	*must*
A *daimen-icker* in a *thrave*	*occasional ear of corn; 24 sheaves*
'S a sma' request;	*small*
I'll get a blessin wi' the lave,	*rest*
An' never miss't!	
Thy wee-bit *housie*, too, in ruin!	*little house*
It's silly wa's the win's are strewin!	*walls; winds; strewing*
An' naething, now, to big a new ane,	*nothing; build; one*
O' foggage green!	*grass*
An' bleak *December's winds* ensuin,	*ensuing*
Baith snell an' keen!	*both sharp*
Thou saw the fields laid bare an' wast,	*waste*
An' weary *Winter* comin fast,	*coming*
An' cozie here, beneath the blast,	*cosy*
Thou thought to dwell,	
Till crash! the cruel *coulter* past	*ploughshare*
Out thro' thy cell.	

That wee-bit heap o' leaves an' stibble,	*little; of; stubble*
Has cost thee monie a weary nibble!	*many*
Now thou's turn'd out, for a' thy trouble,	*all*
But house or hald,	*without; dwelling*
To thole the Winter's *sleety dribble*,	*endure*
An' *cranreuch* cauld!	*hoar-frost cold*
But Mousie, thou art no thy-lane,	*not alone*
In proving *foresight* may be vain:	
The best laid schemes o' *Mice* an' *Men*,	*of*
Gang aft agley,	*go often wide of the aim*
An' lea'e us nought but grief an' pain,	*and leave*
For promis'd joy!	
Still, thou art blest, compared wi' *me!*	*with*
The *present* only toucheth thee:	
But Och! I *backward* cast my e'e,	*ah; eye*
On prospects drear!	
An' *forward*, tho' I canna *see*,	*cannot*
I *guess* an' *fear!*	

The Holy Fair.

A robe of seeming truth and trust
Hid crafty observation;
And secret hung, with poison'd crust,
The dirk of Defamation:
A mask that like the gorget show'd,
Dye-varying, on the pigeon;
And for a mantle large and broad,
He wrapt him in Religion.
HYPOCRISY A-LA-MODE.

Upon a simmer Sunday morn,	*summer*
When Nature's face is fair,	
I walked forth to view the corn,	
An' snuff the callor air.	*fresh*
The rising sun, our GALSTON Muirs,	*over*
Wi' glorious light was glintan;	*with; glinting*
The hares were hirplan down the furrs,	*limping; furrows*
The lav'rocks they were chantan	*larks; chanting*
Fu' sweet that day.	*full, very*
As lightsomely I glowr'd abroad,	*pleasantly; stared*
To see a scene sae gay,	*so*
Three *hizzies*, early at the road,	*women; on the road*
Cam skelpan up the way.	*came skipping*
Twa had manteeles o' dolefu' black,	*two; mantles; doleful*
But ane wi' lyart lining;	*one with red and white*
The third, that gaed a wee a-back,	*went a little behind*
Was in the fashion shining	
Fu' gay that day.	*full, very*
The *twa* appear'd like sisters twin,	*two*
In feature, form an claes;	*and clothes*
Their visage wither'd, lang an' thin,	*long*
An' sour as ony slaes:	*any sloes*

The *third* cam up, hap-step-an'-loup, *came; hop, step and jump*
As light as ony lambie, *any lamb*
An' wi' a curchie low did stoop, *with a curtsey*
As soon as e'er she saw me,
Fu' kind that day. *full, very*

Wi' bonnet aff, quoth I, 'Sweet lass, *off*
I think ye seem to ken me; *know*
I'm sure I've seen that bonie face, *pretty*
But yet I canna name ye.' *cannot*
Quo' she, an' laughan as she spak, *said; laughing; spoke*
An' taks me by the han's, *takes; hands*
'Ye, for my sake, hae gien the feck *have given the majority*
Of a' the *ten comman's* *all; Commandments*
A screed some day. *tear, rip*

My name is FUN—your cronie dear,
The nearest friend ye hae; *have*
An' this is SUPERSTITION here,
An' that's HYPOCRISY.
I'm gaun to [Mauchline] *holy fair*, *going*
To spend an hour in daffin: *larking about*
Gin ye'll go there, yon runkl'd pair, *if; that wrinkled*
We will get famous laughin
At them this day.'

Quoth I, 'With a' my heart, I'll do't; *with all*
I'll get my sunday's sark on, *shirt*
An' meet you on the holy spot;
Faith, we'se hae fine remarkin!' *we shall have*
Then I gaed hame at crowdie-time, *went home; porridge-time (breakfast)*
An' soon I made me ready;
For roads were clad, frae side to side, *from*
Wi' monie a wearie body, *many*
In droves that day.

Here, farmers gash, in ridin graith, *smart; dress*
Gaed hoddan by their cotters; *went jogging; tenants*
There, swankies young, in braw braid-claith, *strapping lads; fine broad-cloth*

Are springan owre the gutters. — *jumping over*
The lasses, skelpan barefit, thrang, — *skipping barefoot; throng*
In silks an' scarlets glitter;
Wi' *sweet-milk cheese*, in monie a whang, — *with; many; slice*
An' *farls*, bak'd wi' butter, — *oatcakes*
Fu' crump that day. — *full, very; crisp*

When by the *plate* we set our nose, — *offering or collection plate*
Weel heaped up wi' ha'pence, — *well; with halfpennies*
A greedy glowr *black-bonnet* throws, — *glare; the church elder*
An' we maun draw our tippence. — *must; two-pence*
Then in we go to see the show,
On ev'ry side they're gath'ran; — *gathering*
Some carryan dails, some chairs an' stools, — *carrying planks*
An' some are busy bleth'ran — *chattering*
Right loud that day.

Here stands a shed to fend the show'rs,
An' screen our countra Gentry; — *country*
There, *racer Jess*, an' twathree wh[o]res, — *two or three*
Are blinkan at the entry. — *smirking*
Here sits a raw o' tittlan jads, — *row of gossiping women*
Wi' heaving breasts an' bare neck;
An' there, a batch o' *Wabster lads*, — *weaver*
Blackguarding frae K[ilmarno]ck — *from*
For *fun* this day.

Here, some are thinkan on their sins, — *thinking*
An' some upo' their claes; — *upon; clothes*
Ane curses feet that fyl'd his shins, — *one; dirtied*
Anither sighs an' prays: — *another*
On this hand sits an *Elect* swatch, — *sample, group*
Wi' screw'd-up, grace-proud faces;
On that, a set o' chaps, at watch, — *of*
Thrang winkan on the lasses — *busy winking*
To *chairs* that day.

O happy is that man, an' blest! — *(from Psalm 146)*
Nae wonder that it pride him! — *no*

Whase ain dear lass, that he likes best, *whose own*
Comes clinkan down beside him! *flopping*
Wi' arm repos'd on the *chair-back*, *with*
He sweetly does compose him;
Which, by degrees, slips round her *neck*,
An's loof upon her *bosom* *and his palm*
Unkend that day. *undetected*

Now a' the congregation o'er *all*
Is silent expectation;
For [Sawney] speels the holy door, *climbs*
Wi' tidings o' s[a]lv[a]t[io]n. *with*
Should *Hornie*, as in ancient days, *the (horned) devil*
'Mang sons o' G[od] present him, *among; of*
The vera sight o' [Moodie]'s face, *very*
To's ain *het hame* had sent him *own hot home*
Wi' fright that day.

Hear how he clears the points o' Faith
Wi' rattlin an' thumpin!
Now meekly calm, now wild in wrath,
He's stampan, an' he's jumpan! *stamping; jumping*
His lengthen'd chin, his turn'd-up snout,
His eldritch squeel an' gestures, *unearthly squeal*
O how they fire the heart devout,
Like *cantharidian* plaisters *Spanish fly (aphrodisiac) plasters*
On sic a day! *such*

But hark! the *tent* has chang'd it's voice;
There's peace an' rest nae langer; *no longer*
For a' the *real judges* rise, *all*
They canna sit for anger. *cannot*
[Smith] opens out his cauld harangues, *cold*
On *practice* and on *morals;*
An' aff the *godly* pour in thrangs, *off; throngs*
To gie the jars an' barrels *give*
A lift that day.

What signifies his barren shine,
  Of *moral pow'rs* an' *reason?*
His English style, an' gesture fine,
  Are a' clean out o' season. *all; of*
Like SOCRATES or ANTONINE,
  Or some auld pagan heathen, *old*
The *moral man* he does define,
  But ne'er a word o' *faith* in *of*
    That's right that day.

In guid time comes an antidote *good*
  Against sic poosion'd nostrum; *such poisoned*
For [Peebles], frae the water-fit, *from; river mouth*
  Ascends the *holy rostrum:*
See, up he's got the word o' G[od],
  An' meek an' mim has view'd it, *prim*
While COMMON-SENSE has taen the road, *taken*
  An' aff, an' up the *Cowgate* *and off*
    Fast, fast that day.

Wee [Miller] niest, the Guard relieves, *little, next*
  An' Orthodoxy raibles, *gabbles*
Tho' in his heart he weel believes, *well*
  An' thinks it auld wives' fables: *old*
But faith! the birkie wants a *Manse*, *fellow; minister's place*
  So, cannilie he hums them; *craftily; fools*
Altho' his *carnal* Wit an' Sense
  Like hafflins-wise o'ercomes him *nearly overcomes*
    At times that day.

Now, butt an' ben, the Change-house fills, *front and back*
  Wi' *yill-caup* Commentators: *with ale-cup*
Here's crying out for bakes an' gills, *biscuits; small measures of whisky*
  An' there the pint-stowp clatters; *tankard*
While thick an' thrang, an' loud an' lang, *throng[ing]; long*
  Wi' *Logic*, an' wi' *Scripture*,
They raise a din, that, in the end,
  Is like to breed a rupture
    O' wrath that day.

Leeze me on Drink! it gies us mair — *I do like drink; gives; more*
  Than either School or Colledge: — *university*
It kindles Wit, it waukens Lear, — *rouses learning*
  It pangs us fou o' Knowledge. — *crams us full of*
Be't *whisky-gill* or *penny-wheep*, — *small beer*
  Or ony stronger potion, — *any*
It never fails, on drinkin deep,
  To kittle up our *notion*, — *stimulate; fancy*
    By night or day.

The lads an' lasses, blythely bent
  To mind baith *saul* an' *body*, — *both soul*
Sit round the table, weel content, — *well*
  An' steer about the *toddy*. — *pass*
On this ane's dress, an' that ane's leuk, — *one's; look*
  They're makin observations; — *making*
While some are cozie i' the neuk, — *in; corner*
  An' forming *assignations*
    To meet some day.

But now the L[ord]'s ain trumpet touts, — *own; toots, sounds*
  Till a' the hills are rairan, — *all; roaring*
An' echos back return the shouts;
  Black [Russel] is na spairan: — *not sparing*
His piercin words, like Highlan swords, — *Highland*
  Divide the joints an' marrow;
His talk o' H[e]ll, whare devils dwell, — *where*
  Our vera 'Sauls does harrow'[1] — *very souls*
    Wi' fright that day!

A vast, unbottom'd, boundless *Pit*,
  Fill'd fou o' *lowan brunstane*, — *full of flaming brimstone*
Whase raging flame, an' scorching heat, — *whose*
  Wad melt the hardest whun-stane! — *would; whin-stone*
The *half asleep* start up wi' fear,
  An' think they hear it roaran, — *roaring*

1 Shakespeare's Hamlet [Burns's note, referring to *Hamlet*, I.v.15].

When presently it does appear,	
’Twas but some neebor *snoran*	*neighbour snoring*
Asleep that day.	
’Twad be owre lang a tale to tell,	*it would; over long*
How monie stories past,	*many*
An’ how they crouded to the yill,	*crowded; ale*
When they were a’ dismist:	*all*
How drink gaed round, in cogs an’ caups,	*went; wooden cups and bowls*
Amang the furms an’ benches;	*among; forms*
An’ *cheese* an’ *bread*, frae women’s laps,	*from*
Was dealt about in lunches,	*chunks*
An’ dawds that day.	*lumps*
In comes a gawsie, gash *Guidwife*,	*jolly, talkative goodwife*
An’ sits down by the fire,	
Syne draws her *kebbuck* an’ her knife;	*then; cheese*
The lasses they are shyer.	
The auld *Guidmen*, about the *grace*,	*old goodmen*
Frae side to side they bother,	*from*
Till some ane by his bonnet lays,	*one*
An’ gies them’t, like a *tether*,	*gives; rope*
Fu’ lang that day.	*very long*
Waesucks! for him that gets nae lass,	*alas; no*
Or lasses that hae naething!	*have nothing*
Sma’ need has he to say a grace,	*small*
Or melvie his braw claithing!	*cover his fine clothing with crumbs*
O *Wives* be mindfu’, ance yoursel,	*mindful; once yourselves*
How bonie lads ye wanted,	*fine*
An’ dinna, for a *kebbuck-heel*,	*do not; cheese-end*
Let lasses be affronted	
On sic a day!	*such*
Now *Clinkumbell*, wi’ rattlan tow,	*rattling bell-rope*
Begins to jow an’ croon;	*toll and sing*
Some swagger hame, the best they dow,	*home; can*
Some wait the afternoon.	

<table>
<tr><td>At slaps the billies halt a blink,</td><td>gaps in walls and hedges; lads; moment</td></tr>
<tr><td>   Till lasses strip their shoon:</td><td>shoes</td></tr>
<tr><td>Wi' faith an' hope, an' love an' drink,</td><td></td></tr>
<tr><td>   They're a' in famous tune</td><td>all</td></tr>
<tr><td>   For crack that day.</td><td>gossip</td></tr>
<tr><td> </td><td></td></tr>
<tr><td>How monie hearts this day converts,</td><td>many</td></tr>
<tr><td>   O' sinners and o' Lasses!</td><td>of</td></tr>
<tr><td>Their hearts o' stane, gin night are gane,</td><td>stone; before; gone, turned</td></tr>
<tr><td>   As saft as ony flesh is.</td><td>soft; any</td></tr>
<tr><td>There's some are fou o' love divine;</td><td>full of</td></tr>
<tr><td>   There's some are fou o' brandy;</td><td></td></tr>
<tr><td>An' monie jobs that day begin,</td><td>many</td></tr>
<tr><td>   May end in Houghmagandie</td><td>fornication</td></tr>
<tr><td>   Some ither day.</td><td>other</td></tr>
</table>

The Twa Dogs, A Tale.

'Twas in that place o' Scotland's isle, *of*
That bears the name o' auld king COIL, *old*
Upon a bonie day in June, *pleasant*
When wearing thro' the afternoon,
Twa Dogs, that were na thrang at hame, *two; not busy; home*
Forgather'd ance upon a time. *met once*

The first I'll name, they ca'd him *Cæsar*, *called*
Was keepet for His Honor's pleasure; *kept*
His hair, his size, his mouth, his lugs, *ears*
Shew'd he was nane o' Scotland's dogs, *showed; none of*
But whalpet some place far abroad, *whelped*
Where sailors gang to fish for Cod. *go*

His locked, letter'd, braw brass-collar *fine*
Shew'd him the *gentleman* an' *scholar*; *showed; and*
But tho' he was o' high degree, *of*
The fient a pride na pride had he, *not a bit of; no*
But wad hae spent an hour caressan, *would have; caressing*
Ev'n wi' a Tinkler-gipsey's *messan:* *with; mongrel*
At Kirk or Market, Mill or Smiddie, *church; smithy*
Nae tawted *tyke*, tho' e'er sae duddie, *no shaggy dog; so ragged*
But he wad stan't, as glad to see him, *would [have] stood*
An' stroan't on stanes an' hillocks wi' him. *and pissed; stones; with*

The tither was a *ploughman's collie*, *other*
A rhyming, ranting, raving billie, *romping; fellow*
Wha for his friend an' comrade had him, *who; and*
And in his freaks had *Luath* ca'd him, *foolishness; called*
After some dog in[1] *Highland sang*, *song*
Was made lang syne, lord knows how lang. *long ago*

1 Cuchullin's dog in Ossian's Fingal [Burns's note, referring to the epic poem 'Fingal' (1762) that James Macpherson (1736–96) claimed to have translated from Scottish Gaelic].

He was a gash an' faithfu' *tyke*, — *shrewd and faithful dog*
As ever lap a sheugh or dyke. — *leapt; ditch; wall*
His honest, sonsie, baws'nt face, — *friendly; with a white patch*
Ay gat him friends in ilka place; — *always got; every*
His breast was white, his towzie back, — *tangled*
Weel clad wi' coat o' glossy black; — *well; with; of*
His gawsie tail, wi' upward curl, — *ample*
Hung owre his hurdie's wi' a swirl. — *over; hindquarters with*

Nae doubt but they were fain o' ither, — *no; fond of each other*
An' unco pack an' thick thegither; — *and extraordinarily close; together*
Wi' social nose whyles snuff'd an' snowket; — *with; sometimes; poked*
Whyles mice and modewurks they howket; — *sometimes; moles; dug up*
Whyles scour'd awa in lang excursion, — *rushed away; long*
An' worry'd ither in diversion; — *and worried each other*
Till tir'd at last wi' mony a farce, — *with many*
They set them down upon their arse,
An' there began a lang digression — *long*
About the *lords o' the creation*. — *of*

CÆSAR.

I've aften wonder'd, honest *Luath*, — *often*
What sort o' life poor dogs like you have; — *of*
An' when the *gentry's* life I saw, — *and*
What way *poor bodies* liv'd ava. — *at all*

Our *Laird* gets in his racked rents, — *lord, landowner*
His coals, his kane, an' a' his stents: — *payment in kind; all; duties*
He rises when he likes himsel; — *himself*
His flunkies answer at the bell;
He ca's his coach; he ca's his horse; — *calls*
He draws a bonie, silken purse — *fine*
As lang's my tail, whare thro' the steeks, — *long as; where; stitches*
The yellow letter'd *Geordie* keeks. — *guinea coin peeps out*

Frae morn to een it's nought but toiling, — *from; evening*
At baking, roasting, frying, boiling;
An' tho' the gentry first are steghan, — *stuffing with food*
Yet ev'n the *ha' folk* fill their peghan — *hall folk, servants; stomach*

Wi' sauce, ragouts, an' sic like trashtrie,	*such kind of rubbish*
That's little short o' downright wastrie.	*wastefulness*
Our *Whipper-in*, wee, blasted wonner,	*dogkeeper; little, dwarfish wonder*
Poor, worthless elf, it eats a dinner,	
Better than ony *Tenant-man*	*any*
His Honor has in a' the lan':	*all the land*
An' what poor *Cot-folk* pit their painch in,	*cottage-folk put; paunch*
I own it's past my comprehension.	
Luath.	
Trowth, Cæsar, whyles their fash't enough;	*truth; sometimes they're troubled*
A *Cotter* howkan in a sheugh,	*farm-worker digging; ditch*
Wi' dirty stanes biggan a dyke,	*with; stones building; wall*
Bairan a quarry, an' sic like,	*clearing; and similar things*
Himsel, a wife, he thus sustains,	*himself*
A smytrie o' wee, duddie weans,	*clutch of small, ragged children*
An' nought but his han'-daurk, to keep	*hand-labour*
Them right an' tight in thack an' raep.	*thatch and thatch-rope*
An' when they meet wi' sair disasters,	*sore, severe*
Like loss o' health or want o' masters,	
Ye maist wad think, a wee touch langer,	*almost would; small; longer*
An' they maun starve o' cauld an' hunger:	*must; of cold*
But how it comes, I never kent yet,	*knew*
They're maistly wonderfu' contented;	*mostly wonderful[ly]*
An' buirdly chiels, and clever hizzies,	*burly fellows; girls*
Are bred in sic a way as this is.	*such*
Cæsar.	
But then, to see how ye're negleket,	*neglected*
How huff'd, an' cuff'd, an' disrespeket!	*scorned; disrespected*
L[or]d man, our gentry care as little	
For *delvers*, *ditchers*, an' sic cattle;	*diggers, labourers; and such*
They gang as saucy by poor folk,	*go*
As I wad by a stinkan brock.	*would; stinking badger*
I've notic'd, on our Laird's *court-day*,	*lord's*
An' mony a time my heart's been wae,	*many; woe*
Poor *tenant bodies*, scant o' cash,	*people*
How they maun thole a *factor's* snash;	*must endure; manager's abuse*

He'll stamp an' threaten, curse an' swear,	
He'll *apprehend* them, *poind* their gear;	*impound; possessions*
While they maun stan', wi' aspect humble,	*must stand*
An' hear it a', an' fear an' tremble!	*all*
I see how folk live that hae riches;	*have*
But surely poor-folk maun be wretches!	*must*
Luath.	
They're no sae wretched 's ane wad think;	*not so wretched as one would*
Tho' constantly on poortith's brink,	*poverty's*
They're sae accustom'd wi' the sight,	*so*
The view o't gies them little fright.	*of it gives*
Then chance and fortune are sae guided,	*so*
They're ay in less or mair provided;	*always; more*
An' tho' fatigu'd wi' close employment,	*with*
A blink o' rest's a sweet enjoyment.	*moment of*
The dearest comfort o' their lives,	
Their grushie weans an' faithfu' wives;	*thriving children; faithful*
The *prattling things* are just their pride,	
That sweetens a' their fire side.	*all*
An' whyles twalpennie-worth o' *nappy*	*sometimes; twelvepence-; ale*
Can mak the bodies unco happy;	*make; extraordinarily*
They lay aside their private cares,	
To mind the Kirk and State affairs;	*church*
They'll talk o' *patronage* an' *priests*,	
Wi' kindling fury i' their breasts,	*in*
Or tell what new taxation's comin,	*coming*
An' ferlie at the folk in LON'ON.	*marvel; London*
As bleak-fac'd Hallowmass returns,	*All Saints' Day (1 November)*
They get the jovial, rantan *Kirns*,	*merry harvest-home celebration*
When *rural life*, of ev'ry station,	
Unite in common recreation;	
Love blinks, Wit slaps, an' social Mirth	
Forgets there's *care* upo' the earth.	*upon*

That *merry day* the year begins,
They bar the door on frosty win's; *winds*
The nappy reeks wi' mantling ream, *ale steams; overflowing froth*
An' sheds a heart-inspiring steam;
The luntan pipe, an' sneeshin mill, *smoking; snuff box*
Are handed round wi' right guid will; *good*
The cantie, auld folks, crackan crouse, *cheerful old; chatting cheerfully*
The young anes rantan thro' the house— *ones romping*
My heart has been sae fain to see them, *so glad*
That I for joy hae barket wi' them. *have barked with*

Still it's owre true that ye hae said, *over, very; have*
Sic game is now owre aften play'd; *such; very often*
There's mony a creditable *stock* *many*
O' decent, honest, fawsont folk, *orderly*
Are riven out baith root an' branch, *torn; both*
Some rascal's pridefu' greed to quench, *prideful*
Wha thinks to knit himsel the faster *who; himself*
In favor wi' some *gentle Master*, *with*
Wha aiblins thrang a *parliamentin*, *who perhaps busy a-parliamenting*
For Britain's guid his saul indentin— *good; soul indenting*

CÆSAR.
Haith lad ye little ken about it; *my goodness; know*
For Britain's guid! guid faith! I doubt it. *good*
Say rather, gaun as PREMIERS lead him, *going; prime ministers*
An' saying *aye* or *no*'s they bid him: *yes or no as*
At Operas an' Plays parading,
Mortgaging, gambling, masquerading:
Or maybe, in a frolic daft,
To HAGUE or CALAIS takes a waft,
To make a *tour* an' tak a whirl, *take*
To learn *bon ton* an' see the worl'. *high classiness; world*

There, at VIENNA or VERSAILLES,
He rives his father's auld entails; *tears; old inheritance*
Or by MADRID he takes the rout, *way*
To thrum *guittars* an' fecht wi' nowt; *and fight with cattle*
Or down *Italian Vista* startles,

Wh[o]re-hunting amang groves o' myrtles: — *among*
Then bowses drumlie *German-water*, — *boozes cloudy spa-water*
To mak himsel look fair and fatter, — *make himself*
An' purge the bitter ga's an' cankers, — *galls*
O' curst *Venetian* b[o]res an' ch[a]ncres. — *holes and ulcers*

For Britain's guid! for her destruction! — *good*
Wi' dissipation, feud an' faction!

LUATH.
Hech man! dear sirs! is that the gate, — *hey; way*
They waste sae mony a braw estate! — *so many; fine*
Are we sae foughten and harass'd — *so worn out*
For gear to gang that gate at last! — *possessions; go; way*

O would they stay aback frae courts, — *from*
An' please themsels wi' countra sports, — *themselves; country*
It wad for ev'ry ane be better, — *would; one*
The *Laird*, the *Tenant*, an' the *Cotter!* — *lord, landowner*
For thae frank, rantan, ramblan billies, — *those; ranting, rambling fellows*
Feint haet o' them's ill hearted fellows; — *hardly any of*
Except for breakin o' their timmer, — *breaking; timber*
Or speakin lightly o' their *Limmer*, — *speaking; mistress*
Or shootin of a hare or moorcock, — *shooting*
The ne'er-a-bit they're ill to poor folk.

But will ye tell me, master *Cæsar*,
Sure *great folk's* life's a life o' pleasure?
Nae cauld nor hunger e'er can steer them, — *no cold; disturb*
The vera thought o't need na fear them. — *very; of it; not frighten*

CÆSAR.
L[or]d man, were ye but whyles where I am, — *sometimes*
The *gentles* ye wad neer envy them! — *would never*

It's true, they need na starve or sweat, — *not*
Thro' Winter's cauld, or Summer's heat; — *cold*
They've nae sair-wark to craze their banes, — *no hardship; bones*
An' fill *auld-age* wi' grips an' granes; — *old-; gripes and groans*
But *human-bodies* are sic fools, — *such*

For a' their colledges an' schools,
That when nae *real* ills perplex them, *no*
They *mak* enow themsels to vex them; *make enough themselves*
An' ay the less they hae to sturt them, *always; have; annoy*
In like proportion, less will hurt them.

A country fellow at the pleugh, *plough*
His *acre's* till'd, he's right eneugh; *enough*
A country girl at her wheel, *spinning-wheel*
Her *dizzen's* done, she's unco weel; *dozen is; very well*
But Gentlemen, an' Ladies warst, *and; worst*
Wi' ev'n down *want o' wark* are curst. *lack of work; cursed*
They loiter, lounging, lank an' lazy; *languid*
Tho' deil-haet ails them, yet uneasy; *damned little*
Their days, insipid, dull an' tasteless,
Their nights, unquiet, lang an' restless. *long*

An' ev'n their sports, their balls an' races,
Their galloping thro' public places,
There's sic parade, sic pomp an' art, *such*
The joy can scarcely reach the heart.

The *Men* cast out in *party-matches*, *quarrel; card-contests*
Then sowther a' in deep debauches. *patch up all*
Ae night, they're mad wi' drink an' wh[o]ring, *one*
Niest day their life is past enduring. *next*

The *Ladies* arm-in-arm in clusters,
As great an' gracious a' as sisters; *all*
But hear their *absent thoughts* o' ither, *of [each] other*
They're a' run deils an' jads thegither. *all; devils; hussies together*
Whyles, owre the wee bit cup an' platie, *sometimes; over; little; plate*
They sip the *scandal-potion* pretty;
Or lee-lang nights, wi' crabbet leuks, *live-long; crabbed looks*
Pore owre the devil's *pictur'd beuks*; *over; books (playing cards)*
Stake on a chance a farmer's stackyard,
An' cheat like ony *unhang'd blackguard*. *any*

There's some exceptions, man an' woman;
But this is Gentry's life in common.

By this, the sun was out o' sight,
An' darker gloamin brought the night: *dusk*
The *bum-clock* humm'd wi' lazy drone, *cockchafer beetle*
The kye stood rowtan i' the loan; *cows; bellowing; cattle-track*
When up they gat an' shook their lugs, *got; ears*
Rejoic'd they were na *men* but *dogs;* *not*
An' each took off his several way, *and*
Resolv'd to meet some ither day. *other*

The Cotter's Saturday Night.

Inscribed to R. A[iken], Esq.

Let not Ambition mock their useful toil,
Their homely joys, and destiny obscure;
Nor Grandeur hear, with a disdainful smile,
The short and simple annals of the Poor.

GRAY.

My lov'd, my honor'd, much respected friend,
No mercenary Bard his homage pays;
With honest pride, I scorn each selfish end,
My dearest meed, a friend's esteem and praise: *reward*
To you I sing, in simple Scottish lays,
The *lowly train* in life's sequester'd scene;
The native feelings strong, the guileless ways,
What A[iken] in a *Cottage* would have been;
Ah! tho' his worth unknown, far happier there I ween! *think*

November chill blaws loud wi' angry sugh; *blows; with; roaring*
The short'ning winter-day is near a close;
The miry beasts retreating frae the pleugh; *from; plough*
The black'ning trains o' craws to their repose: *of crows*
The toil-worn COTTER frae his labour goes, *from*
This night his weekly moil is at an end, *toil*
Collects his *spades*, his *mattocks* and his *hoes*,
Hoping the *morn* in ease and rest to spend,
And weary, o'er the moor, his course does hameward bend. *homeward*

At length his lonely *Cot* appears in view, *cottage*
Beneath the shelter of an aged tree;
The expectant *wee-things*, toddlan, stacher through *little-; toddling; stagger*
To meet their *Dad*, wi' flichterin noise and glee. *fluttering like nestlings*
His wee-bit ingle, blinkan bonilie, *small fire; blinking prettily*
His clean hearth-stane, his thrifty *Wifie's* smile, *-stone*
The *lisping infant*, prattling on his knee,
Does a' his weary *kiaugh* and care beguile, *all; anxiety*
And makes him quite forget his labor and his toil.

Belyve, the *elder bairns* come drapping in, *soon; dropping*
At *Service* out, amang the Farmers roun'; *among; round [about]*
Some ca' the pleugh, some herd, some tentie rin *drive; plough; run with care*
A cannie errand to a neebor town: *prudent; neighbour[ing]*
Their eldest hope, their *Jenny*, woman-grown,
In youthfu' bloom, Love sparkling in her e'e, *youthful; eye*
Comes hame, perhaps, to shew a braw new gown, *home; show; fine*
Or deposite her sair-won penny-fee, *sore-*
To help her *Parents* dear, if they in hardship be.

With joy unfeign'd, *brothers* and *sisters* meet,
And each for other's weelfare kindly spiers: *welfare; asks*
The social hours, swift-wing'd, unnotic'd fleet;
Each tells the uncos that he sees or hears. *news*
The Parents partial eye their hopeful years;
Anticipation forward points the view;
The *Mother*, wi' her needle and her sheers, *with; scissors*
Gars auld claes look amaist as weel's the new; *makes old clothes; almost; well*
The *Father* mixes a' wi' admonition due. *all with*

Their Master's and their Mistress's command,
The *youngkers* a' are warned to obey; *youngsters all*
And mind their labors wi' an eydent hand, *with; diligent*
And ne'er, tho' out o' sight, to jauk or play: *never; of; idle*
'And O! be sure to fear the LORD alway!
And mind your *duty*, duely, morn and night! *duly*
Lest in temptation's path ye gang astray, *go*
Implore his *counsel* and assisting *might:*
They never sought in vain that sought the LORD aright.'

But hark! a rap comes gently to the door;
Jenny, wha kens the meaning o' the same, *who knows*
Tells how a neebor lad came o'er the moor, *neighbour[ing]*
To do some errands, and convoy her hame. *home*
The wily Mother sees the *conscious flame*
Sparkle in *Jenny's* e'e, and flush her cheek, *eye*
With heart-struck, anxious care enquires his name,
While *Jenny* hafflins is afraid to speak; *half, partly*
Weel-pleased the Mother hears, it's nae wild, worthless *Rake*. *well-; no*

With kindly welcome, *Jenny* brings him ben; *inside*
A *strappan youth*; he takes the Mother's eye; *strapping*
Blythe *Jenny* sees the *visit's* no ill taen; *not; taken*
The Father cracks of horses, pleughs and kye. *talks; ploughs; cattle*
The *Youngster's* artless heart o'erflows wi' joy, *with*
But blate an' laithfu', scarce can weel behave; *modest; shy; well*
The Mother, wi' a woman's wiles, can spy *with*
What makes the *youth* sae bashfu' and sae grave; *so bashful*
Weel-pleas'd to think her *bairn's* respected like the lave. *well-; child is; rest*

O happy love! where love like this is found!
O heart-felt raptures! bliss beyond compare!
I've paced much this weary, *mortal round*,
And sage EXPERIENCE bids me this declare—
'If Heaven a draught of heavenly pleasure spare,
One *cordial* in this melancholy *Vale*,
'Tis when a youthful, loving, *modest* Pair,
In other's arms, breathe out the tender tale,
Beneath the milk-white thorn that scents the ev'ning gale.'

Is there, in human form, that bears a heart—
A Wretch! a Villain! lost to love and truth!
That can, with studied, sly, ensnaring art,
Betray sweet Jenny's unsuspecting youth?
Curse on his perjur'd arts! dissembling smooth!
Are *Honor*, *Virtue*, *Conscience*, all exil'd?
Is there no Pity, no relenting Ruth,
Points to the Parents fondling o'er their Child?
Then paints the *ruin'd Maid*, and *their* distraction wild!

But now the Supper crowns their simple board,
The halesome *Porritch*, chief of SCOTIA'S food: *wholesome porridge*
The soupe their *only Hawkie* does afford, *drink; cow*
That 'yont the hallan snugly chows her cood: *beyond; partition; chews; cud*
The *Dame* brings forth, in complimental mood,
To grace the lad, her weel-hain'd kebbuck, fell, *well-kept cheese, pungent*
And aft he's prest, and aft he ca's it guid; *often; calls; good*
The frugal *Wifie*, garrulous, will tell,
How 'twas a towmond auld, sin' Lint was i' the bell.
year old, since flax; in flower

The cheerfu' Supper done, wi' serious face, *cheerful*
  They, round the ingle, form a circle wide; *fire*
The Sire turns o'er, with patriarchal grace,
  The big *ha'-Bible*, ance his *Father's* pride: *family-Bible; once*
His bonnet rev'rently is laid aside,
  His *lyart haffets* wearing thin and bare; *grizzled side-locks*
Those strains that once did sweet in ZION glide,
  He wales a portion with judicious care; *chooses*
'*And let us worship GOD*!' he says with solemn air.

They chant their artless notes in simple guise;
  They tune their *hearts*, by far the noblest aim:
Perhaps *Dundee's* wild warbling measures rise, *(a psalm tune)*
  Or plaintive *Martyrs*, worthy of the name; *(a psalm tune)*
Or noble *Elgin* beets the heaven-ward flame, *(a psalm tune); kindles*
  The sweetest far of SCOTIA'S holy lays:
Compar'd with these, *Italian trills* are tame;
  The tickl'd ears no heart-felt raptures raise;
Nae unison hae they, with our CREATOR'S praise. *no; have*

The priest-like Father reads the sacred page,
  How *Abram* was the friend of GOD on high;
Or, *Moses* bade eternal warfare wage,
  With *Amalek's* ungracious progeny;
Or how the *royal Bard* did groaning lye, *King David*
  Beneath the stroke of Heaven's avenging ire;
Or *Job's* pathetic plaint, and wailing cry;
  Or rapt *Isaiah's* wild, seraphic fire;
Or other *Holy Seers* that tune the *sacred lyre*.

Perhaps the *Christian Volume* is the theme,
  How *guiltless blood* for *guilty man* was shed;
How HE, who bore in heaven the second name,
  Had not on Earth whereon to lay His head:
How His first *followers* and *servants* sped;
  The *Precepts sage* they wrote to many a land:
How *he*, who lone in *Patmos* banished, *St John the Divine*
  Saw in the sun a mighty angel stand;
And heard great *Bab'lon's* doom pronounc'd by Heaven's command.

Then kneeling down to HEAVEN'S ETERNAL KING,
The *Saint*, the *Father*, and the *Husband* prays:
Hope 'springs exulting on triumphant wing,'[1]
That *thus* they all shall meet in future days:
There, ever bask in *uncreated rays*,
No more to sigh, or shed the bitter tear,
Together hymning their CREATOR'S praise,
In *such society*, yet still more dear;
While circling Time moves round in an eternal sphere.

Compar'd with *this*, how poor Religion's pride,
In all the pomp of *method*, and of *art*,
When men display to congregations wide,
Devotion's ev'ry grace, except the *heart!*
The POWER, incens'd, the Pageant will desert,
The pompous strain, the sacredotal stole;
But haply, in some *Cottage* far apart,
May hear, well pleas'd, the language of the *Soul;*
And in His *Book of Life* the Inmates poor enroll.

Then homeward all take off their sev'ral way;
The youngling *Cottagers* retire to rest:
The Parent-pair their *secret homage* pay,
And proffer up to Heaven the warm request,
That HE who stills the *raven's* clam'rous nest,
And decks the *lily* fair in flow'ry pride,
Would, in the way *His Wisdom* sees the best,
For *them* and for their *little ones* provide;
But chiefly, in their hearts with *Grace divine* preside.

From scenes like these, old SCOTIA'S grandeur springs,
That makes her lov'd at home, rever'd abroad:
Princes and lords are but the breath of kings,
'An honest man's the noble work of GOD:'
And *certes*, in fair Virtue's heavenly road, *surely*
The *Cottage* leaves the *Palace* far behind:

1 Pope's 'Windsor Forest.' [Burns's note, referring to line 112 of *Windsor-Forest* (1713) by Alexander Pope (1688–1744)].

What is a lordling's pomp? a cumbrous load,
    Disguising oft the *wretch* of human kind,
Studied in arts of Hell, in wickedness refin'd!

O SCOTIA! my dear, my native soil!
    For whom my warmest wish to heaven is sent!
Long may thy hardy sons of *rustic toil*,
    Be blest with health, and peace, and sweet content!
And O may Heaven their simple lives prevent
    From *Luxury's* contagion, weak and vile!
Then howe'er *crowns* and *coronets* be rent,
    A *virtuous Populace* may rise the while,
And stand a wall of fire around their much-lov'd ISLE.

O THOU! who pour'd the *patriotic tide*,
    That stream'd thro' great, unhappy WALLACE' heart;
Who dar'd to, nobly, stem tyrannic pride,
    Or *nobly die*, the second glorious part:
(The Patriot's GOD, peculiarly thou art,
    His *friend*, *inspirer*, *guardian* and *reward!*)
O never, never SCOTIA's realm desert,
    But still the *Patriot*, and the *Patriot-Bard*,
In bright succession raise, her *Ornament* and *Guard!*

Address to the Deil.

O Prince, O chief of many throned pow'rs,
That led th'embattl'd Seraphim to war—
MILTON [*Paradise Lost*, Book I, lines 128–9].

O Thou, whatever title suit thee!
Auld Hornie, Satan, Nick, or Clootie, — *old Horned One; Hoofy*
Wha in yon cavern grim an' sootie, — *who; that; and*
Clos'd under hatches,
Spairges about the brunstane cootie, — *spatters; brimstone basin*
To scaud poor wretches! — *scald*

Hear me, *auld Hangie*, for a wee, — *old hangman; little*
An' let poor, *damned bodies* bee; — *and; be*
I'm sure sma' pleasure it can gie, — *small; give*
Ev'n to a *deil*, — *devil*
To skelp an' scaud poor dogs like me, — *strike and scald*
An' hear us squeel! — *squeal*

Great is thy pow'r, an' great thy fame;
Far kend an' noted is thy name; — *known*
An' tho' yon *lowan heugh's* thy hame, — *flaming cleft is; home*
Thou travels far;
An' faith! thou's neither lag nor lame, — *slow*
Nor blate nor scaur. — *shy nor timid*

Whyles, ranging like a roaran lion, — *sometimes; roaring*
For prey, a' holes an' corners tryin; — *all*
Whyles, on the strong-wing'd Tempest flyin, — *flying*
Tirlan the *kirks;* — *unroofing; churches*
Whyles, in the human bosom pryin, — *prying*
Unseen thou lurks.

I've heard my rev'rend *Graunie* say, — *grandmother*
In lanely glens ye like to stray; — *lonely valleys*
Or where auld, ruin'd castles, gray, — *old*
Nod to the moon,

Ye fright the nightly wand'rer's way,	
Wi' eldritch croon.	*unearthly moaning*
When twilight did my *Graunie* summon,	*grandmother*
To say her pray'rs, douse, honest woman!	*decent*
Aft 'yont the dyke she's heard you bumman,	*often beyond the wall; buzzing*
Wi' eerie drone;	*with*
Or, rustling, thro' the boortrees coman,	*elder trees coming*
Wi' heavy groan.	
Ae dreary, windy, winter night,	*one*
The stars shot down wi' sklentan light,	*slanting*
Wi' you, *mysel*, I gat a fright,	*myself; got*
Ayont the lough;	*beyond; lake*
Ye, like a *rash-buss*, stood in sight,	*clump of rushes*
Wi' waving sugh.	*sigh*
The cudgel in my nieve did shake,	*fist*
Each bristl'd hair stood like a stake,	
When wi' an eldritch, stoor *quaick, quaick*,	*unearthly, hoarse*
Amang the springs,	*among*
Awa ye squatter'd like a *drake*,	*away; splashed*
On whistling wings.	
Let *Warlocks* grim, an' wither'd *Hags*,	*and*
Tell how wi' you on ragweed nags,	*with*
They skim the muirs an' dizzy crags,	*moors*
Wi' wicked speed;	
And in kirk-yards renew their leagues,	*church-yards*
Owre howcket dead.	*over dug up*
Thence, countra wives, wi' toil an' pain,	*country*
May plunge an' plunge the *kirn* in vain;	*churn*
For Oh! the yellow treasure's taen	*taken*
By witching skill;	
An' dawtet, twal-pint *Hawkie's* gane	*the petted, twelve-pint cow has become*
As yell's the Bill.	*dry as the bull*
Thence, mystic knots mak great abuse,	*make*
On *Young-Guidmen*, fond, keen an' croose;	*householders; self-satisfied*

When the best *wark-lume* i' the house, *tool*
By cantraip wit, *magical*
Is instant made no worth a louse, *not*
Just at the bit.

When thowes dissolve the snawy hoord, *thaws; snowy hoard*
An' float the jinglan icy boord, *jingling; surface*
Then, *Water-kelpies* haunt the foord, *water-sprites; ford*
By your direction,
An' nighted Trav'llers are allur'd *and*
To their destruction.

An' aft your moss-traversing *Spunkies* *often; bog-; will-o'-the-wisps*
Decoy the wight that late an' drunk is: *man*
The bleezan, curst, mischievous monkies *blazing; monkeys*
Delude his eyes,
Till in some miry slough he sunk is, *hollow*
Ne'er mair to rise. *never more*

When MASONS' mystic *word* an' *grip*, *freemasons'; handshake*
In storms an' tempests raise you up,
Some cock or cat, your rage maun stop, *must*
Or, strange to tell!
The *youngest Brother* ye wad whip *would*
Aff straught to *H[e]ll.* *off straight*

Lang syne in EDEN'S bonie yard, *long ago; pleasant*
When youthfu' lovers first were pair'd, *youthful*
An' all the Soul of Love they shar'd,
The raptur'd hour,
Sweet on the fragrant, flow'ry swaird, *sward*
In shady bow'r.

Then you, ye auld, snick-drawing dog! *old; latch-lifting, stealthy*
Ye cam to Paradise incog, *came; incognito*
An' play'd on man a cursed brogue, *trick*
(Black be your fa'!) *fall*
An' gied the infant warld a shog, *gave; world; jolt*
'Maist ruin'd a'. *almost; all*

D’ye mind that day, when in a bizz, *remember; bustle*
Wi’ reeket duds, an’ reestet gizz, *smoky clothes; smoked face*
Ye did present your smoutie phiz *smutty face*
’Mang better folk, *among*
An’ sklented on the *man of Uzz*, *aimed sideways*
Your spitefu’ joke? *spiteful*

An how ye gat him i’ your thrall, *and; got; in; power*
An’ brak him out o’ house an’ hal’, *broke; of; hold*
While scabs an’ botches did him gall, *skin-boils*
Wi’ bitter claw, *scratching*
An’ lows’d his ill-tongu’d, wicked *Scawl* *loosed; scold*
Was warst ava? *worst of all*

But a’ your doings to rehearse, *all*
Your wily snares an’ fechtin fierce, *fighting*
Sin’ that day[1] MICHAEL did you pierce, *since*
Down to this time,
Wad ding a’ *Lallan* tongue, or *Erse*, *would overcome; all Lowland; Gaelic*
In Prose or Rhyme.

An’ now, auld *Cloots*, I ken ye’re thinkan, *old; know; thinking*
A certain *Bardie’s* rantin, drinkin, *minor poet’s; roistering, drinking*
Some luckless hour will send him linkan, *tripping*
To your black pit;
But faith! he’ll turn a corner jinkan, *jinking*
An’ cheat you yet.

But fare-you-weel, auld *Nickie-ben*! *farewell, old*
O wad ye tak a thought an’ men’! *would; take; mend*
Ye aiblins might—I dinna ken— *perhaps; do not know*
Still hae a *stake*— *have a chance*
I’m wae to think upo’ yon den, *woe; upon*
Ev’n for your sake!

1 Vide Milton, Book 6th [Burns’s note, referrring to Book 6 of Milton’s *Paradise Lost* (1667), in which the Archangel Michael fights Satan and the rebel angels in Heaven].

Brose and Butter.

Jenny sits up i' the laft, *in; loft*
Jockie wad fain a been at her; *would gladly have*
But there cam a wind out o' the west *came; of*
Made a' the winnocks to clatter. *all; windows*

O gie my love brose, lasses; *give; oatmeal and hot water*
O gie my love brose and butter;
For nane in Carrick wi' him *none; south Ayrshire; with*
Can gie a c[un]t its supper.

The laverock lo'es the grass, *lark loves*
The paetrick lo'es the stibble: *partridge; stubble*
And hey, for the gardiner lad,
To gully awa wi' his dibble! *slash away with; seed-hole maker*
O gie, &c.

My daddie sent me to the hill
To pu' my minnie some heather: *pull; mother*
An drive it in your fill, *and*
Ye're welcome to the leather.
O gie, &c.

The Mouse is a merry wee beast, *little*
The Moudiewart wants the een; *mole; lacks; eyes*
And O for a touch o' the thing,
I had in my nieve yestreen. *fist yesterday evening*
O gie, &c.

We a' were fou yestreen, *drunk yesterday evening*
The night shall be its brither: *tonight; brother*
And hey, for a roaring pin
To nail twa wames thegither! *two stomachs together*
O gie, &c.

To a Louse

On Seeing one on a Lady's Bonnet at Church.

Ha! whare ye gaun, ye crowlan ferlie!	*where are you going; creeping wonder*
Your impudence protects you sairly:	*sorely, thoroughly*
I canna say but ye strunt rarely,	*cannot; strut*
Owre *gawze* and *lace*;	*over gauze*
Tho' faith, I fear ye dine but sparely,	
On sic a place.	*such*
Ye ugly, creepan, blastet wonner,	*creeping, blasted wonder*
Detested, shunn'd, by saunt an' sinner,	*saint and*
How daur ye set your fit upon her,	*dare; foot*
Sae fine a *Lady!*	*so*
Gae somewhere else and seek your dinner,	*go*
On some poor body.	
Swith, in some beggar's haffet squattle;	*quick; hair nestle*
There ye may creep, and sprawl, and sprattle,	*scramble*
Wi' ither kindred, jumping cattle,	*with other*
In shoals and nations;	
Whare *horn* nor *bane* ne'er daur unsettle,	*where; bone (comb); dare*
Your thick plantations.	*colonies*
Now haud you there, ye're out o' sight,	*hold; of*
Below the fatt'rels, snug an' tight,	*ribbon-ends*
Na faith ye yet! ye'll no be right,	*now; not*
Till ye've got on it,	
The vera tapmost, towrin height	*very topmost, towering*
O' *Miss's bonnet*.	
My sooth! right bauld ye set your nose out,	*my word; bold*
As plump an' gray as onie grozet:	*grey; any gooseberry*
O for some rank, mercurial rozet,	*resin*
Or fell, red smeddum,	*strong; powder*
I'd gie ye sic a hearty dose o't,	*give; such; of it*
Wad dress your droddum!	*would; posterior*

I wad na been surpriz'd to spy — *would not [have]*
You on an auld wife's *flainen toy*; — *old; flannel cap*
Or aiblins some bit duddie boy, — *perhaps; ragged*
          On's *wylecoat*; — *on his undervest*
But Miss's fine *Lunardi*, fye! — *elaborate bonnet*
          How daur ye do't? — *dare*

O *Jenny* dinna toss your head, — *do not*
An' set your beauties a' abread! — *all abroad*
Ye little ken what cursed speed — *know*
          The blastie's makin! — *small creature is making*
Thae *winks* and *finger-ends*, I dread, — *those*
          Are notice takin! — *taking*

O wad some Pow'r the giftie gie us — *would; gift give*
To see oursels as others see us! — *ourselves*
It wad frae monie a blunder free us — *would from many*
          An' foolish notion: — *and*
What airs in dress an' gait wad lea'e us, — *would leave*
          And ev'n Devotion!

A Cantata. [Love and Liberty *or* The Jolly Beggars]

Recitativo

When lyart leaves bestrow the yird, *multi-coloured; earth*
Or wavering like the Bauckie-bird[1] *bat*
Bedim cauld Boreas' blast; *cold north wind's*
When hailstanes drive wi' bitter skyte, *hailstones; with; ricochet*
And infant Frosts begin to bite,
In hoary cranreuch drest; *hoar-frost dressed*
Ae night at e'en a merry core *one; evening; party*
O' randie, gangrel bodies, *of riotous, vagrant folk*
In Poosie-Nansie's held the splore, *spree*
To drink their orra duddies: *spare rags*
Wi' quaffing, and laughing, *with*
They ranted an' they sang; *and*
Wi' jumping, an' thumping,
The vera girdle rang, *very [cooking] griddle*

First, niest the fire, in auld, red rags, *next; old*
Ane sat; weel brac'd wi' mealy bags, *one; well*
And knapsack a' in order; *all*
His doxy lay within his arm; *lover*
Wi' usquebae an' blankets warm, *whisky*
She blinket on her Sodger: *gazed; soldier*
An' ay he gies the tozie drab *always; gives; tipsy slut*
The tither skelpan kiss, *another vigorous*
While she held up her greedy gab, *mouth*
Just like an aumous dish: *alms*
Ilk smack still did crack still, *each kiss*
Just like a cadger's whip; *hawker's*
Then staggering, an' swaggering,
He roar'd this ditty up—

1 The old Scotch name for the Bat [Burns's note].

Air — Tune Soldier's joy —

I am a Son of Mars who have been in many wars,
  And show my cuts and scars wherever I come;
This here was for a wench, and that other in a trench,
  When welcoming the French at the sound of the drum.
          Lal de daudle &c.

My Prenticeship I past where my LEADER breath'd his last,
  When the bloody die was cast on the heights of ABRAM;
And I served out my TRADE when the gallant GAME was play'd,
  And the MORO low was laid at the sound of the drum.

I lastly was with Curtis, among the FLOATING BATT'RIES,
  And there I left for witness, an arm and a limb;
Yet let my Country need me, with Elliot to head me,
  I'd clatter on my stumps at the sound of a drum.

And now tho' I must beg, with a wooden arm and leg,
  And many a tatter'd rag hanging over my bum,
I'm as happy with my wallet, my bottle and my Callet, *wench*
  As when I used in scarlet to follow a drum.

What tho', with hoary locks, I must stand the winter shocks,
  Beneath the woods and rocks oftentimes for a home,
When the tother bag I sell, and the tother bottle tell, *other; count*
  I could meet a troop of HELL at the sound of a DRUM.

Recitativo —

He ended; and the kebars sheuk, *rafters shook*
  Aboon the chorus roar; *above*
While frighted rattons backward leuk, *rats; look*
  An' seek the benmost bore: *inmost hole*
A fairy FIDDLER frae the neuk, *from the corner*
  He skirl'd out, ENCORE. *squealed*
But up arose the martial CHUCK, *girlfriend*
  An' laid the loud uproar —

Air. Tune, Sodger laddie —

I once was a Maid tho' I cannot tell when,
And still my delight is in proper, young men:
Some one of a troop of DRAGOONS was my dadie, *father*
No wonder I'm fond of a SODGER LADDIE, *soldier lad*
Sing, lal de lal &c.

The first of my LOVES was a swaggering blade,
To rattle the thundering drum was his trade;
His leg was so tight and his cheek was so ruddy,
Transported I was with my SODGER LADDIE.

But the godly, old Chaplain left him in the lurch,
The sword I forsook for the sake of the church;
He ventur'd the SOUL, and I risked the BODY,
'Twas then I prov'd false to my SODGER LADDIE. *soldier lad*

Full soon I grew sick of my sanctified SOT.
The Regiment AT LARGE for a HUSBAND I got;
From the gilded SPONTOON to the FIFE I was ready, *officer's pike*
I asked no more but a SODGER LADDIE. *soldier lad*

But the PEACE it reduc'd me to beg in despair,
Till I met my old boy in a CUNNINGHAM fair; *(Ayrshire district)*
His RAGS REGIMENTAL they flutter'd so gaudy,
My heart it rejoic'd at a SODGER LADDIE. *soldier lad*

And now I have lived—I know not how long,
And still I can join in a cup and a song:
But whilst with both hands I can hold the glass steady,
Here's to thee, MY HERO, MY SODGER LADDIE. *soldier lad*

Recitative

Poor Merry-andrew, in the neuk, *corner*
  Sat guzzling wi' a Tinkler-hizzie; *tinker-wench*
They mind't na wha the chorus teuk, *not who; took*
  Between themsels they were sae busy: *so*
At length wi' drink an' courting dizzy,
  He stoiter'd up an' made a face; *staggered*

Then turn'd, an' laid a smack on Grizzie, *kiss*
Syne tun'd his pipes wi' grave grimace. *then*

Air. Tune, Auld Sir Symon.

Sir Wisdom's a fool when he's fou; *full, drunk*
Sir Knave is a fool in a Session,
He's there but a prentice, I trow, *apprentice; believe*
But I am a fool by profession.

My Grannie she bought me a beuk, *book*
An' I held awa to the school; *went off*
I fear I my talent misteuk, *mistook*
But what will ye hae of a fool. *have*

For drink I would venture my neck;
A hizzie's the half of my Craft: *hussy*
But what could ye other expect *otherwise*
Of ane that's avowedly daft. *one; crazy*

I, ance, was ty'd up like a stirk, *once; tied; bullock*
For civilly swearing and quaffing;
I, ance, was abus'd i' the kirk, *once; in the church*
For towsing a lass i' my daffin. *fondling; folly*

Poor Andrew that tumbles for sport,
Let nae body name wi' a jeer; *no*
There's even, I'm tauld, i' the Court *told; in*
A Tumbler ca'd the Premier. *called*

Observ'd ye yon reverend lad *that*
Mak faces to tickle the Mob; *make*
He rails at our mountebank squad,
Its rivalship just i' the job.

And now my conclusion I'll tell,
For faith I'm confoundedly dry:
The chiel that's a fool for himsel, *fellow; himself*
Guid L[or]d, he's far dafter than I. *good*

Recitativo—

Then niest outspak a raucle CARLIN, *next; outspoke; coarse woman*
Wha kent fu' weel to cleek the Sterlin; *who knew very well; hook money*
For mony a pursie she had hooked, *many*
An' had in mony a well been douked: *many; ducked*
Her LOVE had been a HIGHLAND LADDIE,
But weary fa' the waefu' woodie! *fall; woeful hanging-rope*
Wi' sighs an' sobs she thus began *with; and*
To wail her braw JOHN HIGHLANDMAN— *fine*

Air. Tune, O an' ye were dead Gudeman—

A highland lad my Love was born,
The lalland laws he held in scorn; *lowland*
But he still was faithfu' to his clan, *faithful*
My gallant, braw John Highlandman. *fine*

Chorus—

Sing hey my braw John Highlandman!
Sing ho my braw John Highlandman!
There's not a lad in a' the lan' *all the land*
Was match for my John Highlandman.

With his Philibeg an' tartan Plaid, *kilt*
An' guid Claymore down by his side, *good broadsword*
The ladies' hearts he did trepan, *beguile*
My gallant, braw John Highlandman.
Sing hey &c.

We ranged a' from Tweed to Spey, *all; (Scottish rivers)*
An' liv'd like lords an' ladies gay:
For a lalland face he feared none, *lowland*
My gallant, braw John Highlandman.
Sing hey &c.

They banish'd him beyond the sea,
But ere the bud was on the tree,
Adown my cheeks the pearls ran,
Embracing my John Highlandman.
Sing hey &c.

But Och! they catch'd him at the last, *alas*
And bound him in a dungeon fast,
My curse upon them every one,
They've hang'd my braw John Highlandman.
Sing hey &c.

And now a Widow I must mourn
The Pleasures that will ne'er return;
No comfort but a hearty can, *drinking vessel*
When I think on John Highlandman.
Sing hey &c.

Recitativo—

A pigmy Scraper wi' his Fiddle, *with*
Wha us'd to trystes an' fairs to driddle, *who; markets; play the fiddle*
Her strappan limb an' gausy middle, *strapping; plump*
(He reach'd nae higher) *no*
Had hol'd his HEARTIE like a riddle, *heart*
An' blawn't on fire. *blown it*

Wi' hand on hainch, and upward e'e, *haunch; eye*
He croon'd his gamut, ONE, TWO, THREE, *wailed*
Then in an ARIOSO key,
The wee APOLLO *small*
Set off wi' ALLEGRETTO glee
His GIGA SOLO—

Air.— Tune, Whistle owre the lave o't.

Let me ryke up to dight that tear, *reach; wipe*
An' go wi' me an' be my DEAR; *and; with*
An' then your every CARE an' FEAR
May whistle owre the lave o't. *over the rest of it*

Chorus—

I am a Fiddler to my trade,
An' a' the tunes that e'er I play'd, *all*
The sweetest still to WIFE or MAID,
Was whistle owre the lave o't. *over the rest of it*

At KIRNS an' WEDDINS we'se be there, — *harvest-homes; weddings; we shall*
An' O sae nicely's we will fare! — *so*
We'll bowse about till Dadie CARE — *drink in turn; Father*
Sing whistle owre the lave o't.
I am &c.

Sae merrily's the banes we'll pyke, — *so; bones; pick*
An' sun oursells about the dyke; — *ourselves; wall*
An' at our leisure when ye like
We'll whistle owre the lave o't.
I am &c.

But bless me wi' your heav'n o' charms, — *with; of*
An' while I kittle hair on thairms — *tickle; guts (fiddle strings)*
HUNGER, CAULD, an' a' sic harms — *cold, and all such*
May whistle owre the lave o't.
I am &c.

Recitativo—

Her charms had struck a sturdy CAIRD, — *tinker*
As weel as poor GUTSCRAPER; — *well*
He taks the Fiddler by the beard, — *takes*
An' draws a roosty rapier— — *rusty*
He swoor by a' was swearing worth — *swore; all [that]*
To speet him like a Pliver, — *spit; plover*
Unless he would from that time forth
Relinquish her for ever:
Wi' ghastly e'e poor TWEEDLEDEE — *eye*
Upon his hunkers bended, — *squatted*
An' pray'd for grace wi' ruefu' face, — *with rueful*
An' so the quarrel ended;
But tho' his little heart did grieve
When round the TINKLER prest her, — *tinker pressed*
He feign'd to snirtle in his sleeve — *snigger*
When thus the CAIRD address'd her—

Air. Tune, Clout the Caudron.—

My bonie lass, I work in brass, — *pretty*
A TINKLER is my station; — *tinker*
I've travell'd round all Christian ground
In this my occupation;
I've ta'en the GOLD an' been enroll'd — *taken; enlisted*
In many a noble squadron;
But vain they search'd when off I march'd
To go an' clout the CAUDRON. — *patch the cauldron*
I've ta'en the gold &c.

Despise that SHRIMP, that wither'd IMP,
With a' his noise an' cap'rin; — *all; capering*
An' take a share, with those that bear
The BUDGET and the APRON! — *bundle*
And *by* that STOWP! my faith an' houpe, — *stoup; hope*
And *by* that dear KILBAIGIE.[2]
If e'er ye want, or meet wi' scant, — *with; scarcity*
May I ne'er WEET MY CRAIGIE! — *wet; throat*
And by that Stowp, &c.

Recitativo—

The Caird prevail'd—th'unblushing fair
In his embraces sunk;
Partly wi' LOVE o'ercome sae sair, — *overcome so sore[ly]*
An' partly she was drunk:
SIR VIOLINO with an air,
That show'd a man o' spunk, — *of fire*
Wish'd UNISON between the PAIR,
An' made the bottle clunk
To their health that night.

But hurchin Cupid shot a shaft, — *urchin*
That play'd a DAME a shavie— — *trick*
The Fiddler RAK'D her, FORE AND AFT,
Behint the Chicken cavie: — *behind; coop*

2 A peculiar sort of Whiskie so called: a great favorite with Poosie Nansie's Clubs [Burns's note].

Her lord, a wight of HOMER'S[3] craft, *man*
Tho' limpan wi' the Spavie, *limping; spavin*
He hirpl'd up an' lap like daft, *hobbled; leapt*
An' shor'd them DAINTY DAVIE *offered*
O' BOOT that night. *into the bargain*

He was a care-defying blade
As ever BACCHUS listed! *Roman god of wine*
Tho' Fortune sair upon him laid, *sore*
His heart she ever miss'd it.
He had no WISH but—to be glad,
Nor WANT but—when he thristed; *thirsted*
He hated nought but—to be sad,
An' thus the Muse suggested
His sang that night. *song*

Air.—Tune. for a' that an' a' that—

I am a BARD of no regard,
Wi' gentle folks an' a' that; *and all*
But HOMER like the glowran byke, *gazing swarm*
Frae town to town I draw that. *from*

Chorus—
For a' that an' a' that, *all*
An' twice as muckle's a' that, *much as all*
I've lost but ANE, I've TWA behin', *one; two behind*
I've WIFE ENEUGH for a' that. *enough*

I never drank the MUSES' STANK, *ditch*
Castalia's burn an' a' that; *stream*
But there it streams an' richly reams, *froths*
My HELICON I ca' that. *call*
For a' that &c.

Great love I bear to all the FAIR,
Their humble slave an' a' that;
But lordly WILL, I hold it still

3 Homer is allowed to be the eldest Ballad singer on record [Burns's note].

A mortal sin to thraw that. *thwart*
For a' that &c.

In raptures sweet this hour we meet,
Wi' mutual love an' a' that;
But for how lang the flie may stang, *long; fly; sting*
Let INCLINATION law that. *determine*
For a' that &c.

Their tricks an' craft hae put me daft, *have*
They've ta'en me in, an' a' that, *taken*
But clear your decks, an' here's the SEX!
I like the jads for a' that. *jades*
For a' that an' a' that
An' twice as muckle's a' that, *much as all*
My DEAREST BLUID to do them guid, *blood; good*
They're welcome till't for a' that. *to it*

Recitativo—

So sang the BARD—and Nansie's waws *walls*
Shook with a thunder of applause
Re-echo'd from each mouth!
They toom'd their pocks, they pawn'd their duds, *emptied; bags; rags*
They scarcely left to coor their fuds, *cover; buttocks*
To quench their lowan drouth; *fiery thirst*
Then owre again the jovial thrang *over; throng*
The Poet did request
To lowse his PACK an' wale a sang, *untie; choose; song*
A ballad o' the best.
He, rising, rejoicing,
Between his TWA DEBORAHS, *two*
Looks round him an' found them
Impatient for the Chorus.

Air.—Tune. Jolly Mortals fill your glasses—

See the smoking bowl before us, *steaming*
Mark our jovial, ragged ring!
Round and round take up the Chorus,
And in raptures let us sing—

Chorus—

A fig for those by LAW protected!
  LIBERTY's a glorious feast!
Courts for Cowards were erected,
  Churches built to please the PRIEST.

What is TITLE, what is TREASURE,
  What is REPUTATION's care?
If we lead a life of pleasure,
  'Tis no matter HOW OR WHERE.
    A fig &c.

With the ready trick and fable
  Round we wander all the day;
And at night, in barn or stable,
  Hug our doxies on the hay.
    A fig for &c.

Does the train-attended CARRIAGE
  Thro' the country lighter rove?
Does the sober bed of MARRIAGE
  Witness brighter scenes of love?
    A fig for &c.

Life is all a VARIORUM, *medley*
  We regard not how it goes;
Let them cant about DECORUM,
  Who have character to lose.
    A fig for &c.

Here's to BUDGETS, BAGS and WALLETS! *bundles*
  Here's to all the wandering train!
Here's our ragged BRATS and CALLETS! *wenches*
  One and all cry out, AMEN!
    A fig for those by LAW protected,
      LIBERTY's a glorious feast!
    COURTS for Cowards were erected,
      CHURCHES built to please the priest.

Finis——

On a Scotch Bard Gone to the West Indies.

A' ye wha live by sowps o' drink, *all; who; sups*
A' ye wha live by crambo-clink, *doggerel*
A' ye wha live and never think,
    Come, mourn wi' me! *with*
Our *billie's* gien us a' a jink, *comrade has given; dodge*
    An' owre the Sea. *and over*

Lament him a' ye rantan core, *all; merry gang*
Wha dearly like a random-splore; *who; party*
Nae mair he'll join the *merry roar*, *no more*
    In social key;
For now he's taen anither shore, *taken another*
    An' owre the Sea!

The bonie lasses weel may wiss him, *pretty; well; wish, desire*
And in their dear *petitions* place him:
The widows, wives, an' a' may bless him, *and all*
    Wi' tearfu' e'e; *with tearful eye*
For weel I wat they'll sairly miss him *well; know; sorely*
    That's owre the Sea!

O Fortune, they hae room to grumble! *have*
Hadst thou taen aff some drowsy bummle, *taken off: bungler*
Wha can do nought but fyke an' fumble, *who; fidget*
    'Twad been nae plea; *it would[have]; no argument*
But he was gleg as onie wumble, *sharp; any gimlet*
    That's owre the Sea!

Auld, cantie KYLE may weepers wear, *old, cheerful; mourning*
An' stain them wi' the saut, saut tear: *salt*
'Twill mak her poor, auld heart, I fear, *it will make; old*
    In flinders flee: *splinters fly*
He was her *Laureat* monie a year, *laureate many*
    That's owre the Sea!

He saw Misfortune's cauld *Nor-west* — *cold*
Lang-mustering up a bitter blast; — *long-*
A Jillet brak his heart at last, — *flirt broke*
    Ill may she be!
So, took a birth afore the mast, — *berth before*
    An' owre the Sea.

To tremble under Fortune's cummock, — *crooked staff*
On scarce a bellyfu' o' *drummock*, — *bellyful of oatmeal and water*
Wi' his proud, independant stomach,
    Could ill agree;
So, row't his hurdies in a *hammock*, — *rolled; haunches*
    An' owre the Sea.

He ne'er was gien to great misguidin, — *never; given; mismanagement*
Yet coin his pouches wad na bide in; — *would not stay*
Wi' him it ne'er was *under hidin;* — *hiding*
    He dealt it free:
The *Muse* was a' that he took pride in, — *all*
    That's owre the Sea.

Jamaica bodies, use him weel, — *fellows; well*
An' hap him in a cozie biel: — *shelter; cosy refuge*
Ye'll find him ay a dainty chiel, — *always; fellow*
    An' fou o' glee: — *and full of*
He wad na wrang'd the vera *Diel*, — *would not [have] wronged; very Devil*
    That's owre the Sea.

Fareweel, my *rhyme-composing billie!* — *farewell; friend*
Your native soil was right ill-willie; — *ill-willed*
But may ye flourish like a lily,
    Now bonilie! — *handsomely*
I'll toast you in my hindmost *gillie*, — *gill-cup*
    Tho' owre the Sea!

To the Author. [Second Epistle to Davie]

AULD NIBOR, *old neighbour*

I'm three times, doubly, o'er your debtor; *over*
For your auld-farrent, frien'ly letter; *old-fashioned, friendly*
Tho' I maun say't, I doubt ye flatter, *must say it*
    Ye speak sae fair; *so*
For my puir, silly, rhymin' clatter *poor; rhyming*
    Some less maun sair. *must serve*

Hale be your heart, hale be your fiddle;
Lang may your elbuck jink an' diddle, *long; elbow; jiggle*
Tae cheer you thro' the weary widdle *to; struggle*
    O' war'ly cares, *of worldly*
Till bairns' bairns kindly cuddle *children's children*
    Your auld, gray hairs. *old*

But DAVIE, lad, I'm red ye're glaikit; *advised; foolish*
I'm tauld the Muse ye hae negleckit; *told; have neglected*
An' gif it's sae, ye sud be licket *and if; so; should; beaten*
    Until ye fyke: *twitch*
Sic hauns as you sud ne'er be faikit, *such hands; should; spared*
    Be hain't wha like. *whoever protects [them]*

For me, I'm on Parnassus' brink,
Rivan the words tae gar them clink; *wrenching; to make; ring, rhyme*
Whyles daez't wi' love, whyles daez't wi' drink, *sometimes dazed with*
    Wi' jads or masons; *women; freemasons*
An' whyles, but ay owre late, I think *sometimes; always too*
    Braw sober lessons. *fine*

Of a' the thoughtless sons o' man, *all; of*
Commen' me to the Bardie clan; *commend; minor poet*
Except it be some idle plan
    O' rhymin' clink, *of rhyming sound*
The devil-haet, that I sud ban, *devil a bit; should curse*
    They never think.

Nae thought, nae view, nae scheme o' livin', *no*
Nae cares tae gie us joy or grievin'; *no; to; grieving*
But just the pouchie put the nieve in, *pocket; fist*
    An' while ought's there, *anything is*
Then, hiltie skiltie, we gae scrivin', *heedless; go writing*
    An' fash nae mair. *and trouble no more*

Leeze me on rhyme! it's ay a treasure, *blessings on; always*
My chief, amaist my only pleasure; *almost*
At hame, a-fiel, at wark or leisure, *afield; work*
    The Muse, poor hizzie! *woman*
Tho' rough an' raploch be her measure, *uncouth*
    She's seldom lazy.

Haud to the Muse, my daintie Davie: *hold*
The warl' may play you a shavie; *world; trick*
But for the Muse, she'll never leave ye,
    Tho' e'er sae puir, *so poor*
Na, even tho' limpan wi' the spavie *no; limping; spavin*
    Frae door tae door. *from; to*

R.B.

[Lines Written on a Bank of Scotland One Guinea Note]

Wae worth thy pow'r, thou cursed leaf! *woe*
Fell source of all my woe and grief! *deadly*
For lake o' thee I've lost my lass; *lack of*
For lake o' thee I scrimp my glass; *restrict my drinking*
I see the children of Affliction
Unaided, thro thy curst restriction;
I've seen th' Oppressor's cruel smile,
Amid his hapless victims' spoil;
And for thy potence vainly wished,
To crush the Villain in the dust:
For lake o' thee I leave this much-lov'd shore, *lack*
Never perhaps to greet old Scotland more!

R.—B.—Kyle.

[Address of Beelzebub]

To the Rt. Honble JOHN, EARL OF BREADALBINE, President of the Rt Honble & Honble the HIGHLAND SOCIETY which met, on the 23^{d} of May last at the Shakespeare, Covent garden, to concert ways & means to frustrate the designs of FIVE HUNDRED HIGHLANDERS who, the Society were informed by Mr M'kenzie of Applecross, were so audacious as to attempt an escape from theire lawful lords & masters whose property they were by emigrating from the lands of Mr M^{c}donald of Glengary to the wilds of CANADA, in search of that fantastic thing—LIBERTY.

Long life, My lord, an' health be yours, *and*
Unskaith'd by hunger'd HIGHLAN BOORS! *unharmed; Highland peasants*
Lord grant, nae duddie, desp'rate BEGGAR, *no ragged*
Wi' durk, claymore or rusty trigger, *knife; broadsword*
May twin auld SCOTLAND o' a life, *deprive old; of*
She likes—as BUTCHERS like a knife.

Faith, you & Applecross were right
To keep the highlan hounds in sight! *highland*
I doubt na, they wad bid nae better *not; would seek no*
Than let them ance out owre the water; *once; over*
Then up amang thae lakes an' seas *among those; and*
They'll mak what rules an' laws they please— *make*

Some daring HANCOCKE, or a FRANKLINE,
May set their HIGHLAN bluid a ranklin; *blood*
Some Washington again may head them,
Or some MONTGOMERY, fearless, lead them;
Till, God knows what may be effected,
When by such HEADS an' HEARTS directed:
Poor dunghill sons of dirt an' mire,
May to PATRICIAN RIGHTS ASPIRE;
Nae sage North, now, nor sager Sackville, *no*
To watch an' premier owre the pack vile! *over*

An' whare will ye get Howes an' Clintons — *where*
To bring them to a right repentance,
To cowe the rebel generation, — *cow*
An' save the honor o' the NATION? — *of*

They! an' be d[a]mn'd! what right hae they — *have*
To Meat or Sleep, or light o' day,
Far less to riches, pow'r, or freedom,
But what your lordships PLEASE TO GIE THEM? — *give*

But, hear me, my lord! Glengary, hear!
Your HAND'S OWRE LIGHT ON THEM, I fear: — *over*
Your FACTORS, GREIVES, TRUSTEES an' BAILIES, — *estate managers*
I canna say but they do gailies; — *cannot; well*
They lay aside a' tender mercies — *all*
An' tirl the HULLIONS to the birses; — *strip; rascals; bristles*
Yet, while they're only poin'd, & herriet, — *impounded; plundered*
They'll keep their stubborn Highlan spirit.

But Smash them! crush them a' to spails! — *all; splinters*
An' rot the DYVORS i' the JAILS! — *debtors*
The young dogs, swinge them to the labour, — *flog*
Let WARK an' HUNGER mak them sober! — *work; make*
The HIZZIES, if they're oughtlins fausont, — *women; in any way decent*
Let them in DRURY LANE be lesson'd!
An' if the wives, an' dirty brats
Come thiggan at your doors an' yetts, — *begging; gates*
Flaffan wi' duds, an' grey wi' beese, — *flapping; rags; lice*
Frightan awa your deucks an' geese, — *frightening away; ducks*
Get out a HORSE WHIP, or a JOWLER, — *hunting dog*
The langest thong, the fiercest growler, — *longest*
An' gar the tatter'd gipseys pack — *make; depart*
Wi' a' their bastarts on their back! — *with all*

Go on, my lord! I lang to meet you, — *long*
An' in my HOUSE at hame to greet you; — *home*
Wi' COMMON LORDS ye shanna mingle: — *shall not*
The benmost newk beside the ingle, — *innermost corner; hearth*

At my right hand, assigned your seat *hand*
'Tween HEROD'S hip, an' POLYCRATE, *between*
Or, if ye on your station tarrow, *hesitate*
Between ALMAGRO & PIZARRO;
A seat, I'm sure ye're weel deservin't; *well deserving it*
An' till ye come—your humble servant,

BEELZEBUB
HELL 1st June Anno Mundi 5790 *year of the world*

A Dream.

Thoughts, words and deeds, the Statute blames with reason;
But surely Dreams *were ne'er indicted Treason.*

ON READING, IN THE PUBLIC PAPERS, THE LAUREATE'S ODE, WITH THE OTHER PARADE OF JUNE 4TH, 1786, THE AUTHOR WAS NO SOONER DROPT ASLEEP, THAN HE IMAGINED HIMSELF TRANSPORTED TO THE BIRTH-DAY LEVEE; AND, IN HIS DREAMING FANCY, MADE THE FOLLOWING ADDRESS.

GUID-MORNIN to your MAJESTY!	*good morning*
May Heaven augment your blisses,	
On ev'ry new *Birth-day* ye see,	
A humble Bardie wishes!	*minor poet*
My Bardship here, at your Levee,	*morning appearance*
On sic a day as this is,	*such*
Is sure an uncouth sight to see,	
Amang thae Birth-day dresses	*among those*
Sae fine this day.	*so*
I see ye're complimented thrang,	*busily*
By many a *lord* an' *lady;*	*and*
'God save the King' 's a cuckoo sang	*song*
That's unco easy said ay:	*uncommonly; always*
The *Poets* too, a venal gang,	
Wi' rhymes weel-turn'd an' ready,	*with; well-turned*
Wad gar you trow ye ne'er do wrang,	*would make; believe; wrong*
But ay unerring steady,	*always*
On sic a day.	*such*
For me! before a Monarch's face,	
Ev'n *there* I winna flatter;	*will not*
For neither Pension, Post, nor Place,	*government job*
Am I your humble debtor:	
So, nae reflection on YOUR GRACE,	*no*
Your Kingship to bespatter;	

There's monie *waur* been o' the Race, *many worse; of*
And aiblins *ane* been better *perhaps one*
Than You this day.

'Tis very true, my sovereign King,
My skill may weel be doubted; *well*
But *Facts* are cheels that winna ding, *fellows; will not be overcome*
An' downa be disputed: *cannot*
Your *royal nest*, beneath *Your* wing,
Is e'en right reft an' clouted, *torn and patched*
And now the third part o' the string, *of*
An' less, will gang about it *go*
Than did ae day. *one*

Far be't frae me that I aspire *from*
To blame your Legislation,
Or say, ye wisdom want, or fire,
To rule this mighty nation;
But faith! I muckle doubt, my SIRE, *greatly*
Ye've trusted 'Ministration, *administration, government*
To chaps, wha, in a *barn* or *byre*, *who; cowshed*
Wad better fill'd their station *would [have]*
Than *courts* yon day. *that*

And now Ye've gien auld *Britain* peace, *given old*
Her broken shins to plaister; *plaster*
Your sair taxation does her fleece, *sore*
Till she has scarce a tester: *sixpence*
For me, thank God, my life's a *lease*,
Nae *bargain* wearing faster, *no; wasting away*
Or faith! I fear, that, wi' the geese, *with*
I shortly boost to pasture *ought*
I' the craft some day. *croft, infield*

I'm no mistrusting *Willie Pit*, *not*
When taxes he enlarges,
(An' *Will's* a true guid fallow's get, *good fellow's offspring*
A Name not Envy spairges) *spatters*
That he intends to pay your *debt*,

An' lessen a' your *charges;* *all*
But, G[o]d-sake! let nae *saving-fit* *no*
Abridge your bonie *Barges* *handsome*
An' *Boats* this day.

Adieu, my LIEGE! may Freedom geck *toss her head in pride*
Beneath your high protection;
An' may Ye rax Corruption's neck, *twist*
And gie her for dissection! *give*
But since I'm here, I'll no neglect,
In loyal, true affection,
To pay your QUEEN, wi' due respect, *with*
My fealty an' subjection
This great Birth-day.

Hail, *Majesty most Excellent!*
While Nobles strive to please Ye,
Will Ye accept a Compliment,
A simple Bardie gies Ye? *poet gives*
Thae bonie Bairntime, Heav'n has lent, *those pretty children*
Still higher may they heeze Ye *raise*
In bliss, till Fate some day is sent,
For ever to release Ye
Frae Care that day. *from*

For you, young Potentate o' W[ales],
I tell your *Highness* fairly,
Down Pleasure's stream, wi' swelling sails, *with*
I'm tauld ye're driving rarely; *told*
But some day ye may gnaw your nails,
An' curse your folly sairly, *sorely*
That e'er ye brak Diana's *pales*, *broke; fence*
Or rattl'd dice wi' *Charlie*
By night or day.

Yet aft a ragged *Cowte's* been known, *often; colt*
To mak a noble *Aiver*; *make; workhorse*
So, ye may dousely fill a Throne, *decently*
For a' their clish-ma-claver: *all; gossip*

There, Him at *Agincourt* wha shone, *who*
  Few better were or braver;
And yet, wi' funny, queer *Sir John*,[1]
  He was an unco shaver *remarkable roisterer*
    For monie a day. *many*

For you, right rev'rend O[snaburg],
  Nane sets the *lawn-sleeve* sweeter, *none; clerical garment*
Altho' a ribban at your lug *although; ribbon; ear*
  Wad been a dress compleater: *would [have]; completer*
As ye disown yon paughty dog, *that haughty*
  That *bears* the Keys of Peter, *the Pope*
Then swith! an' get a *wife* to hug, *quick*
  Or trouth! ye'll stain the *Mitre* *truth*
    Some luckless day.

Young, royal TARRY-BREEKS, I learn, *tarry-breeches, sailor*
  Ye've lately come athwart her;
A glorious *Galley*,[2] stem and stern,
  Weel rigg'd for *Venus barter;* *well*
But first hang out that she'll discern
  Your *hymeneal Charter*, *marriage*
Then heave aboard your *grapple airn*, *iron*
  An', large upon her *quarter*,
    Come full that day.

Ye lastly, bonie blossoms a', *pretty; all*
  Ye *royal Lasses* dainty,
Heav'n mak you guid as well as braw, *make; good; fine*
  An' gie you *lads* a plenty: *give*
But sneer na *British-boys* awa; *no; away*
  For King's are unco scant ay, *extraordinarily rare always*
An' German-Gentles are but *sma'*, *small*
  They're better just than *want ay* *always*
    On onie day. *any*

1 Sir John Falstaff, Vide Shakespeare [Burns's note].

2 Alluding to the Newspaper account of a certain royal Sailor's Amour [Burns's note].

God bless you a'! consider now, *all*
Ye're unco muckle dautet; *very greatly made much of*
But ere the *course* o' life be through, *of*
It may be bitter sautet: *salted*
An' I hae seen their *coggie* fou, *have; dish full*
That yet hae tarrow't at it. *have complained it's not enough*
But or the *day* was done, I trow, *before; believe*
The laggen they hae clautet *bottom of the dish; have scraped*
Fu' clean that day. *full*

The Brigs of Ayr. *A Poem.*

Inscribed to J. B[allantine], *Esq;* Ayr.

The simple Bard, rough at the rustic plough,
Learning his tuneful trade from ev'ry bough;
The chanting linnet, or the mellow thrush,
Hailing the setting sun, sweet, in the green thorn bush,
The soaring lark, the perching red-breast shrill,
Or deep-ton'd plovers, grey, wild-whistling o'er the hill;
Shall he, nurst in the Peasant's lowly shed, *nursed*
To hardy Independence bravely bred,
By early Poverty to hardship steel'd,
And train'd to arms in stern Misfortune's field,
Shall he be guilty of their hireling crimes,
The servile, mercenary Swiss of rhymes?
Or labour hard the panegyric close,
With all the venal soul of dedicating Prose?
No! though his artless strains he rudely sings,
And throws his hand uncouthly o'er the strings,
He glows with all the spirit of the Bard,
Fame, honest fame, his great his dear reward.
Still, if some Patron's gen'rous care he trace,
Skill'd in the secret, to bestow with grace;
When B[allantine] befriends his humble name,
And hands the rustic Stranger up to fame,
With heartfelt throes his grateful bosom swells,
The godlike bliss, to give, alone excels.

'Twas when the stacks get on their winter-hap, *-covering*
And thack and rape secure the toil-won crap; *thatch; rope; crop*
Potatoe-bings are snugged up frae skaith *-heaps; from harm*
Of coming Winter's biting, frosty breath;
The bees, rejoicing o'er their summer-toils,
Unnumber'd buds an' flow'rs' delicious spoils, *and*

Seal'd up with frugal care in massive, waxen piles,
Are doom'd by Man, that tyrant o'er the weak,
The death o' devils, smoor'd wi' brimstone reek: *smothered with; smoke*
The thund'ring guns are heard on ev'ry side,
The wounded coveys, reeling, scatter wide;
The feather'd field-mates, bound by Nature's tie,
Sires, mothers, children, in one carnage lie:
(What warm, poetic heart but inly bleeds,
And execrates man's savage, ruthless deeds!)
Nae mair the flow'r in field or meadow springs; *no more*
Nae mair the grove with airy concert rings, *no more*
Except perhaps the Robin's whistling glee,
Proud o' the height o' some bit half-lang tree: *of; half-length*
The hoary morns precede the sunny days,
Mild, calm, serene, wide-spreads the noon-tide blaze,
While thick the gossamour waves wanton in the rays. *gossamer*

'Twas in that season; when a simple Bard,
Unknown and poor, simplicity's reward,
Ae night, within the ancient brugh of *Ayr*, *one; burgh*
By whim inspir'd, or haply prest wi' care, *pressed with*
He left his bed and took his wayward rout, *course*
And down by *Simpson's*[1] wheel'd the left about:
(Whether impell'd by all-directing Fate,
To witness what I after shall narrate;
Or whether, rapt in meditation high,
He wander'd out he knew not where nor why)
The drowsy *Dungeon-clock*[2] had number'd two,
And *Wallace Tow'r*[2] had sworn the fact was true:
The tide-swoln Firth, with sullen-sounding roar,
Through the still night dash'd hoarse along the shore:
All else was hush'd as Nature's closed e'e; *eye*
The silent moon shone high o'er tow'r and tree:
The chilly Frost, beneath the silver beam,
Crept, gently-crusting, o'er the glittering stream.—

1 A noted tavern at the *Auld Brig* end [Burns's note].

2 The two steeples [Burns's note].

When, lo! on either hand the list'ning Bard,
The clanging sugh of whistling wings is heard; *whizzing*
Two dusky forms dart thro' the midnight air,
Swift as the *Gos*[3] drives on the wheeling hare;
Ane on th' *Auld Brig* his airy shape uprears, *one; old bridge*
The ither flutters o'er the *rising piers:* *other*
Our warlock Rhymer instantly descry'd *observed*
The Sprites that owre the *Brigs of Ayr* preside. *over; bridges*
(That Bards are second-sighted is nae joke, *no*
And ken the lingo of the sp'ritual folk; *know*
Fays, Spunkies, Kelpies, a', they can explain them, *all*
And ev'n the vera deils they brawly ken them). *very devils; well know*
Auld Brig appear'd of ancient Pictish race,
The vera wrinkles Gothic in his face: *very*
He seem'd as he wi' Time had warstl'd lang, *with; wrestled long*
Yet, teughly doure, he bade an unco bang. *toughly hard; [had] endured; special*
New Brig was buskit in a braw, new coat, *dressed; fine*
That he, at *Lon'on*, frae ane *Adams* got; *London from one*
In's hand five taper staves as smooth's a bead,
Wi' virls an' whirlygigums at the head. *ferrules; ornamentation*
The Goth was stalking round with anxious search,
Spying the time-worn flaws in ev'ry arch;
It chanc'd his new-come neebor took his e'e, *neighbour; eye*
And e'en a vex'd and angry heart had he! *even*
Wi' thieveless sneer to see his modish mien, *cold*
He, down the water, gies him this guid-een— *gives; good evening*

AULD BRIG.

I doubt na, frien', ye'll think ye're nae sheep-shank, *not; no mean fellow*
Ance ye were streekit owre frae bank to bank! *once; stretched over from*
But gin ye be a Brig as auld as me, *if; bridge; old*
Tho' faith, that date, I doubt, ye'll never see;
There'll be, if that day come, I'll wad a boddle, *bet tuppence*
Some fewer whigmeleeries in your noddle. *whimsicalities; head*

3 The gos-hawk, or falcon [Burns's note].

New Brig.

Auld Vandal, ye but show your little mense, *old; common sense*
Just much about it wi' your scanty sense; *with*
Will your poor, narrow foot-path of a street,
Where twa wheel-barrows tremble when they meet, *two*
Your ruin'd, formless bulk o' stane and lime, *stone*
Compare wi' bonie *Brigs* o' modern time? *fine bridges*
There's men of taste wou'd tak the *Ducat-stream*,[4] *take*
Tho' they should cast the vera sark and swim, *very shirt*
E'er they would grate their feelings wi' the view
Of sic an ugly, Gothic hulk as you. *such*

Auld Brig.

Conceited gowk! puff'd up wi' windy pride! *fool*
This mony a year I've stood the flood an' tide; *many*
And tho' wi' crazy eild I'm sair forfairn, *old age; sore worn out*
I'll be a *Brig* when ye're a shapeless cairn! *bridge; pile of stones*
As yet ye little ken about the matter, *know*
But twa-three winters will inform ye better. *two-*
When heavy, dark, continued, a'-day rains *all-day*
Wi' deepening deluges o'erflow the plains;
When from the hills where springs the brawling *Coil*,
Or stately *Lugar*'s mossy fountains boil,
Or where the *Greenock* winds his moorland course,
Or haunted *Garpal*[5] draws his feeble source,
Arous'd by blustering winds an' spotting thowes, *thows*
In mony a torrent down the snaw-broo rowes; *many; melted snow rolls*
While crashing ice, borne on the roaring speat, *spate*
Sweeps dams, an' mills, an' brigs, a' to the gate; *bridges; all to ruin*
And from *Glenbuck*,[6] down to the *Ratton-key*,[7]
Auld *Ayr* is just one lengthen'd, tumbling sea; *old*

4 A noted ford, just above the Auld Brig [Burns's note].

5 The banks of *Garpal Water* is one of the few places in the West of Scotland where those fancy scaring beings, known by the name of *Ghaists*, still continue pertinaciously to inhabit [Burns's note].

6 The source of the river of Ayr [Burns's note].

7 A small landing-place above the large key [Burns's note].

Then down ye'll hurl, deil nor ye never rise! *devil*
And dash the gumlie jaups up to the pouring skies. *muddy splashes*
A lesson sadly teaching, to your cost,
That Architecture's noble art is lost!

New Brig.

Fine *architecture*, trowth, I needs must say't o't! *truth; of it*
The L[or]d be thankit that we've tint the gate o't! *lost the way*
Gaunt, ghastly, ghaist-alluring edifices, *ghost-*
Hanging with threat'ning jut like precipices;
O'er-arching, mouldy, gloom-inspiring coves, *vaults*
Supporting roofs, fantastic, stony groves:
Windows and doors in nameless sculptures drest,
With order, symmetry, or taste unblest;
Forms like some bedlam Statuary's dream,
The craz'd creations of misguided whim;
Forms might be worshipp'd on the bended knee,
And still the *second dread command* be free,
Their likeness is not found on earth, in air, or sea.
Mansions that would disgrace the building-taste
Of any mason reptile, bird, or beast;
Fit only for a doited Monkish race, *crazy*
Or frosty maids forsworn the dear embrace,
Or Cuifs of later times, wha held the notion, *fools; who*
That sullen gloom was sterling, true devotion:
Fancies that our guid Brugh denies protection, *good burgh*
And soon may they expire, unblest with resurrection!

Auld Brig.

O ye, my dear-remember'd, ancient yealings, *contemporaries*
Were ye but here to share my wounded feelings!
Ye worthy *Proveses*, an' mony a *Bailie*, *many*
Wha in the paths o' righteousness did toil ay; *who; always*
Ye dainty *Deacons*, an' ye douce *Conveeners*, *respectable*
To whom our moderns are but causey-cleaners; *street-*
Ye godly *Councils* wha hae blest this town; *who have*
Ye godly *Brethren* o' the sacred gown, *clergymen*
Wha meekly gae your *hurdies* to the *smiters*; *meekly; gave; rear-ends*

And (what would now be strange), ye *godly Writers:*   *lawyers*
A' ye douce folk I've borne aboon the broo,   *all; decent; above; flood*
Were ye but here, what would ye say or do!
How would your spirits groan in deep vexation,
To see each melancholy alteration;
And, agonising, curse the time and place
When ye begat the base, degen'rate race!
Nae langer Rev'rend Men, their country's glory,   *no longer*
In plain, braid Scots hold forth a plain, braid story: *broad*
Nae langer thrifty Citizens, an' douce,   *no longer; and decent*
Meet owre a pint, or in the Council-house;   *over*
But staumrel, corky-headed, graceless Gentry,   *clumsy*
The herryment and ruin of the country;   *devastation*
Men, three-parts made by Taylors and by Barbers,
Wha waste your weel-hain'd gear on d[amn']d *new Brigs* and *Harbours!*   *who; well-kept possessions*

New Brig.

Now haud you there! for faith ye've said enough,   *hold*
And muckle mair than ye can mak to through.   *much more; make good*
As for your Priesthood, I shall say but little,
Corbies and *Clergy* are a shot right kittle: *ravens; difficult*
But, under favor o' your langer beard,   *favour; longer*
Abuse o' Magistrates might weel be spar'd;   *well*
To liken them to your auld-warld squad,   *old-world*
I must needs say, comparisons are odd.
In *Ayr*, Wag-wits nae mair can have a handle   *scandal-mongers no more*
To mouth 'A Citizen,' a term o' scandal:
Nae mair the Council waddles down the street,   *no more*
In all the pomp of ignorant conceit;
Men wha grew wise priggin owre hops an' raisins,   *who; haggling over*
Or gather'd lib'ral views in Bonds and Seisins.   *legal acts of possession*
If haply Knowledge, on a random tramp,
Had shor'd them with a glimmer of his lamp,   *offered*
And would to Common-sense for once betray'd them,
Plain, dull Stupidity stept kindly in to aid them.

What farther clishmaclaver might been said, *gossip*
What bloody wars, if Sprites had blood to shed,
No man can tell; but, all before their sight,
A fairy train appear'd in order bright:
Adown the glittering stream they featly danc'd; *nimbly*
Bright to the moon their various dresses glanc'd:
They footed o'er the wat'ry glass so neat,
The infant ice scarce bent beneath their feet:
While arts of Minstrelsy among them rung,
And soul-ennobling Bards heroic ditties sung.

O had *M'Lauchlan*,[8] thairm-inspiring Sage, *gut-*
Been there to hear this heavenly band engage,
When thro' his dear *Strathspeys* they bore with Highland rage;
Or when they struck old Scotia's melting airs,
The lover's raptur'd joys or bleeding cares;
How would his Highland lug been nobler fir'd, *ear*
And ev'n his matchless hand with finer touch inspir'd!
No guess could tell what instrument appear'd,
But all the soul of Music's self was heard;
Harmonious concert rung in every part,
While simple melody pour'd moving on the heart.

The Genius of the Stream in front appears,
A venerable Chief advanc'd in years;
His hoary head with water-lilies crown'd,
His manly leg with garter tangle bound. *sea-weed*
Next came the loveliest pair in all the ring,
Sweet Female Beauty hand in hand with Spring;
Then, crown'd with flow'ry hay, came Rural Joy,
And Summer, with his fervid-beaming eye:
All-chearing Plenty, with her flowing horn,
Led yellow Autumn wreath'd with nodding corn;
Then Winter's time-bleach'd locks did hoary show,
By Hospitality with cloudless brow.
Next follow'd Courage with his martial stride,
From where the *Feal* wild-woody coverts hide:

8 A well known performer of Scottish music on the violin [Burns's note].

Benevolence, with mild, benignant air,
A female form, came from the tow'rs of *Stair:*
Learning and Worth in equal measures trode,
From simple *Catrine*, their long lov'd abode:
Last, white-rob'd Peace, crown'd with a hazle wreath, *hazel*
To rustic Agriculture did bequeath
The broken, iron instruments of Death,
At sight of whom our Sprites forgat their kindling wrath. *forgot*

The Northern Lass.

Tho' cruel fate should bid us part,
  Far as the pole and line; *equator*
Her dear idea round my heart
  Should tenderly entwine.

Tho' mountains rise, and desarts howl,
  And oceans roar between;
Yet, dearer than my deathless soul,
  I still would love my Jean.

Address to Edinburgh.

Edina! *Scotia*'s darling seat! *Edinburgh; Scotland's*
All hail thy palaces and tow'rs,
Where once beneath a Monarch's feet
Sat Legislation's sov'reign pow'rs!
From marking wildly-scatt'red flow'rs,
As on the banks of *Ayr* I stray'd,
And singing, lone, the ling'ring hours,
I shelter in thy honor'd shade.

Here Wealth still swells the golden tide,
As busy Trade his labours plies;
There Architecture's noble pride
Bids elegance and splendor rise;
Here Justice, from her native skies,
High wields her balance and her rod;
There Learning, with his eagle eyes,
Seeks Science in her coy abode.

Thy Sons, *Edina*, social, kind,
With open arms the Stranger hail;
Their views enlarg'd, their lib'ral mind,
Above the narrow, rural vale:
Attentive still to Sorrow's wail,
Or modest Merit's silent claim;
And never may their sources fail!
And never envy blot their name!

Thy Daughters bright thy walks adorn,
Gay as the gilded summer sky,
Sweet as the dewy, milk-white thorn,
Dear as the raptur'd thrill of joy!
Fair B[urnet] strikes th' adoring eye,
Heav'n's beauties on my fancy shine;
I see the *Sire of Love* on high,
And own his work indeed divine!

There, watching high the least alarms,
  Thy rough, rude Fortress gleams afar;
Like some bold Vet'ran, gray in arms,
  And mark'd with many a seamy scar:
The pond'rous wall and massy bar,
  Grim-rising o'er the rugged rock,
Have oft withstood assailing War,
  And oft repell'd the Invader's shock;

With awe-struck thought, and pitying tears,
  I view that noble, stately Dome,
Where *Scotia*'s kings of other years,
  Fam'd heroes! had their royal home:
Alas, how chang'd the times to come!
  Their royal Name low in the dust!
Their hapless Race wild-wand'ring roam!
  Tho' rigid Law cries out, 'twas just!

Wild beats my heart, to trace your steps,
  Whose ancestors, in days of yore,
Thro' hostile ranks and ruin'd gaps
  Old *Scotia's* bloody lion bore:
Ev'n *I* who sing in rustic lore,
  Haply *my Sires* have left their shed,
And fac'd grim Danger's loudest roar,
  Bold-following where your Fathers led!

Edina! Scotia's darling seat!
  All hail thy palaces and tow'rs,
Where once, beneath a Monarch's feet,
  Sat Legislation's sov'reign pow'rs!
From marking wildly-scatt'red flow'rs,
  As on the banks of *Ayr* I stray'd,
And singing, lone, the ling'ring hours,
  I shelter in thy honor'd shade.

To a Haggis.

Fair fa' your honest, sonsie face,	*[be]fall; handsome*
Great Chieftan o' the Puddin-race!	*of; pudding-*
Aboon them a' ye tak your place,	*above; all; take*
Painch, tripe, or thairm:	*entrails; intestines*
Weel are ye wordy of a *grace*	*well; worthy*
As lang's my arm.	*long as*
The groaning trencher there ye fill,	
Your hurdies like a distant hill,	*haunches*
Your *pin* wad help to mend a mill	*skewer would*
In time o' need,	
While thro' your pores the dews distil	
Like amber bead.	
His knife see Rustic-labour dight,	*make ready*
An' cut you up wi' ready slight,	*with; skill*
Trenching your gushing entrails bright	
Like onie ditch;	*any*
And then, O what a glorious sight,	
Warm-reekin, rich!	*-steaming*
Then, horn for horn they stretch an' strive,	*horn-spoon*
Deil tak the hindmost, on they drive,	*devil take*
Till a' their weel-swall'd kytes belyve	*all; well-swollen bellies soon*
Are bent like drums;	
Then auld Guidman, maist like to rive,	*old goodman; most; split*
Bethankit hums.	*God be thanked*
Is there that owre his French *ragout*,	*over*
Or *olio* that wad staw a sow,	*would satiate*
Or *fricassee* wad mak her spew	*would*
Wi' perfect sconner,	*with; disgust*
Looks down wi' sneering, scornfu' view	*scornful*
On sic a dinner?	*such*

Poor devil! see him owre his trash, *over*
As feckless as a wither'd rash, *weak; rush*
His spindle shank a guid whip-lash, *good*
His nieve a nit; *fist; nut*
Thro' bluidy flood or field to dash, *bloody*
O how unfit!

But mark the Rustic, *haggis-fed*,
The trembling earth resounds his tread,
Clap in his walie nieve a blade, *thrust; sturdy fist*
He'll mak it whissle; *make; whistle*
An' legs, an' arms, an' heads will sned, *and; chop off*
Like taps o' thrissle. *tops of thistle*

Ye Pow'rs wha mak mankind your care, *who make*
And dish them out their bill o' fare,
Auld Scotland wants nae skinking ware *old; no watery*
That jaups in luggies; *sloshes; bowls*
But, if ye wish her gratefu' pray'r, *grateful*
Gie her a *Haggis!* *give*

A Fragment. [There was a Lad]

There was a birkie born in Kyle, *fellow; central district of Ayrshire*
But what na day o' what na Style, *on what; by what*
I doubt its hardly worth the while
  To be sae nice wi' *Robin*. *so precise with*

Robin was a rovin' boy, *roving*
  Rantin' rovin', rantin' rovin'; *romping roving*
Robin was a rovin' Boy,
  Rantin' rovin' Robin.

Our Monarch's hindmost year but ane *one*
Was five an' twenty days begun,[1]
'Twas then a blast o' Janwar win' *January wind*
  Blew hansel in on *Robin*. *a first, good-luck gift*

The Gossip keekit in his loof, *godmother looked; palm*
Quo she, wha lives'll see the proof, *said she; who*
This walie boy will be nae coof, *fine; no fool*
  I think we'll ca' him *Robin*. *call*

He'll hae misfortunes great an' sma', *have; and small*
But ay a heart aboon them a'; *always; above; all*
He'll gie his Daddie's name a blaw, *give; boost*
  We'll a' be proud o' *Robin*.

But sure as three times three maks nine, *makes*
I see by ilka score an' line, *every*
This chap will dearly like our kin', *kind*
  So leeze me on thee *Robin*. *blessings*

Guid faith, quo she, I doubt you, Stir, *good; said she*
Ye'll gar the lasses lie aspar *make; legs apart*
But twenty fauts ye may hae waur, *faults; have worse*
  So blessins on thee *Robin*. *blessings*

1 Jan. 25th 1759, the date of my Bardship's vital existence [Burns's note].

[Inscribed around Fergusson's Portrait]

Curse on ungrateful man, that can be pleas'd,
And yet can starve the author of the pleasure!

O thou, my elder brother in Misfortune,
By far my elder Brother in the muse,
With tears I pity thy unhappy fate!
Why is the Bard unfitted for the world;
Yet has so keen a relish of its Pleasures?

[Lines on Fergusson]

Ill-fated genius! Heaven-taught Fergusson!
  What heart that feels and will not yield a tear,
To think life's sun did set ere well begun
  To shed its influence on thy bright career.
O why should truest worth and genius pine,
  Beneath the iron grasp of Want and Wo,
While titled knaves and idiot greatness shine
  In all the splendour Fortune can bestow!

Written by Somebody on the Window of an Inn at Stirling on Seeing the Royal Palace in Ruins.

Here Stewarts once in triumph reign'd;
And laws for Scotland's weal ordain'd;
But now unroof'd their Palace stands,
Their sceptre's fall'n to other hands;
Fallen indeed, and to the earth,
Whence grovelling reptiles take their birth.—
The injur'd Stewart line are gone,
A Race outlandish fill their throne;
An idiot race, to honor lost;
Who know them best despise them most.—

Ca' the Ewes to the Knowes

[First Version]

Ca' the ewes to the knowes *drive; knolls*
  Ca' them whare the heather grows, *where*
Ca' them whare the burnie rowes, *stream rolls*
  My bonnie dearie. *pretty*

As I gaed down the water-side, *went*
  There I met my shepherd-lad,
He row'd me sweetly in his plaid, *rolled; cloak or shawl*
  And he ca'd me his dearie. *called*
    Ca' the ewes &c.

Will ye gang down the water-side *go*
  And see the waves sae sweetly glide *so*
Beneath the hazels spreading wide,
  The moon it shines fu' clearly. *full*
    Ca' the ewes &c.

I was bred up at nae sic school, *no such*
  My shepherd-lad, to play the fool,
And a' the day to sit in dool, *all; grief*
  And nae body to see me: *no*
    Ca' the ewes &c.

Ye sall get gowns and ribbons meet, *shall; fit*
  Cauf-leather shoon upon your feet, *calf-; shoes*
And in my arms ye'se lie and sleep, *you will*
  And ye sall be my dearie. *shall*
    Ca' the ewes &c.

If ye'll but stand to what ye've said,
  I'se gang wi' you, my shepherd lad, *I shall go with*
And ye may rowe me in your plaid, *roll*
  And I sall be your dearie. *shall*
    Ca' the ewes &c.

While waters wimple to the sea; *meander*
While day blinks in the lift sae hie; *shines; sky so high*
Till clay-cauld death sall blin' my e'e, *-cold; shall blind; eye*
Ye sall be my dearie. *shall*
Ca' the ewes &c.

I Love My Jean.

Of a' the airts the wind can blaw, *directions; blow*
I dearly like the west,
For there the bony Lassie lives, *pretty*
The Lassie I lo'e best: *love*
There's wild-woods grow, and rivers row, *roll*
And mony a hill between; *many*
But day and night my fancy's flight
Is ever wi' my Jean. *with*

I see her in the dewy flowers,
I see her sweet and fair;
I hear her in the tunefu' birds, *tuneful*
I hear her charm the air:
There's not a bony flower, that springs *pretty*
By fountain, shaw, or green, *thicket*
There's not a bony bird that sings, *pretty*
But minds me o' my Jean. *reminds*

O, Were I on Parnassus Hill

O were I on Parnassus hill;
Or had o' Helicon my fill; *of*
That I might catch poetic skill,
To sing how dear I love thee.
But Nith maun be my Muses well, *must*
My Muse maun be thy bonie sell; *must; pretty self*
On Corsincon I'll glowr and spell, *stare*
And write how dear I love thee.

Then come, sweet Muse, inspire my lay!
For a' the lee-lang simmer's day, *all; live-long summer*
I couldna sing, I couldna say, *could not*
How much, how dear, I love thee.
I see thee dancing o'er the green,
Thy waist sae jimp, thy limbs sae clean, *so neat; so*
Thy tempting lips, thy roguish een— *eyes*
By Heaven and Earth I love thee.

By night, by day, a-field, at hame, *home*
The thoughts o' thee my breast inflame; *of*
And ay I muse and sing thy name, *always*
I only live to love thee.
Tho' I were doom'd to wander on,
Beyond the sea, beyond the sun,
Till my last, weary sand was run;
Till then—and then I love thee.

Tam Glen.

My heart is a breaking, dear Tittie,
   Some counsel unto me come len', — *lend*
To anger them a' is a pity, — *all*
   But what will I do wi' Tam Glen. — *with*

I'm thinking, wi' sic a braw fellow, — *with such; fine*
   In poortith I might mak a fen; — *poverty; attempt*
What care I in riches to wallow,
   If I mauna marry Tam Glen. — *cannot*

There's Lowrie the laird o' Dumeller, — *lord, landowner of*
   'Gude day to you brute' he comes ben: — *good; in*
He brags and he blaws o' his siller, — *boasts; silver, money*
   But when will he dance like Tam Glen.

My Minnie does constantly deave me, — *mother; deafen*
   And bids me beware o' young men;
They flatter, she says, to deceive me,
   But wha can think sae o' Tam Glen. — *who; so of*

My Daddie says, gin I'll forsake him, — *if*
   He'll gie me gude hunder marks ten: — *good hundred*
But, if it's ordain'd I maun take him, — *must*
   O wha will I get but Tam Glen. — *who*

Yestreen at the Valentines' dealing, — *last night*
   My heart to my mou gied a sten; — *mouth gave; leap*
For thrice I drew ane without failing, — *one*
   And thrice it was written, Tam Glen.

The last Halloween I was waukin — *watching over*
   My droukit sark-sleeve, as ye ken; — *soaking shirt-; know*
His likeness cam up the house staukin, — *came; stalking*
   And the very grey breeks o' Tam Glen. — *breeches*

Come counsel, dear Tittie, don't tarry;
  I'll gie you my bonie black hen, *give; pretty*
Gif ye will advise me to Marry *if*
  The lad I lo'e dearly, Tam Glen. *love*

Auld Lang Syne.

Should auld acquaintance be forgot *old*
And never brought to mind?
Should auld acquaintance be forgot,
And auld lang syne! *old long ago*

For auld lang syne my jo, *dear*
For auld lang syne,
We'll tak a cup[1] o' kindness yet *take; of*
For auld lang syne.

And surely ye'll be your pint stowp! *flagon*
And surely I'll be mine!
And we'll tak a cup o' kindness yet,
For auld lang syne.
For auld, &c.

We twa hae run about the braes, *two have; hills*
And pou'd the gowans fine; *pulled; daisies*
But we've wander'd mony a weary fitt, *many; foot*
Sin auld lang syne. *since*
For auld, &c.

We twa hae paidl'd in the burn, *two have paddled; stream*
Frae morning sun till dine; *from; dinnertime*
But seas between us braid hae roar'd, *broad have*
Sin auld lang syne.
For auld, &c.

And there's a hand, my trusty fiere! *friend*
And gie's a hand o' thine. *give me*
And we'll tak a right gude-willie-waught, *take; generous drink*
For auld lang syne.
For auld, &c.

1 Some Sing, Kiss, in place of Cup [Burns's note].

Louis What Reck I by Thee.

Louis what reck I by thee, — *Louis XVI, King of France; heed*
  Or Geordie on his ocean: — *George III, King of Britain*
Dyvor, beggar louns to me, — *bankrupt; fellows*
  I reign in Jeanie's bosom.

Let her crown my love her law,
  And in her breast enthrone me:
Kings and nations, swith awa! — *quick away*
  Reif randies I disown ye! — *thieving beggars*

Robin Shure in Hairst.

Robin shure in hairst, *reaped; autumn*
    I shure wi' him *with*
Fint a heuk had I, *the devil a hook*
    Yet I stack by him. *stuck*

I gaed up to Dunse, *went*
    To warp a wab o' plaiden *weave; fabric; tartan cloth*
At his daddie's yet, *gate*
    Wha met me but Robin. *who*
            Robin shure &c.

Was na Robin bauld, *not; bold*
    Tho' I was a cotter, *tenant-farmer*
Play'd me sic a trick *such*
    And me the Eller's dochter? *[church-]elder's daughter*
            Robin shure &c.

Robin promis'd me
    A' my winter vittle, *all; victual*
Fient haet he had but three *devil of it*
    Goos feathers and [a] whittle. *goose; knife*
            Robin shure &c.

Nine Inch Will Please a Lady.

Come rede me, dame, come tell me, dame, — *advise*
My dame, come tell me truly,
What length o' graith, when weel ca'd hame, — *equipment; well driven home*
Will sair a woman duly? — *serve*
The carlin clew her wanton tail, — *old woman; clawed*
Her wanton tail sae ready; — *so*
I learn't a sang in Annandale, — *song*
Nine inch will please a lady.

But for a coontrie c[un]t like mine, — *country*
In sooth we're nae sae gentle; — *truth; not so*
We'll tak' twa thumb-bread to the nine, — *take; two; -breadth*
And that's a sonsie p[intl]e. — *handsome penis*
O leeze me on my Charlie-lad! — *my blessings*
I'll ne'er forget my Charlie!
Twa roarin' handfu' and a daud, — *two; handful; thud*
He nidg't it in fu' rarely. — *squeezed; full, most*

But weary fa' the laithern doup, — *fall; lazy rump*
And may it ne'er ken thrivin'; — *never know*
It's no the length that gars me loup, — *makes; jump*
But its the double drivin'.
Come nidge me Tam, come nodge me Tam, — *squeeze; nudge*
Come nidge me o'er the nyvle; — *navel*
Come louse and lug your batterin' ram, — *loose; pull out*
And thrash him at my gyvel. — *gable, crotch*

Afton Water.

Flow gently sweet Afton among thy green braes, *hills*
Flow gently, I'll sing thee a song in thy praise;
My Mary's asleep by thy murmuring stream,
Flow gently, sweet Afton, disturb not her dream.

Thou stock dove whose echo resounds thro' the glen, *valley*
Ye wild whistling blackbirds in yon thorny den,
Thou green crested lapwing thy screaming forbear,
I charge you disturb not my slumbering Fair.

How lofty, sweet Afton, thy neighbouring hills,
Far mark'd with the courses of clear, winding rills;
There daily I wander as noon rises high,
My flocks and my Mary's sweet Cot in my eye. *cottage*

How pleasant thy banks and green vallies below, *valleys*
Where wild in the woodlands the primroses blow;
There oft as mild ev'ning weeps over the lea,
The sweet scented birk shades my Mary and me. *birch*

Thy chrystal stream, Afton, how lovely it glides, *crystal*
And winds by the cot where my Mary resides; *cottage*
How wanton thy waters her snowy feet lave,
As gathering sweet flowerets she stems thy clear wave.

Flow gently, sweet Afton, among thy green braes, *hills*
Flow gently, sweet River, the theme of my lays;
My Mary's asleep by thy murmuring stream,
Flow gently, sweet Afton, disturb not her dream.

[Epistle to Dr Blacklock]

My Rev^{d}. & dear Friend

Wow, but your letter made me vauntie!	*proud*
And are ye hale, & weel, and cantie?	*well; cheerful*
I kend it still your wee bit jauntie	*knew; small; journey*
Wad bring ye to:	*would*
Lord send you ay as weel's I want ye,	*always; well as*
And then ye'll do.	
The ILL-THIEF blaw the HERON south!	*devil blow*
And never drink be near his drouth!	*thirst*
He tald mysel, by word o' mouth,	*told myself; of*
He'd tak my letter;	*take*
I lippen'd to the chiel in trouth,	*depended on; fellow; truth*
And bade nae better.—	*asked no*
But aiblins honest Master Heron	*perhaps*
Had a' the time some dainty FAIR ONE,	*all*
To ware his theologic care on,	*employ*
And holy study;	
And tired o' SAULS to waste his lear on,	*souls; learning*
E'en tried the BODY.—	
But what d'ye think, my trusty Fier,	*friend*
I'm turn'd a Gauger—Peace be here!	*exciseman*
Parnassian QUINES I fear, I fear;	*girls*
Ye'll now disdain me,	
And then my fifty pounds a year	
Will little gain me.—	
Ye glaiket, gleesome, dainty DAMIES,	*stupid, merry*
Wha by Castalia's wimplin streamies	*who; rippling*
Lowp, sing, and lave your pretty limbies,	*leap*
Ye ken, Ye ken,	*know*
That strang Necessity supreme is	*strong*
'Mang sons o' Men.—	*among*

I hae a wife and twa wee laddies, *have; two small*
They maun hae brose & brats o' duddies; *must have; scraps of clothing*
Ye ken yoursels my heart right proud is, *know yourselves*
    I need na vaunt *not boast*
But I'll sned boosoms and thraw saugh-woodies, *chop brooms; twist*
        Before they want.— *[willow ropes*

Lord help me thro' this warld o' care! *world*
I'm weary sick o't late and air! *of it; early*
Not but I hae a richer share *have*
    Than monie ithers; *many others*
But why should ae man better fare, *one*
    And a' Men brithers! *all; brothers*

Come, FIRM RESOLVE take thou the van, *lead*
Thou stalk o' carl-hemp in man! *stubborn element*
And let us mind, faint heart ne'er wan *remember; won*
    A lady fair:
Wha does the utmost that he can *who[ever]*
    Will whyles do mair.— *sometimes; more*

But to conclude my silly rhyme,
(I'm scant o' verse and scant o' time,) *short*
To make a happy fireside clime
    To weans & wife, *children*
That's the true PATHOS & SUBLIME
    Of Human life.—

My Compliments to Sister Beckie;
And eke the same to honest Lucky, *also*
I wat she is a dainty Chuckie *know; sweet-heart*
    As e'er tread clay! *trod*
And gratefully my gude auld Cockie *good old cock*
    I'm yours for ay.— *ever*

Robt Burns

Ellisland
21$^{st.}$ Oct. 1789

On Capt$^{n.}$ Grose's present peregrinations through Scotland collecting the antiquities of that kingdom

Hear, Land of Cakes & brither Scots, *brother*
Frae Maiden-kirk to Johnie Groats! *from*
If there's a hole in a' your coats *all*
I rede you tent it: *advise; attend to*
A chiel's amang you taking notes, *fellow is among*
And faith he'll print it!

If in your bounds ye chance to light
Upon a fine, fat, fodgel wight, *plump and good-humoured*
Of stature short, but genius bright,
That's he, mark weel: *well*
And wow! he has an unco slight *extraordinary skill*
O' cauk and keel.— *of chalk and red-ochre [for drawing]*

At some auld, houlet-haunted biggin, *old, owl-; building*
Or kirk deserted by its riggin, *church; roofing*
It's ten to ane ye'll find him snug in *one*
Some eldritch part, *eerie*
Wi' deils, they say, L[o]rd safe's, colleaguin *with devils; save us; conspiring*
At some black art.—

Ilk ghaist that haunts auld ha' or chaumer; *each ghost; old hall; chamber*
Ye gipsey gang that deal in glaumor, *enchantment*
And you deep-read in h[e]ll's black grammar, *occult learning*
Warlocks & witches,
Ye'll quake at his conjuring hammer,
Ye midnight b[i]tches.

It's tauld he was a Sodger bred, *told; soldier*
And ane wad rather faun than fled; *one would [have]; fallen*
But now he's quat the spurtle blade *quitted; porridgestick*
And dog-skin wallet,
And taen the—Antiquarian trade *taken*
I think they call it.—

He has a fouth of auld nick-nackets;	*abundance; old bits and pieces*
Rousty airn caps & jinglin jackets	*rusty iron; jingling*
Wad had the Lothians three in tackets	*would hold; hobnails*
A towmont gude,	*twelvemonth good*
And pirratch-pats, and auld saut-backets	*porridge-pots; old salt-boxes*
Afore the Flood.	*before*
Of Eve's first fire he has a cinder;	
Auld Tubal-cain's fire-shool & fender;	*old; fire-shovel*
That which distinguished the gender	
Of Balaam's ass;	
A broom-stick o' the Witch of Endor,	*of*
Weel-shod wi' brass.—	*well-; with*
Besides, he'll cut you aff fu' gleg	*off full brisk[ly]*
The shape of Adam's philibeg;	*kilt*
The knife that nicket Abel's craig,	*nicked; throat*
He'll prove you fully	
If 'twas a faulding jocteleg,	*folding clasp-knife*
Or lang-kail gully.—	*long-cole knife*
But wad ye see him in his glee,	*would*
For meikle glee & fun has he,	*much*
Then set him down, & twa or three	*two*
Gude fallows wi' him,	*good fellows with*
And Port, O Port! shine thou a wee,	*little*
And *then* ye'll see him!	
Now, by the powers o' Verse & Prose,	*of*
Thou art a dainty chiel O Grose!	*fellow*
Whae'er o' thee shall ill suppose,	*whoever*
They sair misca' thee:	*sore[ly] miscall, slander*
I'd tak the rascal by the nose,	*take*
Wad say, Shame fa' thee.	*[who] would; fall*

My Love She's but a Lassie Yet.

My love she's but a lassie yet,
My love she's but a lassie yet,
We'll let her stand a year or twa, *two*
She'll no be half sae saucy yet. *so*

I rue the day I sought her O,
I rue the day I sought her O,
Wha gets her needs na say he's woo'd, *who; not*
But he may say he's bought her O.

Come draw a drap o' the best o't yet, *drop of; of it*
Come draw a drap o' the best o't yet:
Gae seek for pleasure whare you will, *go; where*
But here I never misst it yet. *missed*

We're a' dry wi' drinking o't, *all; with; of it*
We're a' dry wi' drinking o't:
The minister kisst the fidler's wife, *kissed; fiddler's*
He could na preach for thinkin o't. *not; thinking*

My Heart's in the Highlands.

My heart's in the Highlands, my heart is not here;
My heart's in the Highlands a chasing the deer;
A chasing the wild deer, and following the roe,
My heart's in the Highlands, wherever I go.
Farewell to the Highlands, farewell to the north,
The birth place of Valour, the country of Worth,
Wherever I wander, wherever I rove,
The hills of the Highlands for ever I love.

Farewell to the mountains high cover'd with snow;
Farewell to the straths and green vallies below: *[river] valleys*
Farewell to the forests and wild hanging woods;
Farewell to the torrents and loud pouring floods.
My heart's in the Highlands, my heart is not here,
My heart's in the Highlands a chasing the deer:
Chasing the wild deer, and following the roe;
My heart's in the Highlands, wherever I go.

John Anderson my Jo.

John Anderson my jo, John, *sweetheart*
When we were first Acquent; *acquaint[ed]*
Your locks were like the raven,
Your bony brow was brent; *handsome; smooth*
But now your brow is beld, John, *bald*
Your locks are like the snaw; *snow*
But blessings on your frosty pow, *head*
John Anderson my Jo.

John Anderson my jo, John,
We clamb the hill the gither; *climbed; together*
And mony a canty day John, *many; cheerful*
We've had wi' ane anither: *with one another*
Now we maun totter down, John, *must*
And hand in hand we'll go;
And sleep the gither at the foot, *together*
John Anderson my Jo.

Tam o' Shanter. A Tale.

Of Brownyis and of Bogillis full is this buke.

GAWIN DOUGLAS.

When chapmen billies leave the street, — *pedlar fellows*
And drouthy neebors, neebors meet, — *thirsty neighbours*
As market-days are wearing late,
An' folk begin to tak the gate; — *and; take the road*
While we sit bousing at the nappy, — *drinking strong ale*
And getting fou and unco happy, — *full, drunk; uncommonly*
We think na on the lang Scots miles, — *not: long*
The mosses, waters, slaps, and styles, — *peat-bogs; hedge-gaps*
That lie between us and our hame, — *home*
Whare sits our sulky sullen dame, — *where*
Gathering her brows like gathering storm,
Nursing her wrath to keep it warm.

This truth fand honest *Tam o' Shanter*, — *found*
As he frae Ayr ae night did canter, — *from; one*
(Auld Ayr, wham ne'er a town surpasses, — *old*
For honest men and bonny lasses.) — *pretty*

O *Tam!* hadst thou but been sae wise, — *so*
As ta'en thy ain wife *Kate*'s advice! — *taken; own*
She tauld thee weel thou was a skellum, — *told; well; scoundrel*
A blethering, blustering, drunken blellum; — *babbling; gasbag*
That frae November till October, — *from*
Ae market-day thou was nae sober; — *one; not*
That ilka melder, wi' the miller, — *every grinding-day, with*
Thou sat as lang as thou had siller; — *long; silver, money*
That ev'ry naig was ca'd a shoe on, — *horse; fixed*
The smith and thee gat roaring fou on; — *got; drunk*
That at the L[or]d's house, even on Sunday,
Thou drank wi' Kirkton Jean till Monday. — *with*
She prophesied that late or soon,

Thou would be found deep drown'd in Doon; *would*
Or catch'd wi' warlocks in the mirk, *with*
By *Aloway*'s auld haunted kirk. *old*

Ah, gentle dames! it gars me greet, *makes; weep*
To think how mony counsels sweet, *many*
How mony lengthen'd sage advices,
The husband frae the wife despises! *from*

But to our tale: Ae market-night, *one*
Tam had got planted unco right; *extraordinarily*
Fast by an ingle, bleezing finely, *fireside; blazing*
Wi' reaming swats, that drank divinely; *foaming ale*
And at his elbow, Souter *Johnny*, *shoemaker*
His ancient, trusty, drouthy crony; *thirsty crony*
Tam lo'ed him like a vera brither; *loved; very brother*
They had been fou for weeks thegither. *drunk; together*
The night drave on wi' sangs and clatter; *drove; with songs; chatter*
And ay the ale was growing better: *always*
The landlady and *Tam* grew gracious,
Wi' favours, secret, sweet, and precious: *with*
The Souter tauld his queerest stories; *shoemaker told*
The landlord's laugh was ready chorus:
The storm without might rair and rustle, *outside; roar*
Tam did na mind the storm a whistle. *not*

Care, mad to see a man sae happy, *so*
E'en drown'd himsel amang the nappy: *himself among; strong ale*
As bees flee hame wi' lades o' treasure, *fly home, with loads of*
The minutes wing'd their way wi' pleasure:
Kings may be blest, but *Tam* was glorious,
O'er a' the ills o' life victorious! *all; of*

But pleasures are like poppies spread,
You seize the flower, its bloom is shed;
Or like the snow falls in the river,
A moment white—then melts for ever;
Or like the borealis race, *Aurora Borealis or Northern Lights*
That flit ere you can point their place;

Or like the rainbow's lovely form
Evanishing amid the storm.— *vanishing*
Nae man can tether time or tide; *no*
The hour approaches Tam maun ride; *must*
That hour, o' night's black arch the key-stane, *of; key-stone*
That dreary hour he mounts his beast in;
And sic a night he taks the road in, *such; takes*
As ne'er poor sinner was abroad in.

The wind blew as 'twad blawn its last; *it would [have] blown*
The rattling showers rose on the blast;
The speedy gleams the darkness swallow'd;
Loud, deep, and lang, the thunder bellow'd: *long*
That night, a child might understand,
The Deil had business on his hand. *devil*

Weel mounted on his gray mare, *Meg*, *well; grey*
A better never lifted leg,
Tam skelpit on thro' dub and mire, *dashed; puddle; bog*
Despising wind, and rain, and fire;
Whiles holding fast his gude blue bonnet; *sometimes; good*
Whiles crooning o'er some auld Scots sonnet; *humming; old*
Whiles glowring round wi' prudent cares, *staring; with*
Lest bogles catch him unawares: *phantoms*
Kirk-Alloway was drawing nigh, *near*
Whare ghaists and houlets nightly cry.— *where ghosts; owls*

By this time he was cross the ford, *across*
Whare, in the snaw, the chapman smoor'd; *where; snow; pedlar; smothered*
And past the birks and meikle stane, *birches; large stone*
Whare drunken *Charlie* brak's neck-bane; *where; broke his neck-bone*
And thro' the whins, and by the cairn, *gorse; heap of stones*
Whare hunters fand the murder'd bairn; *where; found; child*
And near the thorn, aboon the well, *above*
Whare *Mungo*'s mither hang'd hersel.— *where; mother; herself*
Before him *Doon* pours all his floods;
The doubling storm roars thro' the woods;
The lightnings flash from pole to pole;

Near and more near the thunders roll:
When, glimmering thro' the groaning trees,
Kirk-Alloway seem'd in a bleeze; — *blaze*
Thro' ilka bore the beams were glancing; — *every crack*
And loud resounded mirth and dancing.—

Inspiring bold *John Barleycorn!* — *alcoholic drink*
What dangers thou canst make us scorn!
Wi' tippenny, we fear nae evil; — *small beer; no*
Wi' usquabae, we'll face the devil!— — *whisky*
The swats sae ream'd in *Tammie*'s noddle, — *beer so foamed; head*
Fair play, he car'd na deils a boddle. — *no devils; tuppence*
But *Maggie* stood right sair astonish'd, — *sore[ly]*
Till, by the heel and hand admonish'd,
She ventured forward on the light;
And, vow! *Tam* saw an unco sight! — *wow; extraordinary*
Warlocks and witches in a dance;
Nae cotillion brent new frae *France*, — *no; brand; from*
But hornpipes, jigs, strathspeys, and reels,
Put life and mettle in their heels.
A winnock-bunker in the east, — *window-seat*
There sat auld Nick, in shape o' beast; — *old Nick [the Devil]*
A towzie tyke, black, grim, and large, — *shaggy dog*
To gie them music was his charge: — *give*
He screw'd the pipes and gart them skirl, — *bagpipes; made; squeal*
Till roof and rafters a' did dirl.— — *all; reverberate*
Coffins stood round, like open presses, — *cupboards*
That shaw'd the dead in their last dresses: — *showed*
And by some devilish cantraip slight — *magic trick*
Each in its cauld hand held a light.— — *cold*
By which heroic *Tam* was able
To note upon the haly table, — *holy*
A murderer's banes in gibbet airns; — *bones; irons*
Twa span-lang, wee, unchristen'd bairns; — *two; -long; small; children*
A thief, new-cutted frae a rape, — *from; rope*
Wi' his last gasp his gab did gape; — *with; mouth*
Five tomahawks, wi' blude red-rusted; — *blood*
Five scymitars, wi' murder crusted;

A garter, which a babe had strangled;
A knife, a father's throat had mangled,
Whom his ain son o' life bereft, *own; of*
The grey hairs yet stack to the heft; *stuck*
Wi' mair o' horrible and awefu', *more; awful*
Which even to name wad be unlawfu'. *would; unlawful*

As *Tammie* glowr'd, amaz'd, and curious, *stared*
The mirth and fun grew fast and furious:
The piper loud and louder blew;
The dancers quick and quicker flew;
They reel'd, they set, they cross'd, they cleekit, *linked(arms)*
Till ilka carlin swat and reekit, *every hag sweated; steamed*
And coost her duddies to the wark, *threw off; rags; work*
And linket at it in her sark! *capered; shift*

Now *Tam*, O *Tam!* had thae been queans, *those; girls*
A' plump and strapping in their teens, *all; vigorous*
Their sarks, instead o' creeshie flannen, *shifts; of greasy flannel*
Been snaw-white seventeen hunder linnen! *snow-; hundred*
Thir breeks o' mine, my only pair, *these breeches*
That ance were plush, o' gude blue hair, *once; good*
I wad hae gi'en them off my hurdies, *would have given; backside*
For ae blink o' the bonie burdies! *one glimpse; pretty darlings*

But wither'd beldams, auld and droll, *hags, old*
Rigwoodie hags wad spean a foal, *bony; would wean*
Lowping and flinging on a crummock, *leaping; capering; crook*
I wonder didna turn thy stomach. *did not*

But *Tam* kend what was what fu' brawlie, *knew; full well*
There was ae winsome wench and wawlie, *one; sturdy*
That night enlisted in the core, *company*
(Lang after kend on *Carrick* shore; *long; known*
For mony a beast to dead she shot, *many; death*
And perish'd mony a bony boat, *many; handsome*
And shook baith meikle corn and bear, *both much oats and barley*
And kept the country-side in fear.)
Her cutty sark, o' Paisley harn, *short shift; coarse linen*

That while a lassie she had worn,
In longitude tho' sorely scanty,
It was her best, and she was vauntie.— *proud*
Ah! little kend thy reverend grannie, *knew; grandmother*
That sark she coft for her wee Nannie, *shift; bought; little*
Wi' twa pund Scots, ('twas a' her riches), *two pound Scots; all*
Wad ever grac'd a dance of witches!

But here my Muse her wing maun cour; *must lower*
Sic flights are far beyond her pow'r; *such*
To sing how Nannie lap and flang, *leapt; capered*
(A souple jade she was, and strang), *supple girl; strong*
And how *Tam* stood, like ane bewitch'd, *one*
And thought his very een enrich'd; *eyes*
Even Satan glowr'd, and fidg'd fu' fain, *stared; was restlessly excited*
And hotch'd and blew wi' might and main: *jerked; with*
Till first ae caper, syne anither, *one; then another*
Tam tint his reason a' thegither, *lost; altogether*
And roars out, 'Weel done, Cutty-sark!' *well; short-shift*
And in an instant all was dark:
And scarcely had he Maggie rallied,
When out the hellish legion sallied.

As bees bizz out wi' angry fyke, *buzz; commotion*
When plundering herds assail their byke; *farmboys; hive*
As open pussie's mortal foes, *hare's*
When, pop! she starts before their nose;
As eager runs the market-crowd,
When 'Catch the thief!' resounds aloud;
So Maggie runs, the witches follow,
Wi' mony an eldritch skreech and hollow. *many; unearthly screech; shout*

Ah, *Tam!* Ah, *Tam!* thou'll get thy fairin! *what you deserve*
In hell they'll roast thee like a herrin! *herring*
In vain thy *Kate* awaits thy comin! *coming*
Kate soon will be a woefu' woman! *woeful*

Now, do thy speedy utmost, Meg,
And win the key-stane[1] of the brig; *key-stone; bridge*
There at them thou thy tail may toss,
A running stream they dare na cross. *not*
But ere the key-stane she could make, *key-stone*
The fient a tail she had to shake! *the devil a*
For Nannie, far before the rest,
Hard upon noble Maggie prest, *pressed*
And flew at Tam wi' furious ettle; *effort*
But little wist she Maggie's mettle— *knew*
Ae spring brought off her master hale, *one*
But left behind her ain grey tail: *own*
The carlin claught her by the rump, *woman clutched*
And left poor Maggie scarce a stump.

Now, wha this tale o' truth shall read, *who*
Ilk man and mother's son, take heed: *each*
Whene'er to drink you are inclin'd,
Or cutty-sarks run in your mind, *short-shifts*
Think, ye may buy the joys o'er dear,
Remember Tam o' Shanter's mare.

1 It is a well known fact that witches, or any evil spirits, have no power to follow a poor wight any farther than the middle of the next running stream.—It may be proper likewise to mention to the benighted traveller, that when he falls in with *bogles*, whatever danger may be in his going forward, there is much more hazard in turning back [Burns's note].

The Banks o' Doon.

Ye Banks and braes o' bonie Doon, *slopes; of pretty*
  How can ye bloom sae fresh and fair; *so*
How can ye chant, ye little birds,
  And I sae weary fu' o' care! *so; full*
Thou'll break my heart thou warbling bird,
  That wantons thro' the flowering thorn:
Thou minds me o' departed joys, *reminds; of*
  Departed never to return.

Oft hae I rov'd by bonie Doon, *have; pretty*
  To see the rose and woodbine twine;
And ilka bird sang o' its luve, *every; love*
  And fondly sae did I o' mine. *so*
Wi' lightsome heart I pu'd a rose, *with; carefree; pulled*
  Fu' sweet upon its thorny tree; *full*
And my fause luver staw my rose, *false lover stole*
  But, ah! he left the thorn wi' me. *with*

Ae Fond Kiss.

Ae fond kiss, and then we sever; *one*
Ae farewell and then for ever!
Deep in heart-wrung tears I'll pledge thee,
Warring sighs and groans I'll wage thee. *pay*
Who shall say that fortune grieves him
While the star of hope she leaves him?
Me, nae cheerfu' twinkle lights me; *no cheerful*
Dark despair around benights me.

I'll ne'er blame my partial fancy,
Naething could resist my Nancy: *nothing*
But to see her, was to love her;
Love but her, and love for ever.
Had we never lov'd sae kindly, *so*
Had we never lov'd sae blindly,
Never met—or never parted,
We had ne'er been broken-hearted.

Fare thee weel, thou first and fairest! *well*
Fare thee weel, thou best and dearest!
Thine be ilka joy and treasure, *every*
Peace[,] Enjoyment, Love and Pleasure!
Ae fond kiss, and then we sever; *one*
Ae fareweel, Alas: for ever! *one farewell*
Deep in heart-wrung tears I'll pledge thee,
Warring sighs and groans I'll wage thee. *pay*

Such a Parcel of Rogues in a Nation.

Farewell to a' our Scotish fame, *all; Scottish*
  Fare weel our ancient glory; *well*
Fareweel even to the Scotish name, *farewell*
  Sae fam'd in martial story. *so*
Now Sark rins o'er the Solway sands, *runs*
  And Tweed rins to the ocean
To mark where Englands province stands,
  Such a parcel of rogues in a nation.

What force or guile could not subdue,
  Thro' many warlike ages,
Is wrought now by a coward few,
  For hireling traitors wages.
The English steel we could disdain,
  Secure in valour's station;
But English gold has been our bane,
  Such a parcel of rogues in a nation!

O would, or I had seen the day *before*
  That treason thus could sell us,
My auld grey head had lien in clay *old; lain*
  Wi' Bruce and loyal Wallace! *with*
But pith & power, till my last hour,
  I'll mak this declaration;
We're bought & sold for English gold
  Such a parcel of rogues in a nation!

The De'il's Awa wi' th' Exciseman.

The de'il cam fiddlin thro' the town, *devil came fiddling*
    And danc'd awa wi' th' Exciseman; *away with*
And ilka wife cries, auld Mahoun, *every; old*
    I wish you luck o' the prize, man. *of*
The de'il's awa the de'il's awa *devil's away*
The de'il's awa wi' th' Exciseman,
He's danc'd awa he's danc'd awa
He's danc'd awa wi' th' Exciseman.

We'll mak our maut and we'll brew our drink, *make; malt*
    We'll laugh, sing, and rejoice, man;
And mony braw thanks to the meikle black de'il, *many fine; great*
    That danc'd awa wi' th' Exciseman. *away with*
The de'il's awa, &c.

There's threesome reels, there's foursome reels,
    There's hornpipes and strathspeys, man,
But the ae best dance e'er cam to the Land *one; ever came*
    Was, the de'il's awa wi' th' Exciseman.
The de'il's awa, &c.

Highland Mary

Ye banks & braes, & streams around — *slopes*
The castle o' Montgomery,
Green be your woods, & fair your flowers,
Your waters never drumlie! — *muddy*
There Simmer first unfald her robes, — *summer; unfold[s]*
And there the langest tarry: — *longest*
For there I took the last Fareweel — *farewell*
O' my sweet Highland Mary. — *of*

How sweetly bloom'd the gay green birk — *birch*
How rich the hawthorn's blossom;
As underneath their fragrant shade,
I clasp'd her to my bosom!
The golden Hours, on angel wings,
Flew o'er me & my Dearie; — *darling*
For dear to me as light & life
Was my sweet Highland Mary.

Wi' mony a vow, & lock'd embrace, — *with; many*
Our parting was fu' tender; — *full*
And pledging aft to meet again, — *oft[en]*
We tore oursels asunder: — *ourselves*
But Oh, fell Death's untimely frost, — *fierce*
That nipt my Flower sae early! — *nipped; so*
Now green's the sod, & cauld's the clay, — *cold is*
That wraps my Highland Mary.

O pale, pale now, those rosy lips
I aft hae kiss'd sae fondly. — *oft have; so*
And clos'd for ay, the sparkling glance, — *ever*
That dwalt on me sae kindly — *dwelt; so*
And mouldering now in silent dust,
That heart that lo'ed me dearly! — *loved*
But still within my bosom's core
Shall live my Highland Mary.

The Rights of Woman

Spoken by Miss Fontenelle on her benefit n[igh]t[, November 26, 1792].

While Europe's eye is fix'd on mighty things,
The fate of Empires, & the fall of Kings;
While quacks of State must each produce his plan,
And even children lisp The Rights of Man;
Amid this mighty fuss, just let me mention,
The Rights of Woman merit some attention—

First, in the Sexes' intermixed connection,
One sacred Right of Woman is, Protection!
The tender flower that lifts its head, elate, *exultant*
Helpless, must fall before the blasts of Fate,
Sunk on the earth, defaced its lovely form,
Unless *your Shelter* ward th' impending storm—

Our second Right—but needless here is caution,
To keep that Right inviolate's the fashion.
Each man of sense has it so full before him
He'd die before he'd wrong it—'tis Decorum—
There was indeed, in far less polished days,
A time when rough, rude man had naughty ways:
Would swagger, swear, get drunk, kick up a riot,
Nay even thus invade a lady's quiet.—
Now, thank our Stars! these Gothic times are fled,
Now well-bred men (and you are all well-bred)
Most justly think (and we are much the gainers)
Such conduct neither spirit, wit, nor manners.—

For Right the third, our last, our best, our dearest,
That Right to fluttering Female hearts the nearest,
Which even the Rights of Kings, in low prostration
Most humbly own—'tis dear, dear ADMIRATION!
In that blest sphere alone we live & move;
There taste that life of life, IMMORTAL LOVE.—
Smiles, glances, sighs, tears, fits, flirtations, airs,

'Gainst such an host, what flinty savage dares—
When aweful Beauty joins in all her charms,
Who is so rash as rise in rebel arms?

But truce with kings, & truce with Constitutions,
With bloody armaments, & Revolutions;
Let Majesty your first attention summon,
Ah, ça ira! THE MAJESTY OF WOMAN!!!

Why Should Na Poor People Mow

While Princes & Prelates & het-headed zealots *hot-*
All Europe hae set in a lowe, *have; flame*
The poor man lies down, nor envies a crown,
And comforts himsel with a mow. *fuck*

And why should na poor people mow, mow, mow, *should not*
And why should na poor people mow,
The great folk hae siller, & houses, & land, *have silver, money*
Poor bodies hae naething but mow. *nothing*

Whan Brunswick's great Prince cam a cruising to France, *when; came*
Republican billies to cowe, *fellows; cow*
Bauld Brunswick's great Prince wad hae shawn better sense *would; shown*
At hame with his Princess to mow. *home*

Out over the Rhine proud Prussia wad shine, *would*
To spend his best blood he did vow;
But Frederic had better ne'er forded the water,
But spent as he docht in a mow. *could*

By sea & by shore! the Emperor swore,
In Paris he'd kick up a rowe; *row*
But Paris sae ready, just leugh at the laddie, *so; laughed*
And bade him gae tak him a mow *go take*

Auld Kate laid her claws on poor Stanislaus, *old*
And Poland has bent like a bow;
May the deil in her a[rse] ram a huge pr[i]ck o' brass, *devil*
And damn her in hell with a mow.—

But truce with commotions & new-fangled notions,
A bumper I trust you'll allow: *toast*
Here's George our good king, & lang may he ring, *good; long; reign*
And Charlotte & he tak a mow— *take*
And why should na &c.

Whistle & I'll Come to You My Lad.

O whistle & I'll come to ye, my lad,
O whistle & I'll come to ye, my lad;
Tho' father & mither & a' should gae mad, — *mother; all; go*
Whistle & I'll come to ye, my lad.

But warily tent, when ye come to court me, — *heed*
And come na unless the back-yett be ajee; — *not; back-gate; ajar*
Syne o'er the back-style & let naebody see, — *then; nobody*
And come as ye were na comin to me— — *not; coming*
O come as ye were na comin to me.
O whistle & I'll &c.

At kirk, or at market, whare'er ye meet me, — *church; wherever*
Gae by me as tho' that ye car'd nae a flie; — *go; not a fly*
But steal me a blink o' your bonie black e'e, — *handsome; eye*
Yet look as ye were na lookin at me— — *not looking*
O look as ye were na lookin at me.—
O whistle &c.—

Ay vow & protest that ye care na for me, — *always; not*
And whyles ye may lightly my beauty a-wee; — *sometimes; disparage; a little*
But court nae anither, tho' jokin ye be, — *not another; joking*
For fear that she wyle your fancy frae me— — *wile; from*
For fear that she wyle your fancy frae me!
O, whistle & I'll &c.

Ode [for General Washington's Birthday]

No Spartan tube, no Attic shell,
No lyre Eolian I awake;
'Tis Liberty's bold note I swell,
Thy harp, Columbia, let me take.
See gathering thousands, while I sing,
A broken chain, exulting, bring,
And dash it in a tyrant's face!
And dare him to his very beard,
And tell him, he no more is feared,
No more the Despot of Columbia's race.
A tyrant's proudest insults braved,
They shout, a People freed! They hail an Empire saved.

Where is Man's godlike form?
Where is that brow erect & bold,
That eye that can, unmoved, behold
The wildest rage, the loudest storm,
That e'er created fury dared to raise?
Avaunt! thou caitiff, servile, base,
That tremblest at a Despot's nod,
Yet, crouching under th'iron rod,
Canst laud the arm that struck th'insulting blow!
Art thou of man's imperial line?
Dost boast that countenance divine?
Each sculking feature answers, NO! *skulking*
But come, ye sons of Liberty,
Columbia's offspring, brave as free,
In danger's hour still flaming in the van:
Ye know, & dare maintain, The Royalty of Man.

Alfred, on thy starry throne,
Surrounded by the tuneful choir,
The Bards that erst have struck the patriot lyre,
And roused the freeborn Briton's soul of fire,

No more thy England own.—
Dare injured nations form the great design,
To make detested tyrants bleed?
Thy England execrates the glorious deed!
Beneath her hostile banners waving,
Every pang of honor braving,
England in thunder calls—'The Tyrant's cause is mine!'
That hour accurst, how did the fiends rejoice.
And hell thro' all her confines raise th'exulting voice,
That hour which saw the generous English name
Linkt with such damned deeds of everlasting shame! *linked*

Thee, Caledonia, thy wild heaths among,
Famed for the martial deed, the heaven-taught song,
To thee I turn with swimming eyes—
Where is that soul of Freedom fled?
Immingled with the mighty Dead!
Beneath that hallow'd turf where WALLACE lies!
Hear it not, Wallace, in thy bed of death!

Ye babbling winds in silence sweep,
Disturb not ye the hero's sleep,
Nor give the coward secret breath.—
Is this the ancient Caledonian form,
Firm as her rock, resistless as the storm?
Show me that eye which shot immortal hate,
Blasting the Despot's proudest bearing:
Show me that arm which, nerved with thundering fate,
Braved Usurpation's boldest daring!
Dark-quenched as yonder sinking star,
No more that glance lightens afar;
That palsied arm no more whirls on the waste of war.

Bruce to his Troops on the Eve of the Battle of Bannock-burn.

Scots, wha hae wi' WALLACE bled, *who have with*
Scots, wham BRUCE has aften led; *whom; often*
Welcome to your gory bed,
Or to victorie.

Now's the day, and now's the hour;
See the front o' battle lour; *of*
See approach proud Edward's power—
Chains and slaverie!

Wha will be a traitor-knave? *who*
Wha can fill a coward's grave?
Wha sae base as be a slave? *so*
Let him turn and flee!

Wha for SCOTLAND's king and law *who*
Freedom's sword will strongly draw,
FREE-MAN stand, or FREE-MAN fa', *fall*
Let him follow me!

By oppression's woes and pains!
By your sons in servile chains!
We will drain our dearest veins,
But they shall be free!

Lay the proud usurpers low!
Tyrants fall in every foe!
LIBERTY's in every blow!
Let us DO, or DIE!

Act Sederunt o' the Court o' Session.

In Embrugh town they've made a law, *Edinburgh*
In Embrugh at the court o' session; *of*
That stanin' p[ric]ks are fau'tors a', *standing; wrongdoers all*
An' guilty o' a high transgression. *and*
Decreet o' the court o' session. *judgment of*
Act sederunt o' the session.
That stanin' p[ric]ks are fau'tors a',
An' guilty o' a high transgression.

An' they've provided dungeons deep, *and*
Ilk lass has ane in her possession; *each; one*
Until the fau'tors wail an' weep, *wrongdoers*
They their shall lie for there transgression. *there; their*
Decreet o' the court of session,
Act sederunt o' the session,
The rogues in pouring tears shall weep,
By act sederunt o' the session.

A Red Red Rose.

O my Luve's like a red, red rose, *love is*
  That's newly sprung in June;
O My Luve's like the melodie
  That's sweetly play'd in tune.

As fair art thou, my bonie lass, *pretty*
  So deep in luve am I; *love*
And I will luve thee still, my dear,
  Till a' the seas gang dry. *all; go*

Till a' the seas gang dry, my Dear,
  And the rocks melt wi' the sun: *with*
O I will love thee still my dear,
  While the sands o' life shall run. *of*

And fare thee weel, my only Luve! *well; love*
  And fare thee weel, a while!
And I will come again, my Luve,
  Tho' it were ten thousand mile!

Ca' the Yowes to the Knowes

[Second Version]

Ca' the yowes to the knowes, *drive; ewes; knolls*
Ca' them whare the heather growes, *where*
Ca' them whare the burnie rowes, *stream rolls*
My bonie dearie. *pretty*

Hark, the mavis' evening sang *thrush's evening song*
Sounding Clouden's woods amang;[1] *among*
Then a faulding let us gang, *sheep-folding; go*
My bonie dearie.
Ca' the, &c.

We'll gae down by Clouden side, *go*
Thro' the hazels spreading wide,
O'er the waves, that sweetly glide
To the moon sae clearly. *so*
Ca' the, &c.

Yonder Clouden's silent towers,
Where at moonshine midnight hours,
O'er the dewy bending flowers,
Fairies dance sae cheary. *so; cheer[full]y*
Ca' the, &c.

Ghaist nor bogle shalt thou fear; *ghost; phantom*
Thou'rt to love and heaven sae dear, *so*
Nocht of ill may come thee near, *naught, nothing*
My bonie dearie.
Ca' the, &c.

Fair and lovely as thou art,
Thou hast stown my very heart; *stolen*
I can die—but canna part, *cannot*
My bonie dearie.
Ca' the, &c.

1 The river Clouden, a tributary stream to the Nith [Burns's note].

For a' that & a' that.

Is there, at honest Poverty
  That hings his head, & a' that? *hangs; all*
A coward slave, we pass him by,
  We dare be poor for a' that! *all*
For a' that, & a' that,
  Our toils obscure, & a' that;
The rank is but the guinea's stamp,
  The Man's the gowd for a' that.— *gold*

What tho' on hamely fare we dine, *homely*
  Wear hoddin grey, & a' that; *homespun cloth*
Gie fools their silks, & knaves their wine, *give*
  A Man's a Man for a' that.—
For a' that, & a' that,
  Their tinsel show, & a' that;
The honest man, tho' e'er sae poor, *ever so*
  Is king o' men for a' that.— *of*

Ye see yon birkie ca'd, a Lord, *smart fellow called*
  Wha struts & stares & a' that; *who*
Tho' hundreds worship at his word,
  He's but a coof for a' that.— *fool*
For a' that, & a' that,
  His ribband, star, & a' that;
The man of independant mind
  He looks & laughs at a' that.—

A Prince can mak a belted knight, *make*
  A marquis, duke, & a' that,
But an honest man's aboon his might, *above*
  Gude faith he mauna fa' that! *good; must not claim*
For a' that, & a' that,
  Their dignities & a' that;

The pith o' Sense, & pride o' Worth,
  Are higher rank for a' that.—

Then let us pray, that come it may,
  As come it will for a' that,
That Sense & Worth, o'er a' the earth, *over all*
  May bear the gree & a' that.— *win the prize*
For a' that, & a' that,
  Its comin yet for a' that, *coming*
That Man to Man, the warld o'er, *world*
  Shall brothers be for a' that.—

The Dumfries Volunteers.

Does haughty Gaul invasion threat, *France*
   Then let the louns beware, Sir, *rogues*
There's wooden walls upon our seas, *(warships)*
   And Volunteers on shore, Sir.
The Nith shall rin to Corsincon, *run*
   The Criffel sink in Solway,
E're we permit a foreign foe, *before*
   On British ground to rally,
We'll ne'er permit a foreign foe,
   On British ground to rally.

O let us not, like snarling curs,
   In wrangling be divided,
Till, slap! come in an unco loun, *suddenly; foreign fellow*
   And wi' a rung decide it: *with; cudgel*
Be Britain still to Britain true,
   Amang oursels united: *among ourselves*
For never but by British hands
   Maun British wrangs be righted. *must; wrongs*
      For never but &c.

The kettle o' the Kirk and State, *of*
   Perhaps a clout may fail in't; *patch; in it*
But deil a foreign tinkler loun *devil; tinker fellow*
   Shall ever ca' a nail in't: *drive*
Our fathers blude the kettle bought, *blood*
   And wha wad dare to spoil it, *who would*
By Heavens, the sacrilegious dog
   Shall fuel be to boil it!
      By Heav'ns, &c.

The wretch that would a Tyrant own,
   And the wretch, his true sworn brother,
Who would set the Mob above the throne,
   May they be damn'd together.

Who will not sing, God save the king;
Shall hang as high's the steeple;
But while we sing, God save the king,
We'll ne'er forget the People.
But while we sing &c.

The Heron Ballads I

Wham will we send to London town, *whom*
To Parliament, & a' that. *all*
Wha maist in a' the country round, *who most*
For worth & sense may fa' that? *deserve*
For a' that & a' that *all*
Thro' Galloway & a' that,
Whilk is the Laird, or belted Knight, *which; lord, landowner*
That best deserves to fa' that? *have*

Wha sees Kirouchtree's open yett *who; gate*
And wha is't never saw that, *who is it*
Or wha e'er wi' Kirouchtree met *with*
That has a doubt of a' that *all*
For a' that & a' that
Here's Heron yet for a' that,
The independant Patriot,
The Honest Man, & a' that

Tho' wit & worth, in either sex,
Saint Mary's Isle can shaw that; *show*
Wi' Lords & Dukes let Selkirk mix
For weel does Selkirk fa' that. *well; deserve*
For a' that & a' that,
Here's Heron yet for a' that;
An independant Commoner
Maun bear the gree & a' that. *must take the prize*

To paughty Lordlings shall we jouk, *haughty; bow*
And it against the law that:
For even a Lord may be a gowk, *fool*
Tho' sprung frae kings & a' that. *from*
For a' that & a' that,
Here's Heron yet for a' that;
A lord may be a lousy loun, *rogue*
Wi' ribband, star & a' that. *with*

Yon beardless boy comes o'er the hills
Wi's uncle's gowd, & a' that; *with his; gold*
But we'll hae ane frae 'mang oursels, *have one from among ourselves*
A man we ken & a' that.— *know*
For a' that & a' that,
Here's Heron yet for a' that;
We are na to the market come *not*
Like nowt & naigs & a' that. *cattle; nags*

If we are to be knaves & fools,
And bought & sauld & a' that, *sold*
A truant callan frae the schools *lad from*
It's ne'er be said did a' that
For a' that, & a' that,
Here's Heron yet for a' that;
And Master Dicky, thou shalt get
A gird & stick to ca' that. *hoop; drive*

Then let us drink the Stewartry,
Kerroughtree's laird, an' a' that,
Our representative to be,
For weel he's worthy a' that. *well*
For a' that, an' a' that,
Here's Heron yet for a' that!
A House of Commons such as he,
They would be blest that saw that.

To the Tooth-Ach.

My curse upon your venom'd stang — *sting*
That shoots my tortur'd gooms alang, — *gums along*
An' thro my lug gies sic a twang, — *and; ear; gives such; sharp pain*
        Wi' gnawing vengeance, — *with*
Tearing my nerves wi' bitter pang,
        Like racking engines.

When fevers burn, or agues freeze us,
Rheumatics gnaw, or colics squeeze us,
Our neebor's sympathy does ease us — *neighbour's*
        Wi' pitying moan;
But thee, thou hell of a' diseases! — *all*
        They mock our groan.

Adown my beard the slavers trickle; — *saliva*
I throw the wee stools owre the meickle; — *small; over; big*
While round the fire the giglets keckle, — *girls cackle*
        To see me loup; — *jump*
An' raving-mad I wish a heckle — *flax-comb*
        Were in their doup. — *bottom*

In a' the num'rous human dools, — *sorrows*
Ill Har'sts, daft bargains, cutty-stools, — *bad harvests*
Or worthy friends rak'd i' the mools, — *grave*
        Sad sight to see!
The tricks o' knaves or fash o'fools, — *annoyance*
        Thou bears the gree. — *take first prize*

Whare'er that place be Priests ca' hell, — *wherever; call*
Where a' the tones o' Misery yell, — *all*
An' ranked plagues their numbers tell,
        In dreadfu' raw; — *dreadful row*
Thou, Tooth-Ach, surely bears the bell — *wins the prize*
        Amang them a'. — *among*

O thou grim, mischief-making Chiel, *fellow*
Wha gars the notes o' Discord squeel, *who makes; squeal*
Till daft Mankind aft dance a reel, *often; Scottish dance*
        In gore a shoe-thick;
Gie a' the Faes of Scotland's weel, *give all; foes; weal*
        A TOWMOND'S TOOTH-ACH! *twelve-month's*

[Oh Wert Thou in the Cauld Blast]

Oh wert thou in the cauld blast, *cold*
  On yonder lea, on yonder lea;
My plaidie to the angry airt, *cloak; direction*
  I'd shelter thee, I'd shelter thee:
Or did misfortune's bitter storms
  Around thee blaw, around thee blaw, *blow*
Thy bield should be my bosom, *shelter*
  To share it a', to share it a'. *all*

Or were I in the wildest waste,
  Sae black and bare, sae black and bare, *so*
The desart were a paradise,
  If thou wert there, if thou wert there.
Or were I monarch o' the globe,
  Wi' thee to reign, wi' thee to reign; *with*
The brightest jewel in my crown,
  Wad be my queen, wad be my queen. *would*

The Solemn League and Covenant

The Solemn League and Covenant
    Now brings a smile, now brings a tear.
But sacred Freedom, too, was theirs:
    If thou'rt a slave, indulge thy sneer.

The Selkirk Grace.

Some hae meat and canna eat, *have; cannot*
    And some wad eat that want it; *would*
But we hae meat and we can eat,
    And sae the Lord be thanket. *so; thanked*

Tam Lin.

O I forbid you, maidens a' *all*
That wear gowd on your hair, *gold*
To come or gae by Carterhaugh, *go*
For young Tam Lin is there.

There's nane that gaes by Carterhaugh *none; goes*
But they leave him a wad; *pledge*
Either their rings, or green mantles,
Or else their maidenhead.

Janet has belted her green kirtle, *gown*
A little aboon her knee, *above*
And she has broded her yellow hair *braided*
A little aboon her bree; *above; brow*
And she's awa to Carterhaugh *away*
As fast as she can hie.

When she came to Carterhaugh
Tom-Lin was at the well,
And there she fand his steed standing *found*
But away was himsel. *himself*

She had na pu'd a double rose, *not pulled*
A rose but only twa, *two*
Till up then started young Tam-Lin,
Says, Lady, thou's pu' nae mae. *shall pull no more*

Why pu's thou the rose, Janet, *pulls*
And why breaks thou the wand!
Or why comes thou to Carterhaugh
Withoutten my command? *without*

Carterhaugh it is my ain, *own*
My daddie gave it me;
I'll come and gang by Carterhaugh *go*
And ask nae leave at thee. *no*

Janet has kilted her green kirtle, *gown*
A little aboon her knee, *above*
And she has snooded her yellow hair, *tied back*
A little aboon her bree, *above; brow*
And she is to her father's ha, *hall*
As fast as she can hie.

Four and twenty ladies fair,
Were playing at the ba, *ball*
And out then cam the fair Janet, *came*
Ance the flower amang them a'. *once; among; all*

Four and twenty ladies fair,
Were playing at the chess,
And out then cam the fair Janet, *came*
As green as onie glass. *any*

Out then spak an auld grey knight, *spoke; old*
Lay o'er the castle wa', *over; wall*
And says, Alas, fair Janet for thee,
But we'll be blamed a'. *all*

Haud your tongue, ye auld fac'd knight, *hold; old*
Some ill death may ye die,
Father my bairn on whom I will, *child*
I'll father nane on thee. *none*

Out then spak her father dear, *spoke*
And he spak meek and mild,
And ever alas, sweet Janet, he says,
I think thou gaes wi' child. *goes with*

If that I gae wi' child, father, *go with*
Mysel maun bear the blame; *myself must*
There's ne'er a laird about your ha, *lord; hall*
Shall get the bairn's name. *child's*

If my Love were an earthly knight,
As he's an elfin grey;
I wad na gie my ain true-love *would not give; own*
For nae lord that ye hae. *no; have*

The steed that my true-love rides on,
Is lighter than the wind;
Wi' siller he is shod before, *with silver*
Wi' burning gowd behind. *gold*

Jenet has kilted her green kirtle *gown*
A little aboon her knee; *above*
And she has snooded her yellow hair *tied back*
A little aboon her brie; *above; brow*
And she's awa to Carterhaugh *away*
As fast as she can hie

When she cam to Carterhaugh, *came*
Tam-Lin was at the well;
And there she fand his steed standing, *found*
But away was himsel. *himself*

She had na pu'd a double rose, *not pulled*
A rose but only twa, *two*
Till up then started young Tam-Lin,
Says, Lady thou pu's nae mae. *pulls no more*

Why pu's thou the rose Janet, *pulls*
Amang the groves sae green, *among; so*
And a' to kill the bonie babe *all; pretty*
That we gat us between. *got*

O tell me, tell me, Tam-Lin she says,
For's sake that died on tree, *for his sake; (the cross)*
If e'er ye was in holy chapel,
Or Christendom did see.

Roxbrugh he was my grandfather,
Took me with him to bide *stay*
And ance it fell upon a day *once*
That wae did me betide. *woe*

And ance it fell upon a day, *once*
A cauld day and a snell, *cold; bitter*
When we were frae the hunting come *from*
That frae my horse I fell.

The queen o' Fairies she caught me, *of*
  In yon green hill to dwell,
And pleasant is the fairy-land;
  But, an eerie tale to tell!

Ay at the end of seven years *always*
  We pay a tiend to hell. *tithe*
I am sae fair and fu' o' flesh *so; full of*
  I'm fear'd it be mysel. *myself*

But the night is Halloween, lady, *tonight*
  The morn is Hallowday; *All Saints' Day (1 November)*
Then win me, win me, an ye will, *if*
  For weel I wat ye may. *well; know*

Just at the mirk and midnight hour *dark*
  The fairy folk will ride;
And they that wad their truelove win, *would*
  At Milescross they maun bide. *must wait*

But how shall I thee ken Tam-Lin, *know*
  Or how my true love know.
Amang sae mony unco knights, *among so many strange*
  The like I never saw.

O first let pass the black Lady,
  And syne let pass the brown; *then*
But quickly run to the milk white steed,
  Pu ye his rider down. *pull*

For I'll ride on the milk-white steed.
  And ay nearest the town. *always*
Because I was an earthly knight
  They gie me that renown. *give*

My right hand will be glov'd lady,
  My left hand will be bare
Cockt up shall my bonnet be, *cocked*
  And kaim'd down shall my hair, *combed*

And thae's the takens I gie thee,   *those are; tokens; give*
  Nae doubt I will be there.   *no*

They'll turn me in your arms lady,
  Into an esk and adder,   *newt*
But hald me fast and fear me not,   *hold*
  I am your bairn's father.   *child's*

They'll turn me to a bear sae grim,   *so*
  And then a lion bold,
But hold me fast and fear me not,
  As ye shall love your child.

Again they'll turn me in your arms,
  To a red het gaud of airn.   *hot bar; iron*
But hold me fast and fear me not,
  I'll do to you nae harm.   *no*

And last they'll turn me in your arms,
  Into the burning lead;
Then throw me into well water,
  O throw me in wi' speed.   *with*

And then I'll be your ain true love,   *own*
  I'll turn a naked knight.
Then cover me wi' your green mantle,   *with*
  And cover me out o' sight.   *of*

Gloomy, gloomy was the night,
  And eerie was the way,
As fair Jenny in her green mantle
  To Milescross she did gae.   *go*

About the middle o' the night,   *of*
  She heard the bridles ring;
This lady was as glad at that
  As any earthly thing.

First she let the black pass by,
  And syne she let the brown;   *then*

But quickly she ran to the milk white steed,
  And pu'd the rider down. *pulled*

Sae weel she minded what he did say *so well; remembered*
  And young Tam Lin did win;
Syne cover'd him wi' her green mantle *then; with*
  As blythe's a bird in spring. *happy as*

Out then spak the queen o' fairies, *spoke; of*
  Out of a bush o broom; *of*
Them that has gotten young Tam Lin,
  Has gotten a stately groom.

Out then spak the queen o' fairies, *spoke; of*
  And an angry queen was she;
Shame betide her ill-far'd face, *ill-favoured, ugly*
  And an ill death may she die,
For she's ta'en awa the boniest knight *taken away; finest*
  In a' my companie, *all*

But had I kend Tam Lin, she says, *known*
  What now this night I see.
I wad hae taen out thy twa grey een, *would have taken; two; eyes*
  And put in twa een o' tree. *two eyes of wood*

Comin thro' the Rye.

Comin thro' the rye, poor body *coming*
  Comin thro' the rye
She draigl't a' her petticoatie *bedraggled with water all*
  Comin thro' the rye.
Oh Jenny's a' weet poor body, *all wet*
  Jenny's seldom dry
She draigl't a' her petticoatie
  Comin thro the rye.

Gin a body meet a body *if*
  Comin thro' the rye,
Gin a body kiss a body
  Need a body cry
Oh Jenny's a' weet, &c.

Gin a body meet a body *if*
  Comin thro' the glen;
Gin a body kiss a body
  Need the warld ken! *world know*
Oh Jenny's a' weet, &c.

Charlie He's my Darling.

'Twas on a monday morning,
  Right early in the year,
That Charlie came to our town,
  The young Chevalier.
An' Charlie he's my darling, my darling, my darling,
Charlie he's my darling the young Chevalier.

As he was walking up the street,
  The city for to view,
O there he spied a bonie lass *pretty*
  The window looking thro'.
An' Charlie &c.

Sae light's he jimped up the stair, *so; jumped*
  And tirled at the pin; *rattled; latch*
And wha sae ready as hersel, *who so; herself*
  To let the laddie in.
An' Charlie, &c.

He set his Jenny on his knee,
  All in his Highland dress;
For brawlie weel he ken'd the way *very well; knew*
  To please a bonie lass.
An' Charlie, &c. *pretty*

It's up yon hethery mountain, *heathery*
  And down yon scroggy glen, *bushy*
We daur na gang a milking, *dare not go*
  For Charlie and his men.
An' Charlie, &c.

The Trogger.

As I cam down by Annan side, *came*
Intending for the border,
Amang the Scroggie banks and braes, *among; scrubland; hills*
Wha met I but a trogger. *who; pedlar*
He laid me down upon my back,
I thought he was but jokin', *joking*
Till he was in me to the hilts,
O the deevil tak sic troggin! *devil take such peddling*

What could I say, what could I do,
I bann'd and sair misca'd him, *cursed; sore[ly] miscalled*
But whiltie-whaltie gae'd his a[rs]e *thumpity-thump went*
The mair that I forbade him: *more*
He stell'd his foot against a stane, *braced; stone*
And doubl'd ilka stroke in, *every*
Till I gaed daft amang his hands, *went; among*
O the deevil tak sic troggin!

Then up we raise, and took the road, *rose*
And in by Ecclefechan,
Where the brandy-stoup we gart it clink, *flagon; made*
And the strang-beer ream the quech in. *strong-; foam; bowl*
Bedown the bents o' Bonshaw braes, *moors; hills*
We took the partin' yokin'; *parting yoking*
But I've claw'd a sairy c[un]t synsine, *scratched; sorry; since then*
O the deevil tak sic troggin!

The Tree of Liberty.

Heard ye o' the tree o' France,   *of*
  I watna what's the name o't;   *know not; of it*
Around it a' the patriots dance,   *all*
  Weel Europe kens the fame o't.   *well; knows*
It stands where ance the Bastile stood,   *once*
  A prison built by kings, man,
When Superstition's hellish brood   *the Church*
  Kept France in leading-strings, man.

Upo' this tree there grows sic fruit,   *upon; such*
  Its virtues a' can tell, man;   *all*
It raises man aboon the brute,   *above*
  It maks him ken himsel', man.   *makes; know himself*
Gif ance the peasant taste a bit,   *if once*
  He's greater than a lord, man,
And wi' the beggar shares a mite   *with*
  O' a' he can afford, man.   *of all*

This fruit is worth a' Afric's wealth,   *all*
  To comfort us 'twas sent, man:
To gie the sweetest blush o' health,   *give; of*
  And mak us a' content, man.   *make; all*
It clears the een, it cheers the heart,   *eyes*
  Maks high and low guid friends, man;   *makes; good*
And he wha acts the traitor's part,   *who*
  It to perdition sends, man.

My blessings aye attend the chiel,   *forever; fellow*
  Wha pitied Gallia's slaves, man,   *who; France's*
And staw a branch, spite o' the deil,   *stole; of the devil*
  Frae yont the western waves, man.   *from beyond*
Fair Virtue watered it wi' care,   *with*
  And now she sees wi' pride, man,
How weel it buds and blossoms there,   *well*
  Its branches spreading wide, man.

But vicious folk aye hate to see *always*
The works o' Virtue thrive, man;
The courtly vermin's banned the tree,
And grat to see it thrive, man; *wept*
King Loui' thought to cut it down,
When it was unco sma', man; *very small*
For this the watchman cracked his crown,
Cut aff his head and a', man. *off; all*

A wicked crew syne, on a time, *then*
Did tak a solemn aith, man, *take; oath*
It ne'er should flourish to its prime,
I wat they pledged their faith, man. *know*
Awa' they gaed wi' mock parade, *away; went with*
Like beagles hunting game, man,
But soon grew weary o' the trade,
And wished they'd been at hame, man. *home*

Fair Freedom, standing by the tree,
Her sons did loudly ca', man; *call*
She sang a sang o' liberty, *song*
Which pleased them ane and a', man. *one and all*
By her inspired, the new-born race
Soon drew the avenging steel, man;
The hirelings ran—her foes gied chase, *gave*
And banged the despot weel, man. *beat; well*

Let Britain boast her hardy oak,
Her poplar and her pine, man,
Auld Britain ance could crack her joke, *old; once*
And o'er her neighbours shine, man.
But seek the forest round and round,
And soon 'twill be agreed, man,
That sic a tree can not be found *such*
'Twixt London and the Tweed, man. *between*

Without this tree, alake this life *alas*
Is but a vale o' wo, man; *of woe*
A scene o' sorrow mixed wi' strife, *with*
Nae real joys we know, man. *no*

We labour soon, we labour late,
  To feed the titled knave, man;
And a' the comfort we're to get, *all*
  Is that ayont the grave, man. *beyond*

Wi' plenty o' sic trees, I trow, *with; such*
  The warld would live in peace, man; *world*
The sword would help to mak a plough, *make*
  The din o' war wad cease, man. *of; would*
Like brethren in a common cause,
  We'd on each other smile, man;
And equal rights and equal laws
  Wad gladden every isle, man. *would*

Wae worth the loon wha wadna eat *woe; fellow who would not*
  Sic halesome dainty cheer, man; *such wholesome*
I'd gie my shoon frae aff my feet, *give; shoes from off*
  To taste sic fruit, I swear, man. *such*
Syne let us pray, auld England may *then; old*
  Sure plant this far-famed tree, man;
And blithe we'll sing, and hail the day *happily*
  That gave us liberty, man.

Rediscovered Poems

The Rediscovered Poems in this Book

The Best Laid Schemes contains several poems and fragments newly printed from manuscripts in the collection of the National Trust for Scotland's Robert Burns Birthplace and Museum at Alloway (RBBM). While he was working on *The Bard: Robert Burns, A Biography* (2009) Robert Crawford tracked these down through extensive digital searching of the National Burns Collection (NBC) online catalogue of Burns manuscripts which revealed mention of several items which earlier editors appear either to have ignored or dismissed. When Crawford followed up on descriptions of these, photocopies of the originals were supplied through the kind offices of Mr David Hopes (Curator, RBBM) and Mr Kenneth Dunn of the National Library of Scotland, where the originals have been stored during construction work on the Alloway Burns Museum. All the manuscripts are in Burns's hand.

The most substantial of these is the poem which begins 'My steps Fate on a mad conjuncture thrust'. Accompanied by a note in another (probably late-eighteenth or early-nineteenth–century) hand, explaining that the manuscript comprises 'Noble verses by the Bard to Clarinda – on an occasion when she had said that "they must part" &c.', this is the fullest extant version of the poem which appears in James Kinsley's three-volume *Poems and Songs of Robert Burns* (Oxford: Clarendon Press, 1968) as '[Passion's Cry]'. The second half of Kinsley's 26-line principal text corresponds to the conclusion of the poem as printed from manuscript in the present book. Kinsley also notes that P. Hately Waddell published six further lines in his 1867 *Life and Works of Robert Burns*. Though repunctuated, these correspond to the last six lines of the second stanza of the poem as published here. It seems almost certain the 42-line manuscript which provides the text printed in *The Best Laid Schemes* is the manuscript mentioned in Kinsley's textual note on page 710 of his second volume: '*The 42-line MS listed in E. C. Bigmore's reprint of the 1861 sale catalogue has not been traced.*'

In terms of length, the next most substantial manuscript in this group of 'new' poems is 'Logie o' Buchan'. Again in Burns's hand, the manuscript is a version of a Scottish song and the wording corresponds exactly with that of 'Logie o' Buchan' as it appears in the fourth (1792) volume of James Johnson's *Scots Musical Museum*. Though this poem is not attributed to Burns there or in any other printed edition, and it might be argued that it is simply a song transcription, rather than Burns's own recasting of traditional material, an astute, anonymous typed note which accompanies the manuscript in the Alloway collection points out that a different version of this song appears in the 1853 edition of William Stenhouse's *Illustrations of the Lyric Poetry and Music of Scotland.* The version in Stenhouse is said to derive from the collection of James Sibbald, and Stenhouse (who thinks the original lyric was by Lady Anne Lindsay) contends that 'Burns has made several alterations on the old verses', though he does not consider them all to be improvements. The author of the RBBM typed note also points out that Peter Buchan had printed the original song in his 1825 *Gleanings of Scarce Old Ballads* and was said to have attributed it to George Halket, schoolmaster at Rathen in 1736. 'Later anthologies in which the poem appears print the original rather than the Burns version'. The differences between the two are not very extensive. A substantially different version of the song was printed in the anonymous *Colin and Phoebe's Garland, containing some of the Choicest New Songs* ([?Newcastle],[?1770]). The balance of probability would appear to indicate that Burns, as he often did, has recast (albeit slightly) a traditional song. His manuscript carries a footnote: 'Note, there is but one strain in the tune, so it is just repeated in the Chorus'.

The Jacobite song, 'Here is to the king, Sir', is also a version of a traditional piece. The manuscript in Burns's hand is almost identical to that printed in the second (1788) volume of James Johnson's *Scots Musical Museum*, though where in the second line of the chorus Burns writes 'all', Johnson prints 'a''. In Johnson the song is set to the tune 'Hey Tutti Taiti'. Though he uses a different tune, James Hogg follows Johnson's text in his 1819 *Jacobite Relics of Scotland (First Series)*. That work's modern editor, Murray G. H. Pittock, apparently unaware that a version exists in Burns's hand, draws attention on page 458 of his 2002 Edinburgh University Press edition to a 'very similar set' of verses in 'NLS Adv. MS. 19.3.44 p. 68'. However, this manuscript collection of songs, apparently connected with a family named Fraser, offers a version of the song which is quite substantially different from both Burns's manuscript and the text printed by Johnson and by Hogg. The National Library of Scotland manuscript is in English rather than Scots and includes, for instance, a stanza about 'the royall Spainard' which is not in Burns's manuscript nor in Johnson or Hogg, while Burns's version contains two stanzas not in the substantially earlier NLS manuscript which predates the Battle of Culloden and appears to date from the early eighteenth century. Again, it seems likely that Burns has recast a traditional Jacobite song, perhaps one that he collected while touring the Highlands in 1787.

The cancelled fragment, 'I courted a lassie', is in Burns's hand on the verso of his manuscript of the song 'O Gude yill comes, & gude yill goes', while the fragment beginning 'Tho life's gay scenes delight no more' accompanies the quatrain 'On Chloris [Jean Lorimer] requesting me to give her a spray of a sloe-thorn in full bloom' which begins, 'From the white-blossom'd sloe, my dear Chloris requested'. These fragments are again from the RBBM collection.

Though it is offered here only as an addition to Burns's 'Dubia', a previously unnoticed Burns attribution which at least deserves modern discussion occurs in the *Caledonian Mercury* for Monday, June 19, 1826 (issue 16354):

> Upon the 22d Nov. 1820, Mr John Anderson, engraver in Edinburgh, presented a fragment of a song, in the holograph of Robert Burns, to Mr R. A. Smith. On the 5th Jan. 1821, Mr Smith presented this relic of the poet to Mr Robert Allan, Kilbarchan. Mr Allan states that the verses have never appeared in print. They are as under: –

The Highlander's Lament

A soldier for gallant achievements renown'd,
  Revolv'd in despair the campaigns of his youth;
Then, beating his bosom, and sighing profound,
  That malice itself might have melted to ruth,
Are these, he exclaimed, the results of my toil?
  In want and obscurity thus to retire?
For this did compassion restrain me from spoil,
  When earth was all carnage, and Heaven all fire?

Among nineteenth-century Burns attributions, this one is particularly interesting, in part because Robert Allan was wrong about the 'verses ... never' having 'appeared in print'. An almost identical text (with minor differences in punctuation, and ending with the words 'on fire' rather than 'all fire') appears in the sixth (1803) volume of Johnson's *Scots Musical Museum*, where it is followed by eight further lines:

The sun's bright effulgence, the fragrance of air
The vari'd horizon henceforth I abhore.
Give me death the sole boon of a wretch in despair,
Which fortune can offer or nature implore.

To madness impell'd by his griefs as he spoke,
And darting around him a look of disdain,
Down headlong he leapt from a heaven towring rock,
And sleeps where the wretched forbear to complain.

A note adds the words, 'Supposed to have been written in the year 1746.'

The detailed provenance of the supposed Burns manuscript mentioned by Allan takes it back to 'John Anderson, engraver in Edinburgh'. George Herbert Bushnell in his *Scottish Engravers: A Biographical Dictionary* (Oxford University Press, 1949) records that Anderson, a music printer and engraver, was apprenticed to James Johnson. This provides a link which could connect the manuscript to Burns's friend, the editor of the *Scots Musical Museum*; Johnson, more used than most people to handling Burns's manuscripts, died in 1811, by which time Anderson's apprenticeship was long over. The line of the manuscript's transmission through Johnson's apprentice Anderson to the Paisley musician Robert Archibald Smith (a friend of Burns's admirer the Paisley poet Robert Tannahill), who edited the song collection the *Scotish Minstrel* (1821–24), and then from R. A. Smith to his friend and Tannahill's, the Renfrewshire weaver and songwriter Robert Allan (1774–1841), sounds credible. The *Oxford Dictionary of National Biography* records that Allan died almost immediately after emigrating to New York. The 'holograph of Robert Burns' that apparently provided the text for the *Caledonian Mercury* in 1826 appears long lost. Unlike in the cases of the other 'new' poems in the present volume, manuscript evidence cannot be supplied. Yet the provenance and circumstances surrounding 'The Highlander's Lament' make it one of the stronger contenders among rediscovered Burns poems. It may not be a great work, but its Jacobite sympathies and despairing tone are consonant with the views of the bard who visited Culloden and who, like Robert Fergusson in an earlier generation, often carried with him his own sense of being 'a wretch in despair.'

Logie o' Buchan

O Logie o' Buchan, O Logie the laird, *of; landowner*
They've taen awa Jamie that wrought in the yard; *taken away*
Wha play'd on the pipe wi' the viol sae sma', *who; with; so small*
They've taen awa Jamie the flower o' them a'.— *all*

O think na lang, lassie, tho' I be awa, *not long; away*
An' think na lang, lassie, tho' I be awa; *and*
The simmer is come & the winter's awa, *summer; away*
And I'll come & see thee in spite o' them a'.— *of; all*

O Sandy has owsen, & siller, & kye, *oxen; silver; cattle*
A house & a haddin, & a' things forbye, *holding; all; besides*
But I wad hae Jamie wi's bonnet in's hand, *would have; with his; in his*
Before I'd hae Sandy wi' houses & land.— *have; with*
O think &c.

My daddie was sulkie, my minnie was sour, *mother*
They gloom'd on my Jamie because he was poor; *frowned*
But daddie & minnie altho' that they be,
There's nane o' them a' like my Jamie to me.— *none of; all*
O think &c.

I'll sit on my sunkie & spin at my wheel, *stool*
And sing o' my Jamie wha loes me sae weel; *who loves; so well*
He took a white saxpence & brak it in twa, *sixpence; broke; two*
And gae me the hauf o't when he gaed awa. *gave; half of it; went away*

Sayin, think upon't lassie when I am awa, *saying; away*
An' think upon't lassie when I am awa: *and*
The simmer is come, & the winter's awa, *summer; away*
And I'll come & see thee in spite o' them a'.— *of; all*

I Courted a Lassie

[Cancelled fragment]

I courted a lassie, I courted her lang, *long*
The lassie she did comply;
But she has prov'd fickle & broken her vow,
And e'en let her gang, say I! *even; go*
And e'en let gang—& e'en let her gang,
And e'en let her gang—say I—

* * *

My Steps Fate on a Mad Conjuncture Thrust

My steps Fate on a mad conjuncture thrust,
'Twas grav'd in ir'n, the stern decree, 'You Must!'—
Ah, no! the plume pluck'd from the am'rous dove,
The Sentence flam'd in golden lines of love.—
Wild erring from the path by Virtue shown,
I snatch'd a flower in Virtue's ways unknown,
With charms methought to raptur'd sense more sweet
Than aught in Virtue's walks I e'er could meet:—
The lovely Flower fond in my bosom worn,
I knew, or heeded not, its poison'd thorn.—

O, why is bitter mem'ry so alive,
When Pleasures, Friendships, Loves, nor Hopes survive!
O'er joys no more, fond recollection burns;
Thy image haunts & blesses me by turns.—
The desp'rate barbs are flesh'd deep in my heart,
Death, & Death only, can extract the dart:—
His bowl alone can drug my soul to rest:
But be thou happy! be thou ever blest!
Mild zephyrs waft thee to life's farthest shore,
Nor think of me, or my distresses more!—
Falsehood accursed!— No! still I beg a place,
Still near thy heart some little, little trace,
For that dear trace, the world I would resign,
Oh, let me live—and die— & think it mine!

Thou despot, Love, whom all my powers obey,
Why lord it thus with such tyrannic sway!
In vain the Laws his feeble force oppose;
Chain'd at his feet, they groan Love's vanquish'd foes:
In vain Religion meets my shrinking eye;
I dare not combat—but I turn & fly:
Conscience in vain upbraids th'unhallow'd fire;
Love grasps her scorpions, stifled they expire:
Reason drops headlong from his sacred throne,

Thy dear idea reigns & reigns alone: *image*
Each thought intoxicated homage yields,
And riots, wanton, in forbidden fields.

By all on high, adoring mortals know!
By all the conscious Villain fears below!
By, what, Alas! much more my soul alarms,
My doubtful hopes once more to fill thy arms!
E'en should'st thou, false, forswear the guilty tie,
Thine, & thine only, I must live & die!!!

Here is to the king, Sir

Here is to the king, Sir,
Ye ken wha I mean, Sir, *know who*
And to every honest man
That will do't again. *do it*
Fill up your bumpers high
We'll drink all your barrels dry
Out upon them fy, fy,
That winna do't again. *will not*

Here's to the Chieftans *chieftains*
Of the Scots Highland clans
They hae done it mair than ance *have; more; once*
And will do't again.
Fill up &c

When ye hear the trumpets sound
Tuti taity to the drum,
Up your swords and down your guns
And to the louns again. *fellows*
Fill up &c

Here's to the king o' Swedes *of*
Fresh laurels crown his head
Pox on every sneaking blade
That winna do't again. *will not*
Fill &c

But to make a' things right now, *all*
He that drinks must fight too
To shew his heart's upright too *show*
And that he'll do't again.

Tho' Life's Gay Scenes Delight No More

[Fragment]

Tho' Life's gay scenes delight no more,
Still much is left behind,
Still rich art thou in nobler store,
The comforts of the Mind.—

Thine is the self-approving glow,
On conscious Honor's part:
And

* * *

Prose

Five Extracts from Burns's First Commonplace Book, 1783–85

1 [April, 1783]

Observations, Hints, Songs, Scraps of Poetry &c. by Rob[t] Burness; a man who had little art in making money, and still less in keeping it; but was, however, a man of some sense, a great deal of honesty, and unbounded good-will to every creature rational or irrational.—As he was but little indebted to scholastic education, and bred at a plough-tail, his performances must be strongly tinctured with his unpolished, rustic way of life; but as I believe, they are really his own, it may be some entertainment to a curious observer of human-nature to see how a plough-man thinks, and feels, under the pressure of Love, Ambition, Anxiety, Grief with the like cares and passions, which, however diversified by the Modes, and Manners of life, operate pretty much alike I believe, in all the Species——

2 [March, 1784]

I have often observed in the course of my experience of human life that every man even the worst, have something good about them, though very often nothing else than a happy tempermant of constitution inclining them to this or that Virtue; on this likewise, depend a great many, no man can say how many of our vices; for this reason no man can say in what degree any other person besides himself can be, with strict justice called Wicked.— Let any of the strictest character for regularity of conduct among us, examine impartially how many of his virtues are owing to constitution & education; how many vices he has never been guilty of, not from any care or vigilance, but from want of opportunity, or some accidental circumstance intervening; how many of the weakness's of mankind he has escaped because he was out of the line of such temptation; and, what often, if not always, weighs more than all the rest; how much he is indebted to the World's good opinion, because the World does not know all; I say any man who can thus think, will scan the failings, nay the faults & crimes of mankind around him, with a brother's eye.

March—84}

I have often coveted the acquaintance of that part of mankind commonly known by the ordinary phrase of BLACKGUARDS, sometimes farther than was consistent with the safety of my character; those who by thoughtless Prodigality, or headstrong Passions have been driven to ruin:— though disgraced by follies, nay sometimes 'Stain'd with guilt, and crimson'd o'er with crimes;' I have yet found among them, in not a few instances, some of the noblest Virtues, Magnanimity Generosity, disinterested friendship and even modesty, in the highest perfection.—

3 [April, 1784]

I think the whole species of young men may be naturally enough divided in two grand Classes, which I shall call the Grave, and the Merry; tho' by the bye these terms do not with propriety enough express my ideas.— There are indeed, some exceptions; some part of the species who, according to my ideas of these divisions, come under neither of them; such are those individuals whom Nature turns off her hand, oftentimes, very like blockheads, but generally, on a nearer inspection, have somethings surprisingly clever about them.— They are more properly Men of Conceit, than Men of Genius; men whose heads are filled, and whose faculties are engrossed, by some whimsical notions in some art, or science; so that they cannot think, nor speak with pleasure, on any other subject.— Besides this pedantic species, Nature has always produced some meer, insipid blockeads, who may be said to live a vegetable life, in this world.

The Grave, I shall cast into the usual division of those who are goaded on, by the love of money; and those whose darling wish, is, to make a figure in the world.— The Merry, are the men of Pleasure, of all denominations; the jovial lads who have too much fire & spirit to have any settled rule of action; but without much deliberation, follow the strong impulses of nature: the thoughtless, the careless, the indolent; and in particular He, who, with a happy sweetness of natural temper, and a cheerful vacancy of thought, steals through life, generally indeed, in poverty & obscurity; but poverty & obscurity are only evils to him, who can sit gravely down, and make a repining comparison between his own situation and that of others; and lastly to grace the quorum, such are, generally, the men whose heads are capable of all the towerings of Genius, and whose hearts are warmed with the delicacy of Feeling.—

4 [August 1785]

However I am pleased with the works of our Scotch Poets, particularly the excellent Ramsay, and the still more excellent Ferguson, yet I am hurt to see other places of Scotland, their towns, rivers, woods, haughs, &c. immortalized in such celebrated performances, whilst my dear native country, the ancient Bailieries of Carrick, Kyle, & Cunningham, famous both in ancient & modern times for a gallant, and warlike race of inhabitants; a country where civil, & particularly religious Liberty have ever found their first support, & their last asylum; a country, the birthplace of many famous Philosophers, Soldiers, & Statesmen, and the scene of many important events recorded in Scottish History, particularly a great many of the actions of the GLORIOUS WALLACE, the SAVIOUR of his Country; Yet, we have never had one Scotch Poet of any eminence, to make the fertile banks of Irvine, the romantic woodlands & sequestered scenes on Aire, and the heathy, mountainous source, & winding sweep of Doon emulate Tay, Forth, Ettrick, Tweed, &c. this is a complaint I would gladly remedy, but Alas! I am far unequal to the task, both in native genius & education.— Obscure I am, & obscure I must be, though no young Poet, nor young Soldier's heart ever beat more fondly for fame than mine—

5 [September 1785]

There is a certain irregularity in the old Scotch Songs, a redundancy of syllables with respect to that exactness of accent & measure that the English Poetry requires, but which glides in, most melodiously with the respective tunes to which they are set. For instance, the fine old Song of The Mill Mill O, to give it a plain prosaic reading it halts prodigiously out of measure; on the other hand, the Song set to the same tune in Bremner's collection of Scotch Songs which begins 'To Fanny fair could I impart &c.' it is most exact measure, and yet, let them be both sung before a real Critic, one above the biasses of prejudice, but a thorough Judge of Nature,—how flat & spiritless will the last appear, how trite, and tamely methodical, compared with the wild-warbling cadence, the heart-moving melody of the first.— This particularly is the case with all those airs which end with a hypermetrical syllable.— There is a degree of wild irregularity in many of the compositions & Fragments which are daily sung to them by my compeers, the common people— a certain happy arrangement of old Scotch syllables, & yet, very frequently, nothing, not even *like* rhyme, or sameness of jingle at the ends of the lines.— This has made me sometimes imagine that perhaps, it might be possible for a Scotch Poet, with a nice, judicious ear, to set compositions to many of our most favorite airs, particularly that class of them mentioned above, independent of rhyme altogether.—

There is a noble Sublimity, a heart-melting tenderness in some of these ancient fragments, which show them to be the work of a masterly hand; and it has often given me many a heart ake to reflect that such glorious old Bards—Bards, who, very probably, owed all their talents to native genius, yet have described the exploits of Heroes, the pangs of Disappointment, and the meltings of Love with such fine strokes of Nature, and, O mortifying to a Bard's vanity, their very names are 'buried 'mongst the wreck of things which were.'—

O ye illustrious Names unknown! who could feel so strongly and describe so well, the last, the meanest of the Muses train—one who, though far inferiour to your flights, yet eyes your path, and with trembling wing would sometimes soar after you—a poor, rustic Bard unknown, pays this sympathetic pang to your memory! Some of you tell us, with all the charms of Verse, that you have been unfortunate in the world—unfortunate in love; he too, has felt all the unfitness of a Poetic heart for the struggle of a busy, bad world; he has felt the loss of his little fortune, the loss of friends, and worse than all, the loss of the woman he adored!— Like you, all his consolation was his Muse—She taught him in rustic measures to complain—Happy, could he have done it with your strength of imagination, and flow of Verse! May the turf rest lightly on your bones! And may you now enjoy that solace and rest which this world rarely gives to the heart tuned to all the feeling of POESY AND LOVE!——

Preface

[to *Poems, Chiefly in the Scottish Dialect*, 1786]

The following trifles are not the production of the Poet, who, with all the advantages of learned art, and perhaps amid the elegancies and idlenesses of upper life, looks down for a rural theme, with an eye to Theocrites or Virgil. To the Author of this, these and other celebrated names their countrymen are, in their original languages, 'A fountain shut up, and a book sealed.' Unacquainted with the necessary requisites for commencing Poet by rule, he sings the sentiments and manners, he felt and saw in himself and his rustic compeers around him, in his and their native language. Though a Rhymer from his earliest years, at least from the earliest impulses of the softer passions, it was not till very lately, that the applause, perhaps the partiality, of Friendship, wakened his vanity so far as to make him think any thing of his was worth showing; and none of the following works were ever composed with a view to the press. To amuse himself with the little creations of his own fancy, amid the toil and fatigues of a laborious life; to transcribe the various feelings, the loves, the griefs, the hopes, the fears, in his own breast; to find some kind of counterpoise to the struggles of a world, always an alien scene, a task uncouth to the poetical mind; these were his motives for courting the Muses, and in these he found Poetry to be it's own reward.

Now that he appears in the public character of an Author, he does it with fear and trembling. So dear is fame to the rhyming tribe, that even he, an obscure, nameless Bard, shrinks aghast, at the thought of being branded as 'An impertinent blockhead, obtruding his nonsense on the world; and because he can make a shift to jingle a few doggerel, Scotch rhymes together, looks upon himself as a Poet of no small consequence forsooth.'

It is an observation of that celebrated Poet,[1] whose divine Elegies do honor to our language, our nation, and our species, that 'Humility has depressed many a genius to a hermit, but never raised one to fame.' If any Critic catches at the word *genius*, the Author tells him, once for all, that he certainly looks upon himself as possest of some poetic abilities, otherwise his publishing in the manner he has done, would be a manœuvre below the worst character, which, he hopes, his worst enemy will ever give him: but to the genius of a Ramsay, or the glorious dawnings of the poor, unfortunate Ferguson, he, with equal unaffected sincerity, declares, that, even in his highest pulse of vanity, he has not the most distant pretensions. These two justly admired Scotch Poets he has often had in his eye in the following pieces; but rather with a view to kindle at their flame, than for servile imitation.

To his Subscribers, the Author returns his most sincere thanks. Not the mercenary bow over a counter, but the heart-throbbing gratitude of the Bard, conscious how much he is indebted to Benevolence and Friendship, for gratifying him, if he deserves it, in that dearest wish of every poetic bosom—to be distinguished. He begs his readers, particularly the Learned and the Polite, who may honor him with a perusal, that they will make every allowance for Education and Circumstances of Life: but, if after a fair, candid, and impartial criticism, he shall stand convicted of Dulness and Nonsense, let him be done by, as he would in that case do by others—let him be condemned, without mercy, to contempt and oblivion.

Dedication

[to *Poems, Chiefly in the Scottish Dialect*, 1787]

TO THE

NOBLEMEN AND GENTLEMEN

OF THE

CALEDONIAN HUNT.

My Lords, and Gentlemen,

A Scottish Bard, proud of the name, and whose highest ambition is to sing in his Country's service, where shall he so properly look for patronage as to the illustrious Names of his native Land; those who bear the honours and inherit the virtues of their Ancestors?—The Poetic Genius of my Country found me as the prophetic bard Elijah did Elisha—at the plough; *and threw her inspiring* mantle *over me. She bade me sing the loves, the joys, the rural scenes and rural pleasures of my natal Soil, in my native tongue: I tuned my wild, artless notes, as she inspired.—She whispered me to come to this ancient metropolis of Caledonia, and lay my Songs under your honoured protection: I now obey her dictates.*

Though much indebted to your goodness, I do not approach you, my Lords and Gentlemen, in the usual stile of dedication, to thank you for past favours; that path is so hackneyed by prostituted Learning, that honest Rusticity is ashamed of it.—Nor do I present this Address with the venal soul of a servile Author, looking for a continuation of those favours: I was bred to the Plough, and am independent. I come to claim the common Scottish name with you, my illustrious Countrymen; and to tell the world that I glory in the title.—I come to congratulate my Country, that the blood of her ancient heroes still runs uncontaminated; and that from your courage, knowledge, and public spirit, she may expect protection, wealth, and liberty.—In the last place, I come to proffer my warmest wishes to the Great Fountain of Honour, the Monarch of the Universe, for your welfare and happiness.

When you go forth to waken the Echoes, in the ancient and favourite amusement of your Forefathers, may Pleasure ever be of your party; and may Social-joy await your return! When harassed in courts or camps with the justlings of bad men and bad measures, may the honest consciousness of injured Worth attend your return to your native Seats; and may Domestic Happiness, with a smiling welcome, meet you at your gates! May Corruption shrink at your kindling indignant glance; and may tyranny in the Ruler and licentiousness in the People equally find you an inexorable foe!

I have the honour to be,

With the sincerest gratitude and highest respect,

MY LORDS AND GENTLEMEN,

Your most devoted humble servant,

ROBERT BURNS.

EDINBURGH,
April 4. 1787.

Extract from Burns's Journal of his Border Tour

[9 May 1787]

Dine with Captn. Rutherford. The Captn. a specious polite fellow, very fond of money in his farming way, but showed a particular respect to My Bardship—his lady exactly a proper matrimonial second part for him—Miss Rutherford a beautiful girl, but too far gone woman to expose so much of so fine a swelling bosom—her face tho' very fine rather inanimately heavy—return to Jedburgh—walk up Jed with some ladies to be shown Love-lane & Black-burn two fairy scenes—introduced to Mr Potts, Writer, a very clever fellow; & Mr Somerville the clergyman of the place, a man & a gentleman but sadly addicted to punning—The walking Partie of ladies—Mrs F[air] & miss Lookup her sister before-mentioned N.B. these two appear still more comfortably ugly & stupid,—and bore me most shockingly—Two Miss Fairs, tolerably agreable but too much of the Mother's half-ell mouth & hag-like features—Miss Hope, a tolerably pretty girl, fond of laughing & fun—Miss Lindsay a good-humor'd amiable girl; rather short et embonpoint, but handsome and extremely graceful — beautiful hazle eyes full of spirit & sparkling with delicious moisture—an engaging face & manner, un tout ensemble that speaks her of the first order of female minds—her sister, a bonie, strappan, rosy, sonsie lass—Shake myself loose, after several unsuccessful efforts, of M^rs^ F[ai]r & Miss L[ooku]p and somehow or other get hold of Miss Lindsay's arm—my heart thawed into melting pleasure after being so long frozen up in the Greenland bay of Indifference amid the noise and nonsense of Edin^{r}—Miss seems very well pleased with my Bardship's distinguishing her, and after some slight qualms which I could easily mark, she sets the titter round at defiance, and kindly allows me to keep my hold; and when parted by the ceremony of my introduction to Mr Somerville she met me half to resume my situation—NOTA BENE—The Poet within a point and a half of being damnably in love.—I am afraid my bosom still nearly as much tinder as ever——

The old, cross-grained, Whiggish, ugly, slanderous hag, Miss Lookup with all the poisonous spleen of a disappointed, ancient maid, stops me very unseasonably to ease her hell-rankling bursting breast by falling abusively foul on the Miss Lindsays, particularly on my Dulcinea; I hardly refrain from cursing her to her face—May she, for her pains, be curst with eternal desire and damn'd with endless disappointment! Hear me, O Heavens, and give ear, O Earth! may the burden of antiquated Virginity crush her down to the lowest regions of the bottomless Pit! for daring to mouth her calumnious slander on one of the finest pieces of the workmanship of Almighty Excellence. Sup at M$^{r.}$ F[air's] vexed that the Miss Lindsays are not of the supper party as they only are wanting. M^{rs} F[ai]r & Miss L[ooku]p still improve infernally on my hands——

Letter to Dr John Moore

2 August 1787

Sir,

For some months past I have been rambling over the country, partly on account of some little business I have to settle in various places; but of late I have been confined with some lingering complaints originating as I take it in the stomach. To divert my spirits a little in this miserable fog of Ennui, I have taken a whim to give you a history of MYSELF.— My name has made a small noise in the country; you have done me the honor to interest yourself very warmly in my behalf; and I think a faithful account of what character of a man I am, and how I came by that character, may perhaps amuse you in an idle moment.— I will give you an honest narrative though I know it will be at the expence of frequently being laughed at, for I assure you, Sir I have, like

Solomon whose character excepting the trifling affair of WISDOM, I sometimes think I resemble I have I say like him 'Turned my eyes to behold Madness and Folly', and like him too frequently shaken hands with their intoxicating friendship.— In the very polite letter Miss Williams did me the honor to write me, she tells me you have got a complaint in your eyes.— I pray God that it may be removed; for considering that lady and you are my common friends, you will probably employ her to read this letter; and then goodnight to that esteem with which she was pleased to honor the Scotch Bard.—After you have perused these pages, should you think them trifling and impertinent, I only beg leave to tell you that the poor Author wrote them under some very twitching qualms of conscience, that, perhaps he was doing what he ought not to do: a predicament he has more than once been in before. —

I have not the most distant pretensions to what the pye-coated guardians of escutcheons call, A Gentleman.— When at Edin[r.] last winter, I got acquainted in the Herald's Office, and looking through that granary of Honors I there found almost every name in the kingdom; but for me,

> '—My ancient but ignoble blood
> Has crept thro' Scoundrels ever since the flood'

Gules, Purpure, Argent, &c, quite disowned me.— My Fathers rented land of the noble Kieths of Marshal, and had the honor to share their fate.— I do not use the word, Honor, with any reference to Political principles; loyal and disloyal I take to be merely relative terms in that ancient and formidable court known in this Country by the name of CLUB-LAW.— Those who dare welcome Ruin and shake hands with Infamy for what they sincerely believe to be the cause of their God or their KING— 'Brutus and Cassius are honorable men.'—I mention this circumstance because it threw my father on the world at large where after many years wanderings and sojournings, he pickt up a pretty large quantity of Observation and Experience, to which I am indebted for most of my little pretensions to wisdom.— I have met with few who understood 'Men, their manners and their ways' equal to him, but stubborn, ungainly Integrity, and headlong, ungovernable Irrascibillity are disqualifying circumstances: consequently I was born a very poor man's son.— For the first six or seven years of my life, my father was gardiner to a worthy gentleman of small estate in the neighbourhood of Ayr — Had my father continued in that situation, I must have marched off to be one of the little underlings about a farm-house; but it was his dearest wish and prayer to have it in his power to keep his children under his own eye till they could discern between good and evil; so with the assistance of his generous Master my father ventured on a small farm in his estate.— At these years I was by no means a favorite with any body.— I was a good deal noted for a retentive memory, a stubborn, sturdy something in my disposition, and an enthusiastic, idiot piety.— I say idiot piety, becaus I was then but a child.— Though I cost the schoolmaster some thrashings, I made an excellent English scholar; and again at the years of ten or eleven, I was absolutely a Critic in substantives, verbs and particles.— In my infant and boyish days too, I owed much to an old Maid of my Mother's, remarkable for her ignorance, credulity and superstition.— She had, I suppose, the largest collection in the country of tales and songs concerning devils, ghosts, fairies, brownies, witches, warlocks, spunkies, kelpies, elf-candles, dead-lights, wraiths, apparitions, cantraips, giants, enchanted towers, dragons and other trumpery.— This cultivated the latent seeds of Poesy; but had so strong an effect on my imagination, that to this hour in my nocturnal rambles, I sometimes keep a sharp look-out in suspicious places; and though nobody can be more sceptical in these matters than I yet it often takes an effort of Philosophy to shake off these idle terrors.— The earliest thing of Composition that I recollect taking pleasure in was The Vision of Mirza and a hymn of Addison's beginning— 'How are Thy servants blest, O Lord!' I particularly remember one half-stanza which was music to my boyish ear—

'For though in dreadful whirls we hung,
High on the broken wave'—

I met with these pieces in Mason's English Collection, one of my school-books.— The two first books I ever read in private, and which gave me more pleasure than any two books I ever read again, were, the life of Hannibal and the history of Sir William Wallace.— Hannibal gave my young ideas such a turn that I used to strut in raptures up and down after the recruiting drum and bagpipe, and wish myself tall enough to be a soldier; while the story of Wallace poured a Scotish prejudice in my veins which will boil along there till the flood-gates of life shut in eternal rest.— Polemical divinity about this time was putting the country half mad; and I ambitious of shining in conversation parties on sundays between sermons, funerals, &c, used in a few years more to puzzle Calvinism with so much heat and indiscretion that I raised a hue and cry of heresy against me which has not ceased to this hour.—

My vicinity to Ayr was of great advantage to me— My social disposition not checked by some modification of spited pride like our catechism definition of

Infinitude was 'without bounds or limits.[']— I formed many connections with other Youngkers who possessed superiour advantages; the youngling Actors who were busy with the rehearsal of PARTS in which they were shortly to appear on that STAGE where, Alas, I was destined to drudge behind the SCENES.— It is not commonly at these green years that the young Noblesse and Gentry have a just sense of the immense distance between them and their ragged Playfellows.— It takes a few dashes into the world to give the young Great man that proper, decent, unnoticing disregard for the poor, insignificant, stupid devils, the mechanics and peasantry around him; who perhaps were born in the same village.— My young Superiours never insulted the clouterly appearance of my ploughboy carcase, the two extremes of which were often exposed to all the inclemencies of all the seasons.— They would give me stray volumes of books; among them, even then, I could pick up some observations; and ONE, whose heart I am sure not even the MUNNY BEGUMS scenes have tainted, helped me to a little French.— Parting with these, my young friends and benefactors, as they dropped off for the east or west Indies, was often to me a sore affliction; but I was soon called to more serious evils.— My father's generous Master died; the farm proved a ruinous bargain; and, to clench the curse, we fell into the hands of a FACTOR who sat for the picture I have drawn of one in my Tale of two dogs.— My father was advanced in life when he married, I was the eldest of seven children; and he, worn out by early hardship was unfit for labour.— My father's spirit was soon irritated, but not easily broken.— There was a freedom in his lease in two years more, and to weather these two years we retrenched expences.— We lived very poorly; I was a dextrous Ploughman for my years; and the next eldest to me was a brother, who could drive the plough very well and help me to thrash.— A Novel-Writer might perhaps have viewed these scenes with some satisfaction, but so did not I: my indignation yet boils at the recollection of the scoundrel tyrant's insolent threat[en]ing epistles, which used to set us all in tears.—

This kind of life, the chearless gloom of a hermit with the unceasing moil of a galley-slave, brought me to my sixteenth year; a little before which period I first committed the sin of RHYME.— You know our country custom of coupling a man and woman together as partners in the labors of Harvest.— In my fifteenth autumn, my Partner was a bewitching creature who just counted an autumn less.— My scarcity of English denies me the power of doing her justice in that language; but you know the Scotch idiom, she was a bonie, sweet, sonsie lass.— In short, she altogether unwittingly to herself, initiated me in a certain delicious Passion, which in spite of acid Disappointment, gin-horse

Prudence and bookworm Philosophy, I hold to be the first of human joys, our dearest pleasure here below.— How she caught the contagion I can't say; you medical folks talk much of infection by breathing the same air, the touch, &c. but I never expressly told her that I loved her.— Indeed I did not well know myself, why I liked so much to loiter behind with her, when returning in the evening from our labors; why the tones of her voice made my heart strings thrill like an Eolian harp; and particularly, why my pulse beat such a furious ratann when I looked and fingered over her hand, to pick out the nettle stings and thistles.— Among her other love-inspiring qualifications, she sung sweetly; and 'twas her favorite reel to which I attempted giving an embodied vehicle in rhyme.— I was not so presumtive as to imagine that I could make verses like printed ones, composed by men who had Greek and Latin; but my girl sung a song which was said to be composed by a small country laird's son, on one of his father's maids, with whom he was in love, and I saw no reason why I might not rhyme as well as he, for excepting smearing sheep and casting peats his father living in the moors, he had no more scholarcraft than I had.—

Thus with me began Love and Poesy; which at times have been my only and till within this last twelvemonth have been my highest enjoyment.— My father struggled on till he reached the freedom in his lease, when he entered on a larger farm about ten miles farther in the country.— The nature of the bargain was such as to throw a little ready money in his hand at the commencement; otherwise the affair would have been impractible.— For four years we lived comfortably here; but a lawsuit between him and his Landlord commencing, after three years tossing and whirling in the vortex of Litigation, my father was just saved from absorption in a jail by phthisical consumption, which after two years promises, kindly stept in and snatch'd him away— 'To where the wicked cease from troubling, and where the weary be at rest.'—

It is during this climacterick that my little story is most eventful.— I was, at the beginning of this period, perhaps the most ungainly, aukward being in the parish.— No Solitaire was less acquainted with the ways of the world.— My knowledge of ancient story was gathered from Salmon's and Guthrie's geographical grammars; my knowledge of modern manners, and of literature and criticism I got from the Spectator.— These with Pope's works, some plays of Shakespear, Tull and Dickson on Agriculture, The Pantheon, Locke's Essay on the human understanding, Stackhouse's history of the bible, Justice's British Gardiner's directory, Boyle's lectures, Allan Ramsay's works, Taylor's scripture doctrine of original sin, a select Collection of English songs and Harvey's meditations had been the extent of my reading.— The Collection of Songs was my vade mecum.— I pored over them, driving my cart or walking to labor, song by song, verse by verse; carefully noting the true tender or sublime from affectation and fustian.— I am convinced I owe much to this for my critic-craft such as it is.—

In my seventeenth year, to give my manners a brush, I went to a country dancing school.— My father had an unaccountable antipathy against these meetings; and my going was, what to this hour I repent, in absolute defiance of his commands.— My father, as I said before, was the sport of strong passions; from that instance of rebellion he took a kind of dislike to me, which, I believe was one cause of that dissipation which marked my future years.— I say, Dissipation, comparative with the strictness and sobriety of Presbyterian country life; for though the will-o'-wisp meteors of thoughtless Whim were almost the sole lights of my path, yet early ingrained Piety and Virtue never failed to point me out the line of Innocence.— The great misfortune of my life was never to have AN AIM.— I had felt early some stirrings of Ambition, but they were the blind gropins of Homer's Cyclops round the walls of his cave: I saw my father's situation entailed on me perpetual labor.— The only two doors by which I could enter the fields of fortune were, the most niggardly economy, or the little chicaning art of bargain-making: the first is so contracted an aperture I never could squeeze myself into it; the last I always hated the contamination of the threshold.— Thus abandoned of aim or view in life; with a strong appetite for sociability, as well from native hilarity as from a pride of observation and remark; a constitutional hypochondriac taint which made me fly solitude; add to all these incentives to social life my reputation for bookish knowledge a certain wild, logical talent, and a strength of thought something like the rudiments of good sense, made me generally a welcome guest; so 'tis no great wonder that always 'where two or three were met together, there was I in the midst of them.'— But far beyond all the other impulses of my heart was, an penchant à l'adorable moitiée du genre humain.— My heart was compleatly tinder, and was eternally lighted up by some Goddess or other; and like every warfare in this world, I was sometimes crowned with success, and sometimes mortified with defeat.— At the plough, scythe or reap-hook I feared no competitor and set Want at defiance, and as I never cared farther for my labors than while I was in actual exercise I spent the evening in the way after my own heart.— A country lad rarely carries on an amour without an assisting confident.— I possessed a curiosity, zeal and intrepid dexterity in these matters which recommended me a proper Second in duels of that kind; and I dare say, I felt as much pleasure at being in the secret of half the amours in the parish, as ever did Premier at knowing the intrigues of half the courts of Europe.—

The very goose feather in my hand seems instinctively to know the well-worn path of my imagination, the favorite theme of my song; and is with difficulty restrained from giving you a couple of paragraphs on the amours of my Compeers, the humble Inmates of the farm-house and cottage; but the grave sons of Science, Ambition or Avarice baptize these things by the name of Follies.— To the sons and daughters of labor and poverty they are matters of the most serious nature: to them, the ardent hope, the stolen interview, the tender farewell are the greatest and most delicious part of their enjoyments.—

Another circumstance in my life which made very considerable alterations on my mind and manners was I spent my seventeenth summer on a smuggling [coast] a good distance from home at a noted school, to learn Mensuration, Surveying, Dialling, &c. in which I made a pretty good progress:— But I made greater progress in the knowledge of mankind.— The contraband trade was at that time very successful; scenes of swaggering riot and roaring dissipation were as yet new to me; and I was no enemy to social life.— Now, though I learned to look unconcernedly on a large tavern-bill, and mix without fear in a drunken squabble, yet I went on with a high hand in my geometry; till the sun entered Virgo, a month which is always a carnival in my bosom, when a charming Fillette who lived next door to the school overset my Trigonomertry, and set me off in a tangent from the sphere of my studies.— I struggled on with my Sines and Co-sines for a few days more; but stepping out to the garden one charming noon to take the sun's altitude, I met my Angel,

—'Like Proserpine gathering flowers,
Herself a fairer flower'—

It was vain to think of doing any more good at school.— The remaining week I staid, I did nothing but craze the faculties of my soul about her, or steal out to meet with her; and the two last nights of my stay in the country, had sleep been a mortal sin, I was innocent;—

I returned home very considerably improved.— My reading was enlarged with the very important addition of Thomson's and Shenstone's works; I had seen mankind in a new phasis; and I engaged several of my schoolfellows to keep up a literary correspondence with me.— This last helped me much on in composition.— I had met with a collection of letters by the Wits of Queen Ann's reign, and I pored over them most devoutly.— I kept copies of any of my own letters that pleased me and a comparison between them and the composition of most of my correspondents flattered my vanity.— I carried this whim so far that though I had not three farthings worth of business in the world, yet every post brought me as many letters as if I had been a broad plodding son of Day-book & Ledger.—

My life flowed on much in the same tenor till my twenty third year.— Vive l'amour et vive la bagatelle, were my sole principles of action.— The addition of two more Authors to my library gave me great pleasure; Sterne and M'kenzie.— Tristram Shandy and the Man of Feeling were my bosom favorites.— Poesy was still a darling walk for my mind, but 'twas only the humour of the hour.— I had usually half a dozen or more pieces on hand; I took up one or other as it suited the momentary tone of the mind, and dismissed it as it bordered on fatigue.— My Passions when once they were lighted up raged like so many devils, till they got vent in rhyme; and the conning over my verses like a spell soothed all into quiet.— None of the rhymes of those days are in print, except Winter a Dirge the eldest of my printed pieces; The death of Poor Mailie; John Barleycorn, And songs first, second and third: song second was the bullition of that passion which ended the forementioned school-business.—

My twenty third year was to me an important era.— Partly thro' whim, and partly that I wished to set about doing something in life, I joined with a flax-dresser in a neighbouring town to learn his trade and carry on the business of manufacturing and retailing flax. This turned out a sadly unlucky affair.— My Partner was a scoundrel of the first water who made money by the mystery of thieving; and to finish the whole, while we were giving a welcoming carousal to the New year, our shop, by the drunken carelessness of my Partner's wife, took fire and was burnt to ashes; and left me like a true Poet, not worth sixpence.— I was oblidged to give up business; the clouds of misfortune were gathering thick round my father's head, the darkest of which was, he was visibly far gone in a consumption; and to crown all, a belle fille whom I adored and who had pledged her soul to meet me in the field of matrimony jilted me with peculiar circumstances of mortification.— The finishing evil that brought up the rear of this infernal file was my hypochondriac complaint being irritated to such a degree, that for three months I was in diseased state of body and mind, scarcely to be envied by the hopeless wretches who have just got their mittemus. 'Depart from me ye Cursed.'—

From this adventure I learned something of a town-life. But the principal thing which gave my mind a turn was, I formed a bosom friendship with a young fellow, the first created being I had ever seen, but a hapless son of misfortune.— He was the son of a plain mechanic; but a great Man in the neighbourhood taking him under his patronage gave him a genteel education with a view to bettering his situation in life.—The Patron dieing just as he was ready to launch forth into the world, the poor fellow in despair went to sea; where after a variety of good and bad fortune, a little before I was acquainted with him, he had been set ashore by an American Privateer on the wild coast of Connaught, stript of every thing.— I cannot quit this poor fellow's story without adding that he is at this moment Captain of a large westindiaman belonging to the Thames.

This gentleman's mind was fraught with courage, independance, Magnanimity, and every noble, manly virtue.— I loved him, I admired him to a degree of enthusiasm; and I strove to imitate him.— In some measure I succeeded: I had the pride before but he taught it to flow in proper channels.— His knowledge of the world was vastly superiour to mine, and I was all attention to learn.— He was the only man I ever saw who was a greater fool than myself when WOMAN was the presiding star; but he spoke of a certain fashionable failing with levity, which hitherto I had regarded with HORROR.— Here his friendship did me a mischief, and the consequence was that soon after I resumed the plough, I wrote the WELCOME inclosed.— My reading was only increased by two stray volumes of Pamela, and one of Ferdinand Count Fathom, which gave me some idea of Novels.— Rhyme except some religious pieces that are in print, I had given up; but meeting with Fergusson's Scotch Poems, I strung anew my wildly-sounding, rustic lyre with emulating vigour.— When my father died, his all went among the rapacious hell-hounds that growl in the kennel of justice; but we made a shift to scrape a little money in the family amongst us, with which, to keep us together, my brother and I took a neighbouring farm.— My brother wanted my harebrained imagination as well as my social and amorous madness, but in good sense and every sober qualification he was far my superiour.—

I entered on this farm with a full resolution, 'Come, go to I will be wise!'— I read farming books; I calculated crops; I attended markets; and in short, in spite of 'The devil, the world and the flesh,' I believe I would have been a wise man; but the first year from unfortunately buying in bad seed the second from a late harvest, we lost half of both our crops: this overset all my wisdom, and I returned 'Like the dog to his vomit, and the sow that was washed to her wallowing in the mire ['].

I now began to be known in the neighbourhood as a maker of rhymes— The first of my poetic offspring that saw the light was a burlesque lamentation on a quarrel between two rev$^{d.}$ Calvinists, both of them dramatis personæ in my Holy Fair.— I had an idea myself that the piece had some merit; but to prevent the worst I gave a copy of it to a friend who was very fond of these things, and told him I could not guess who was the Author of it, but that I thought it pretty clever.— With a certain side of both clergy and laity it met with a roar of applause. Holy Willie's Prayer next made its appearance, and alarmed the kirk-Session so much that they held three several meetings to look over their holy artillery, if any of it was pointed against profane Rhymers.— Unluckily for me my idle wanderings led me on another side, point blank within the reach of their heaviest metal.— This is the unfortunate story alluded to in my printed poem, The Lament.— 'Twas a shocking affair, which I cannot yet bear to recollect, and had very nearly given [me] one or two of the principal qualifications for a place among those who have lost the chart and mistaken the reckoning of Rationality.— I gave up my part of the farm to my brother, as in truth it was only nominally mine; and made what little preparation was in my power for JAMAICA.— Before leaving my native country for ever, I resolved to publish my Poems.— I weighed my productions as impartially as in my power; I thought they had merit; and 'twas a delicious idea that I would be called a clever fellow even though it should never reach my ears a poor Negro-driver, or perhaps a victim to that inhospitable clime gone to the world of Spirits.— I can truly say that pauvre Inconnu as I then was, I had pretty nearly as high an idea of myself and my works as I have at this moment.— It [was] ever my opinion that the great unhappy mistakes and blunders, both in a rational and religious point of view, of which we see thousands daily guilty, are owing to their ignorance, or mistaken notions of themselves.— To know myself had been all along my constant study.— I weighed myself alone; I balanced myself with others; I watched every means of information how much ground I occupied both as a Man and as a Poet: I studied assiduously Nature's DESIGN where she seem'd to have intended the various LIGHTS and SHADES in my character.— I was pretty sure my Poems would meet with some applause; but at the worst the roar of the Atlantic would deafen the voice of Censure, and the novelty of west-Indian scenes make me forget Neglect.—

I threw off six hundred copies: of which I had got subscriptions for about three hundred and fifty.— My vanity was highly gratified by the reception I met with from the Publick; besides pocketing, all expences deducted, near twenty pounds.— This last came very seasonable, as I was about to indent myself for want of money to pay my freight.— So soon as I was master of nine guineas, the price of wafting me to the torrid zone, I bespoke a passage in the very first ship that was to sail, for

'Hungry wind had me in the wind'—

I had for some time been sculking from covert to covert under all the terrors of a Jail, as some ill-advised, ungrateful people had uncoupled the merciless legal Pack at my heels.— I had taken the last farewel of my few friends; my chest was on the road to Greenock. I had composed my last song I should ever measure in Caledonia, 'The gloomy night is gathering fast,' when a letter from Dr BLACKLOCK to a friend of mine overthrew all my schemes by rousing my poetic ambition.— The Doctor belonged to a set of Critics for whose applause I had not even dared to hope.— His idea that I would meet with every encouragement for a second edition fired me so much that away I posted to Edinburgh without a single acquaintance in town, or a single letter of introduction in my pocket.— The baneful Star that had so long shed its blasting influence in my Zenith, for once made a revolution to the Nadir; and the providential care of a good God placed me under the patronage of one of his noblest creatures, the Earl of Glencairn: 'Oublie moi, Grand Dieu, si jamais je l'oublie!'—

I need relate no farther.— At Edin^r.^ I was in a new world: I mingled among many classes of men, but all of them new to me; and I was all attention 'to catch the manners living as they rise.'

You can now, Sir, form a pretty near guess what sort of a Wight he is whom for some time you have honored with your correspondence.— That Fancy & Whim, keen Sensibility and riotous Passions may still make him zig-zag in his future path of life, is far from being improbable; but come what will, I shall answer for him the most determinate integrity and honor; and though his evil star should again blaze in his meridian with tenfold more direful influence, he may reluctantly tax Friendship with Pity but no more.

My most respectful Compliments to Miss Williams.— Her very elegant and friendly letter I cannot answer at present, as my presence is requisite in Edinburgh, and I set off tomorrow.—

If you will oblidge me so highly and do me so much honor as now and then to drop me a letter, Please direct to me at Mauchline, Ayrshire.—

I have the honor to be,

Sir,

your ever grateful humble serv^t^

ROB^T.^ BURNS.

Mauchline 2^d^ August

1787

Edin$^{r.}$ 23^{d} Sept:
Sir,

the foregoing letter, was unluckily forgot among other papers at Glasgow on my way to Edin$^{r.}$.— Soon after I came to Edin$^{r.}$ I went on a tour through the Highlands and did not recover this letter till my return to town which was the other day.— My ideas I picked up in my pilgrimage, and some rhymes of my earlier years, I shall soon be at leisure to give you at large so soon as I hear from you whether you are in London.—

I am again
Sir,
yours most gratefully
ROB$^{T.}$ BURNS.—

Letter to Agnes McLehose

19 January 1788

Saturday Morning
There is no time, my Clarinda, when the conscious thrilling chords of Love and Friendship give such delight, as in the pensive hours of what our favourite Thomson calls, 'Philosophic Melancholy.' The sportive insects who bask in the sunshine of Prosperity, or the worms that luxuriant crawl amid their ample wealth of earth, they need no Clarinda; they would despise Sylvander— if they durst.— The family of Misfortune, a numerous group of brothers and sisters! they need a resting place to their souls: unnoticed, often condemned by the world; in some degree perhaps condemned by themselves, they feel the full enjoyment of ardent love, delicate tender endearments, mutual esteem and mutual reliance.—

In this light I have often admired Religion.— In proportion as we are wrung with grief, or distracted with anxiety, the ideas of a compassionate Deity, an Almighty Protector are doubly dear.—

> ' 'Tis this, my friend, that streaks our morning bright;
> 'Tis this that gilds the horrors of our night'—

I have been this morning taking a peep thro', as Young finely says, 'the dark postern of time long elaps'd;' and you will easily guess, 'twas a rueful prospect.— What a tissue of thoughtlessness, weakness, and folly! My life reminded me of a ruin'd temple; what strength what proportion in some parts! what unsightly gaps, what prostrate ruins in others! I kneeled down before the Father of mercies and said, 'Father, I have sinned against Heaven and in thy sight, and am no more worthy to be called thy son!['] I rose, eased and strengthened.— I despise the superstition of a Fanatic, but I love the Religion of a Man.— 'The future,' said I to myself, 'is still before me: there let me—

—On Reason build Resolve,
That column of true majesty in man!'—

'I have difficulties many to encounter,' said I; 'but they are not absolutely insuperable: and where is firmness of mind shown but in exertion? mere declamation, is bombast rant.— Besides, wherever I am, or in whatever situation I may be—

—'Tis nought to me:
Since God is ever present, ever felt,
In the void waste as in the city full;
And where He vital breathes, there must be joy!'

Saturday night—half after ten—

What luxury of bliss I was enjoying this time yesternight! My ever-dearest Clarinda, you have stolen away my soul: but you have refined, you have exalted it; you have given it a stronger sense of Virtue, and a stronger relish for Piety.— Clarinda, first of your Sex, if ever I am the veriest wretch on earth to forget you; if ever your lovely image is effaced from my soul;

'May I be lost, no eye to weep my end
And find no earth that's base enough to bury me!'

What trifling silliness is the childish fondness of the every day children of the world! 'tis the unmeaning toying of the younglings of the fields and forests: but where Sentiment and Fancy unite their sweets; where Taste and Delicacy refine; where Wit adds the flavour, and Good-sense gives strength and spirit to all what a delicious draught is the hour of tender endearment! Beauty and Grace in the arms of Truth and Honor in all the luxury of mutual love!

Clarinda, have you ever seen the picture realized? not in all its very richest colouring: but

[']Hope, thou Nurse of young Desire;
Fairy promiser of joy'—

Last night, Clarinda, but for one slight shade, was the glorious Picture—

—Innocence
Look'd, gayly smiling on; while rosy Pleasure
Hid young Desire amid her flowery wreath,
And pour'd her cup luxuriant; mantling high,
The sparkling heavenly vintage, Love and Bliss!

Clarinda, when a Poet and Poetess of Nature's making, two of Nature's noblest productions! when they drink together of the same cup of Love and Bliss—Attempt not, ye coarser stuff of Human nature, profanely to measure enjoyment ye never can know!

Goodnight, my dear Clarinda!

SYLVANDER.

Letter to Agnes McLehose

25 January 1788

Clarinda, my life, you have wounded my soul.— Can I think of your being unhappy, even tho' it be not described in your pathetic elegance of language, without being miserable? Clarinda, can I bear to be told from you, that 'you will not see me to-morrow night—that you wish the hour of parting were come'! Do not let us impose on ourselves by sounds: if in the moment of fond endearment and tender dalliance, I perhaps trespassed against the *letter* of Decorum's law; I appeal even to you whether I ever sinned in the very least degree against the *spirit* of her strictest statute.— But why, My Love, talk to me in such strong terms; every word of which cuts me to the very soul? You know, a hint the slightest signification of your wish, is to me a sacred command.— Be reconciled, My Angel, to your God, your self and me: and I pledge you *Sylvander's honor*, an oath I dare say you will trust without reserve, that you shall never more have reason to complain of his conduct.— Now my Love, do not wound our next meeting with any averted looks or restrained caresses: I have marked the line of conduct, a line I know exactly to your taste and which I will inviolably keep but do not *you* show the least inclination to make boundaries: seeming distrust, where you know you may confide, is a cruel sin against Sensibility.—

'Delicacy, you know it, was what won me to you at once.— *take care* you do not loosen the dearest most sacred tie that unites us'— Clarinda, I would not have stung *your* soul I would not have bruised *your* spirit as that harsh crucifying 'Take care', did *mine*; no, not to have gained heaven! Let me again appeal to your dear Self, if Sylvander, even when he seemingly half-transgressed the laws of Decorum, if he did not shew more chastised, trembling, faultering delicacy than the MANY of the world do in keeping these laws.—

O Love and Sensibility, ye have conspired against My Peace! I love to madness, and I feel to torture! Clarinda, how can I forgive myself, that I ever have touched a single chord in your bosom with pain! would I do it willingly? Would any consideration, any gratification make me [do so?]

Oh, did you love like me, you would not, you could not deny or put off a meeting— with the Man who adores you; who would die a thousands deaths before he would injure you; and who must soon bid you a long farewell!—

I had proposed bringing my bosom friend, M^r. Ainslie, tomorrow evening, at his strong request, to see you: as he only has time to stay with us about ten minutes, for an engagement but—I shall hear from you: this afternoon, for mercy's sake! for till I hear from you I am wretched.— O Clarinda, the tie that binds me to thee, is entwisted incorporated with my dearest threads of life!

Sylvander

Letter to Robert Ainslie

3 March 1788

Mauchline, March 3rd, 1788.

My dear Friend,—

I am just returned from Mr. Millar's farm. My old friend, whom I took with me was highly pleased with the bargain and advised me to accept of it. He is the most intelligent, sensible farmer in the country, and his advice has staggered me a good deal. I have the two plans before me[.] I shall endeavour to balance them to the best of my judgment, and fix on the most eligible. On the whole, if I find Mr. Miller in the same favourable disposition as when I saw him last, I shall in all probability turn farmer.

I have been through sore tribulation and under much buffetting of the Wicked One since I came to this country[.] Jean I found banished like a martyr—forlorn, destitute, and friendless. All for the good old cause. I have reconciled her to her mother. I have taken her a room. I have taken her to my arms. I have given her a mahogany bed. I have given her a guinea, and I have f[ucke]d her till she rejoiced with joy unspeakable and full of glory. But, as I always am on every occasion, I have been prudent and cautious to an astonishing degree. I swore her privately and solemnly never to attempt any claim on me as a husband, even though anybody should persuade her she had such a claim (which she had not), neither during my life nor after my death. She did all this like a good girl, and I took the opportunity of some dry horse litter, and gave her such a thundering scalade that electrified the very marrow of her bones. Oh, what a peacemaker is a guid weel-willy p[int]le! It is the mediator, the guarantee, the umpire, the bond of union, the solemn league and covenant, the plenipotentiary, the Aaron's rod, the Jacob's staff, the prophet Elisha's pot of oil, the Ahasuerus' sceptre, the sword of mercy, the philosopher's stone, the horn of plenty, and Tree of Life between Man and Woman.

I shall be in Edinburgh the middle of next week. My farming ideas I shall keep private till I see. I got a letter from Clarinda yesterday, and she tells me she has got no letter of mine but one. Tell her that I wrote to her from Glasgow, from Kilmarnock, from Mauchline, and yesterday from Cumnoch, as I returned from Dumfries. Indeed she is the only person in Edinburgh I have written to till to-day. How are your soul and body putting up? A little like man and wife, I suppose.

Your faithful friend,
R. B.

Extract from a Letter to Burns from Agnes McLehose

Tuesday Forenoon.

Your attention in writing me before you set out this Morning was one of these delicate Compliments which give a *nameless* pleasure to succeptible minds! I am now *convinced* that, in the wide circle of the universe, there are not two souls so completely form'd for each other as ours.

My Spirits are a little weighted to-day—but I'm not unhappy. Last night I saw you low and Depress'd—my heart was bent upon soothing and raising your Spirits—the Intention was good—But it led me perhaps too far. To-day, I am quite sensible of it—even 'present in the very lap of Love' I was chect at the Idea of impropriety. However, I hope to be enabled to do better in future. Happy, for me, I've learnt not to depend on my own weak resolves—But on the 'Rock of Ages'! I must forgive you. But I wish you may not need to ask it on the same account again. Why do you allow yourself [to sink] in Melancholy Reflections? I trust you are seeking the Divine Blessing on your lawfull Effort for a livelihood—and if so, can you not rely on His Goodness who 'Feeds the Young Ravens when they cry'!

Besides, has not Clarinda's fondest, warmest Friendship been sought ardently after as your Chief Earthly Happiness—and has it not been attained to your utmost wish? Ah! Sylvander, it is indeed attained—it will depend on yourself to *secure* it. While you are the same—Clarinda will be so too—what a Complicated Creature is Man! A little month ago, Clarinda's affections would (you thought) have made your happiness complete—*that* is ensured—and other wishes spring up and command your anxious pursuit. It will be so—till we be united to Infinite Perfection.—I can now carry you with me to God's footstool—there, I pour out my ardent requests for your Success in Life, for your happiness in Eternity!—'tis only since Saturday last, I could do so—and I feel a sensation so delightful, so serene, as makes me almost hope that Heaven itself approves our union.

I tremble for Mary, least she feel an involuntary throb in your favour—I'm not so much afraid of you—amiable and Bonie as she is—I think Clarinda is more entirely Congenial to the Heart of Sylvander.

Why did not you see *Her* first? Young, Blooming, *disengaged*!—but—'tis too late—dear as I love Her—I could not spare her a *Heart* so precious to mine—no, unless *you* wished it! 'twould be an effort more than Human! Come to-morrow evening as soon as you can get off—You'll see no *stars*—*without* at least; *within* you'll find the Star Venus which always attends the Sun you know[. . .]

Yours,

Clarinda.

Letter to Dr John Moore

4 January 1789

Ellisland near Dumfries— Jan. 4$^{th.}$ *1789*
Sir,

As often as I think of writing to you, which has been three or four times every week these six months, it gives me something so like the idea of an ordinary-sized Statue offering at a conversation with the Rhodian Colossus that my mind misgives me; and the affair always miscarries somewhere between Purpose and Resolve.— I have at last got some business with you, and business-letters are written by the Style-book.— I say my business is with you, Sir, for you never had any with me, except the business that Benevolence has in the mansion of Poverty. —

The character and employment of a Poet were formerly my pleasure, but are now my pride.— I know that a very great deal of my late eclat was owing to the singularity of my situation, and the honest prejudice of Scotsmen; but still as I said in the preface to my first Edition, I do look upon myself as having some pretensions from Nature to the Poetic Character.— I have not a doubt but the knack, the aptitude to learn the Muses' trade, is a gift bestowed by Him 'who forms the secret biass of the soul;' but I as firmly believe that *excellence* in the Profession is the fruit of industry, labour, attention and pains.— At least I am resolved to try my doctrine by the test of Experience.— Another appearance from the Press, I put off to a very distant day; a day that may never arrive; but Poesy I am determined to prosecute with all my vigour.— Nature has given very few, if any, of the Profession, the talents of shining in every species of Composition: I shall try, for untill trial it is impossible to know, whether she has qualified me to shine in any one.— The worst of it is, against one has finished a Piece, it has been so often viewed and reviewed before the mental eye that one loses in a good measure the powers of critical discrimination.— Here the best criterion I know is A Friend; not only of abilities to judge, but with good nature enough, like a prudent teacher with a young learner, to give perhaps a little more than is exactly due, lest the thin-skinned animal fall into that most deplorable of all Poetic diseases, heart-breaking despondency of himself.— Dare I, Sir, already immensely indebted to your goodness, ask the additional obligation of your being that Friend to me?

I inclose you an Essay of mine in a walk of Poesy to me entirely new; I mean the Epistle addressed to R— G— Esq. or Robert Graham of Fintry Esquire; a gentleman of uncommon worth, to whom I lie under very great obligations.— The story of the Poem; like most of my Poems, is connected with my own story; and to give you the one, I must give you something of the other.—

I cannot boast of M$^{r.}$ Creech's ingenuous fair-dealing to me.— He kept me hanging on about Edin$^{r.}$ from the 7$^{th.}$ Aug. 1787, untill the 13$^{th.}$ April 1788, before he would condescend to give me a Statement of affairs; nor had I got it even then, but for an angry letter I wrote him which irritated his pride.— 'I could' not a 'tale' but a detail 'unfold'— but what am I that I should speak against the Lord's annointed Bailie of Edinburgh?— I believe I shall in whole, £100 Copy-right included, clear about £400, some little odds; and even part of this depends upon what the gentleman has yet to settle with me.— I give you this information because you did me the honor to interest yourself much in my welfare; but I give it to yourself only, for the world would accuse me of ingratitude, and I am still much in the gentleman's mercy.— Perhaps I injure the man in the idea I am sometimes tempted to have of him—God forbid I should! A little time will try, for in a month I shall go to town to wind up the business— if possible.— To give the rest of my story in brief, I have married 'My Jean', and taken a farm: with the first step I have every day more & more reason to be satisfied; with the last it is rather the reverse.— I have a younger brother who supports my aged mother, another still younger brother & three sisters in a farm.— On my last return from Edin$^{r.}$ it cost me about £180 to save them from ruin.— Not that I have lost so much; I only interposed between my brother and his impending fate by the loan of so much.— I give myself no airs on this, for it was mere selfishness on my part.— I was conscious that that the opposite scale of the balance was pretty heavily charged, and I thought that throwing a little filial piety & fraternal affection into the scale in my favor, might help to smooth matters at the GRAND RECKONING.— There is still one thing would make my circumstances quite easy.— I have an Excise-Officer's Commission, & I live in the midst of a country Division.— My request to M$^{r.}$ Graham, who is one of the Commiss: of Excise, was, if in his power, to procure me that Division.— If I were very sanguine, I might hope that some of my Great Patrons might procure me a Treasury-warrant for Supervisor, Surveyor-general, &c. but thank Heaven I am in a good degree independant.— If farming will not do, a simple petition will get me into employ in the Excise somewhere; & poor as the salary comparatively is, it is luxury to what either my wife or I were in early life taught to expect.— Thus, secure of a livelyhood, 'to thee sweet Poetry, delightful maid,' I consecrate my future days.—

With the highest esteem & warmest gratitude

I have the honor to be, Sir, your most humble serv[t]

Rob[T.] Burns

Extract from a Letter to Mrs Frances Dunlop of Dunlop

12 January 1795

12[th.] Jan[ry.]

You will have seen our worthy & ingenious friend, the Doctor, long ere this.— I hope he is well, & beg to be remembered to him.— I have just been reading over again, I dare say for the hundred & fiftieth time, his 'View of Society & Manners;' & still I read it with unsated delight.— His humour is perfectly original.— It is neither the humour of Addison, nor Swift, nor Sterne, nor any body, but Dr. Moore; & is positively as rich a vein as any of them could boast.— By the bye, you have deprived me of Zeluco: remember *that*, when you are disposed to rake up the sins of my neglect from among the ashes of my laziness.—

He has paid me a pretty compliment, by quoting me, in his last Publication, though I must beg leave to say, that he has not written this last work in his usual happy manner.— Entre nous, you know my Politics; & I cannot approve of the honest Doctor's whining over the deserved fate of a certain pair of Personages.— What is there in the delivering over a perjured Blockhead & an unprincipled Prostitute, into the hands of the hangman that it should arrest for a moment, attention, in an eventful hour, when, as my friend Roscoe in Liverpool gloriously expresses it—'When the welfare of Millions is hung in the scale

And the balance yet trembles with fate!'

But our friend is already indebted to People in power, & still looks forward for his Family, so I can apologise for him; for at bottom I am sure he is a staunch friend to liberty.— Thank God, these London trials have given us a little more breath, & I imagine that the time is not far distant when a man may freely blame Billy Pit, without being called an enemy to his Country.—

Adieu! RBurns

Letter to James Armour

10 July 1796

For Heaven's sake & as you value the we[l]fare of your daughter, & my wife, do, my dearest Sir, write to Fife to M$^{rs.}$ Armour to come if possible.— My wife thinks she can yet reckon upon a fortnight.—The Medical people order me, *as I value my existence*, to fly to seabathing & country quarters, so it is ten thousand chances to one that I shall not be within a dozen miles of her when her hour comes.— What a situation for her, poor girl, without a single friend by her on such a serious moment.—

I have now been a week at salt water, & though I think I have got some good by it yet I have some secret fears—that this business will be dangerous if not fatal.—

Your most affectionate son—

RBurns

July 10th

Notes

Notes

Abbreviations:

1786:	*Poems, Chiefly in the Scottish Dialect*, Kilmarnock, 1786.
1787:	*Poems, Chiefly in the Scottish Dialect*, Edinburgh, 1787.
Currie, 1800:	James Currie, *The Works of Robert Burns, with an Account of his Life, and Criticism on his Writings*, Liverpool, 1800.
Kinsley:	James Kinsley, *The Poems and Songs of Robert Burns*, Oxford, 1968.
SMM:	James Johnson, *The Scots Musical Museum*, Edinburgh, six volumes, 1787, 1788, 1790, 1792, 1796, 1803.

My Father was a Farmer

Text: a facsimile of Burns's manuscript is available in *Robert Burns's Commonplace Book 1783–1785*, first published in 1938 with a transcript and notes by James Cameron Ewing and Davidson Cook, republished in 1965 with an introduction by David Daiches (London: Centaur Press).

Carrick: the southern part of Ayrshire.

Potosi: the richest silver mine in Bolivia from about 1550 to 1800, mentioned also in 'The Vision'.

To Ruin.

Text: 1786.

The Death and Dying Words of Poor Mailie, The Author's Only Pet Yowe, An Unco Mournfu' Tale.

Text: 1786.

Poor Mailie's Elegy.

Text: 1786.

Tweed: the river that forms part of the border between Scotland and England.

Doon: the Ayrshire river near where Burns lived.

Aire: the river Ayr.

Mary Morison

Text: there is a copy of this song in a letter by Burns in the Pierpont Morgan Library, New York.

On a Noisy Polemic.

Text: 1786.

Jamie: James Humphrey (1755–1844), a mason in Mauchline, Ayrshire, who liked to debate matters of religious doctrine.

For the Author's Father.

Text: 1786.

A Fragment. [When Guilford Good our Pilot Stood]

Text: 1787

Guilford: Frederick Guilford, Lord North (1732–92), British Prime Minister throughout the American War of Independence. When he allowed the East India Company to ship tea to America without paying tax on it, some Americans poured three ship-loads of the tea into Boston Harbour in 1773 as a show of defiance of the British government. This act, known as the Boston Tea Party, symbolically began the American revolution against British rule.

Montgomery: Richard Montgomery (1736–75), American general born in Ireland, who captured Montreal in 1775 and then marched down the St Lawrence river to attack Quebec. His death in the unsuccessful assault ended the American campaign in Canada.

Carleton: Sir Guy Carleton (1724–1808), later Lord Dorchester, Governor of Quebec, 1768–78, and British commander-in-chief in America, 1782–83. He led the successful British resistance to the American invasion of Canada in 1775 and after the war succeeded in resettling thousands of British loyalists and former slaves driven out of the United States of America.

Gage: Thomas Gage (1719–87), British commander-in-chief in America, 1763–75. He was virtually besieged in Boston by the American rebel forces.

Howe: William Howe (1729–1814), British general. He defeated the Americans at Breed's Hill (known as the Battle of Bunker Hill, 1775) overlooking Boston before he replaced Gage as commander-in-chief in America. He evacuated Boston and in 1776 recaptured New York, from where he operated successfully against George Washington's Continental Army, taking Philadelphia in 1777. He was however blamed for the British defeat at Saratoga in the same year because he had not marched north from New York to support Burgoyne's advance from Canada.

Burgoyne: John Burgoyne (1722–92), British general who led an army south from Canada in 1777 but was unable to defeat the Americans opposing him and, running out of supplies, was forced to surrender at Saratoga in New York State. This defeat was the turning-point of the war because it persuaded France and Spain to support the Americans and declare war on Britain.

Fraser: Simon Fraser (1729–77), British general, killed in the Battle of Bemis Heights preceding the surrender at Saratoga.

Cornwallis: Charles Cornwallis (1738–1805), British general, commander in the south during the American war. In 1781 he was besieged at Yorktown, Virginia, by American and French forces. When help from the British commander in New York failed to arrive, Cornwallis had to surrender. This defeat led to the fall of Lord North's government in London and an end to the war.

Clinton: Sir Henry Clinton (1738–95), successor to William Howe as British commander in America, 1778–82. He quarrelled with most of the British generals and admirals during the war and his failure to respond to Cornwallis's pleas for help to lift the siege of Yorktown was blamed for the British defeat there and the subsequent loss of the American colonies.

Montague: John Montagu, fourth Earl of Sandwich (1718–1792), First Lord of the Admiralty, 1771–82, the government minister responsible for the British navy during the American War of Independence.

Sackville: George Sackville (1716–85), later Lord Germain, was British Secretary of State for America, 1775–82, in Lord North's government and as such responsible for dealing with the revolt of the American colonies and the war that followed there. In 1759 he had commanded the British cavalry at the Battle of Minden in Germany, when his refusal to follow orders from the army commander Duke Ferdinand of Brunswick to charge the enemy gave him a reputation for cowardice. Burns's phrase 'stood the stoure' is an ironic reference to this incident.

Burke: Edmund Burke (1729–97), Irish (hence Burns's reference to him as Paddy) member of the British parliament and a leading critic of Lord North's conduct of the American War.

Fox: Charles James Fox (1749–1806), British Whig politician. He supported American independence and led the opposition to Lord North's government, thus earning the dislike of King George III. Fox was Foreign Secretary in Lord Rockingham's government after the fall of North's. Fox was usually depicted in political cartoons as a fat, rascally man, fond of eating and gambling.

In 1783 he agreed to form a government with North, despite having been his opponent throughout the American War; this is alluded to in the next stanza of the poem, where 'North an' Fox united stocks'.

Rockingham: Charles Watson-Wentworth, second Marquis of Rockingham (1730–82), leader of the Whig party in opposition to Lord North's government, who became Prime Minister after North in 1782, although he died very soon after. He recognized the independence of the United States of America.

Shelburne: William Petty, second Earl of Shelburne (1737–1805), later Marquis of Lansdowne, became Prime Minister after the death of Lord Rockingham in 1782. Considered devious by contemporaries, Shelburne had planned to improve commercial links between Britain and the new United States, but he lost support in Parliament and his government did not last long.

Saint Stephen's boys: that is, members of the House of Commons, which met in St Stephen's Hall until 1834, when much of the Palace of Westminster was destroyed by fire and had to be replaced with the present building.

Diamond's Ace, of Indian race: a reference to the Pitt Diamond, whose sale in 1717 laid the foundation of the fortune that enabled members of the Pitt family (see next note) to pursue political careers.

Chatham's boy: William Pitt the Younger (1759–1806), the son of the Earl of Chatham (1708–78) and the dominant British political figure in the last decades of the eighteenth century. He took office as Prime Minister in 1783, at the age of 24, and remained in that position until 1801, returning to the post from 1804 until his death. At first, however, Pitt's government did not have support from a majority in Parliament and he was hard pressed by the opposition, led by Fox and North, until the general election of 1784, in which Pitt triumphed.

Grenville: William Grenville (1759–1834), later first Baron Grenville, William Pitt's cousin and supporter.

Dundas: Henry Dundas (1742–1811), first Viscount Melville, Scottish lawyer and politician, whose close management of Scottish affairs for William Pitt's government brought him the nickname 'The Uncrowned King of Scotland'.

Address to the Unco Guid, Or the Rigidly Righteous.

Text: 1787.

O Leave Novels

Text: *SMM*, 1803, with initial upper case letters at lines 4 and 6–8.

Mauchline: Ayrshire town near Burns's farm at Mossgiel.

Tom Jones: the titular hero of Henry Fielding's novel of 1749.

Grandisons: from Samuel Richardson's novel *Sir Charles Grandison* (1753–4).

Green Grow the Rashes. A Fragment.

Text: 1787.

The wisest Man: the Bible's King Solomon.

Epistle to Davie, A Brother Poet.

Text: 1786.

Davie: David Sillar (1760–1830), local poet and fiddler, who published his own poems in 1789.

Ben-Lomond: a mountain in the Scottish Highlands north of Ayrshire, beside Loch Lomond.

Commoners: ordinary people, but also the lower classes who relied for subsistence on common land, owned by the community as a whole. Commoners of air presumably have the right to even less, though Burns may well be punning on the town of Ayr, whose name was variously spelled in the eighteenth century.

Phœbus and the famous Nine: Phœbus Apollo, the god of poetry, and the Nine Muses.

Pegasus: a winged horse in Greek mythology who, by striking his hoof on Mount Helicon, produced the Hippocrene fountain, sacred to the Muses. Pegasus is often used as a symbol of poetic inspiration.

Holy Willie's Prayer

Text: there is one of many manuscript copies in the National Library of Scotland, Edinburgh.

Holy Willie: William Fisher (1737–1809), an elder of Mauchline parish church and as such a member of the Kirk Session, which had the power to examine and punish parishioners accused of offences against church doctrine and moral standards.

Gavin Hamilton: a Mauchline lawyer, Burns's landlord at Mossgiel and a friend and supporter of the poet, who included a dedicatory poem to Hamilton in the first edition of his poems, 1786. Hamilton's liberal views made him, like Burns, a target for self-righteous guardians of public morality such as Fisher.

Auld: William Auld (1709–1891), the Mauchline minister from 1742.

presbytery: in the Church of Scotland parishes are grouped together into presbyteries for administrative purposes; the presbytery can act as a court of appeal against decisions taken by the Kirk Session of a parish.

Robert Aiken: Aiken (1739–1807) was an Ayr lawyer and friend and supporter of Burns.

sax thousand: reckoning from around 4000 BC, the supposed date of the Creation as calculated by many Biblical scholars, notably Archishop James Ussher (1581–1656).

Death and Doctor Hornbook. A True Story.

Text: 1787.

Great lies and nonsense baith to vend: in later editions this line was changed to 'A rousing whid [*lie*] at times to vend'.

Sax thousand years: reckoning from the supposed date of the Creation around 4000 BC.

Epistle to J. L[aprai]k, An Old Scotch Bard.

Text: 1786.

J L[aprai]k: John Lapraik (1727–1807) published *Poems on Several Occasions* in 1788.

Pope: Alexander Pope (1688–1744), English poet.

Steele: Sir Richard Steele (1672–1729), Anglo-Irish writer.

Beattie: James Beattie (1735–1803), Scottish poet and academic.

Muirkirk: a town in Ayrshire about twenty-five miles east of Ayr.

Inverness: a city in the north of Scotland.

Tiviotdale: Teviotdale, one of the river-valleys in the Scottish Borders.

Parnassus: the mountain sacred to the Muses in Greek mythology.

Allan: Allan Ramsay (1685–1758), Scottish poet.

Ferguson: Robert Fergusson (1750–74), Scottish poet.

Mauchline: the Ayrshire town nearest to Burns's farm and about fifteen miles west of Muirkirk.

The Vision.

Text: 1786.

'hair-brain'd, sentimental trace': Burns appears to be quoting from his own poem, 'To J. S[mith]' (1786), line 157.

Fullarton: William Fullarton (1754–1808), Ayrshire landowner.

Dempster: George Dempster (1732–1818) Ayrshire landowner.

Beattie: James Beattie (1735–1803), author of *The Minstrel* (1771–4) and of an attack on the sceptical philosophy of David Hume (1711–76).

Coila: the Latinized name for Kyle, part of Ayrshire.

Thomson: James Thomson (1700–48), Scottish poet, most famous for his nature-poem *The Seasons* (1726–30).

Shenstone: William Shenstone (1714–63), English poet.
Gray: Thomas Gray (1716–71), English poet.
Potosi's mine: a famous source of silver in Bolivia, mentioned also in the song 'My Father was a Farmer'.

To a Mouse

Text: 1786.

The Holy Fair.

Text: 1786.
Hypocrisy a-la-Mode: Burns's note has been taken to refer to a play called *The Stage-Beaux toss'd in a Blanket or, Hypocrisie Alamode* (1704) by Thomas Brown (1663–1704), but the verses in the epigraph do not appear in this text, which is mainly in prose, apart from a prologue and epilogue in couplets. Perhaps the epigraph is by Burns himself.
Galston: a village in Ayrshire a few miles north of Burns's farm at Mossgiel.
Mauchline holy fair: the annual communion at Mauchline, the nearest town in Ayrshire to Burns's farm, where many hundreds of people from several parishes gathered to hear the preachers and take the sacrament.
racer Jess: Janet Gibson, daughter of the Mauchline tavern-keeper Agnes Gibson, the 'Poosie Nansie' of Burns's cantata *Love and Liberty*.
Kilmarnock: the town in Ayrshire where the first edition of Burns's poems was published in 1786.
Elect: that is, chosen, the word used in later editions of the poem. Burns is referring to the Calvinist doctrine of predestination, the idea that God has already chosen which human beings are saved and destined for Heaven, and which are not.
Moodie: Alexander ('Sawney') Moodie (1728–99), minister of Riccarton, south of Kilmarnock. He was a ferocious preacher; in later editions of the poem the word 'salvation' in the next line was replaced with 'damnation'.
Smith: George Smith (died 1823), minister of Galston, a preacher of the moderate party of the Church of Scotland, scorned by the traditional Calvinist 'Auld Lichts' (Old Lights) as too modern and easy on sinners.
Socrates: the ancient Greek philosopher (469–399 BC).
Antonine: Antoninus Pius (AD 86–161), Roman emperor from AD 138, whose reign was peaceful if uneventful.
Peebles: William Peebles (1753–1826), minister of Newton-upon-Ayr.
Miller: Alexander Miller (dates unknown), minister of St Michael's, Ayrshire.

Russel: John Russel (*c.* 1740–1817), minister of Kilmarnock, another fierce Calvinist.

Clinkumbell: the town-crier or bellman

The Twa Dogs, A Tale.

Text: 1786.

king Coil: the legendary king of Kyle, the central part of Ayrshire; Burns was not alone in connecting him with the nursery-rhyme about Old King Cole.

Where sailors gang to fish for Cod: that is, Newfoundland.

Luath: the name of a dog in *Fingal* (1762), a prose-poem translated, according to its author James Macpherson (1736–96), from Scottish Gaelic; the word 'luath' means 'swift' in Gaelic and was the name Burns gave to his own dog.

patronage: the question of who chooses the parish minister, the local landowner or the whole congregation, an issue which caused centuries of argument and division in the Scottish church.

The Cotter's Saturday Night.

Text: 1786.

Gray: Thomas Gray (1716–71); the epigraph consists of lines 29–32 of his 'Elegy written in a Country Churchyard' (1751).

Aiken: Robert Aiken (1739–1807), Ayr lawyer and friend and supporter of Burns.

'An honest man's the noble work of GOD': Alexander Pope, *An Essay on Man* (1733–4), Epistle IV, line 248, with 'noble' for 'noblest'.

Wallace: Sir William Wallace (1272–1305), leader of the resistance to the conquest of Scotland by the English king Edward I (1239–1307), who captured Wallace and had him executed in London.

Address to the Deil.

Text: 1786.

man of Uzz: Job, whose story is told in the Old Testament of the Bible; God agrees to permit Satan to test Job's faith by subjecting him to a series of disasters, including an attack of boils. Job resists the temptation to blame God for his misfortunes but his wife is not so patient and scolds him.

Brose and Butter.

Text: *The Merry Muses of Caledonia*, 1799.

merry wee beast: the printed text has 'wi" for 'wee'.

And O for a touch: the printed text has 'o" for 'O'.

To a Louse

Text: 1786.

Lunardi: Vincenzo Lunardi (1759–1806), an Italian balloonist, made several sensational balloon flights in Scotland in 1784–85 that resulted in a fashion for balloon-shaped ladies' bonnets named after him.

A Cantata. [Love and Liberty *or* The Jolly Beggars]

Text: a manuscript copy is in the Robert Burns Birthplace and Museum, Alloway.

Poosie-Nansie: Agnes Gibson, mother of Racer Jess, who is mentioned in 'The Holy Fair', kept a disreputable tavern in Mauchline. 'Poosie' is Burns's spelling of 'pussy', a disrespectful term for a woman.

heights of Abram: in 1759 a British army commanded by James Wolfe defeated the French, under the Marquis of Montcalm, on the Plains of Abraham outside Quebec. Although Wolf, like Montcalm, died of wounds immediately after the battle, his victory led to the replacement of France by Britain as the ruling power in Canada.

the Moro: the Morro is a fortress guarding the entrance to the harbour at Havana in Cuba, captured by the British in 1762 after a siege costing many casualties, mainly from yellow fever.

Curtis: Admiral Sir Roger Curtis (1746–1816) was in 1782 involved in the defence of Gibraltar against a Spanish attack that used ten old warships converted into floating gun batteries.

Elliot: George Augustus Eliott, first Baron Heathfield (1717–90), Governor of Gibraltar from 1777 to 1787, including the period of the Great Siege of Gibraltar, 1779–83, by France and Spain.

Castalia: in Greek mythology, a sacred fountain, at the foot of Mount Parnassus near Delphi, whose waters gave poetic inspiration.

Helicon: the mountain at whose foot the fountain of Castalia rises.

On a Scotch Bard Gone to the West Indies.

Text: 1786.

Kyle: the central region of Ayrshire.

To the Author. [Second Epistle to Davie]

Text: *Poems by David Sillar* (Kilmarnock 1789), pp. 9–11.

To the Author: this is the title of the poem where it appears as dedicatory verses to David Sillar (1760–1830) in *Poems by David Sillar*. Burns's own

Kilmarnock edition includes an earlier verse 'Epistle to Davie' (see this volume) and so this poem is usually re-titled 'Second Epistle to Davie'.

Parnassus: a mountain sacred to the Muses in Greek mythology.

The warl' may play you a shavie: this line seems too short and so the word 'mony' (= many) is often added before 'a shavie', although it is conceivable that Burns gave the 'r' of 'warl'' syllabic force.

[Lines Written on a Bank of Scotland One Guinea Note]

Text: facsimile image from Robert Burns Birthplace and Museum, Alloway. Burns's verses are written on the back of the bank note, which is dated Edinburgh, 1st March 1780.

[Address of Beelzebub]

Text: there is a manuscript in the National Library of Scotland, Edinburgh.

Breadalbine: John Campbell (1762–1834), Earl of Breadalbane in the south-west Highlands of Scotland.

M'Kenzie of Applecross: Thomas Mackenzie of Applecross in the north-west Highlands.

Macdonald of Glengary: presumably Alasdair Ranaldson MacDonell of Glengarry (1771–1828), fifteenth chief of the MacDonells of Glengarry, a branch of the MacDonald clan. During his chieftainship many of his clansmen emigrated in the process known as the Highland Clearances.

Hancocke: John Hancock (1737–93), a leading American revolutionary and, as President of the Continental Congress, the first to sign the Declaration of Independence, 4 July 1776.

Frankline: Benjamin Franklin (1706–90), the American writer and scientist; from 1776–85 he served as an ambassador in Paris, bringing about the alliance with France that led to the success of the American Revolution.

Washington: George Washington (1732–99), American general and first President of the USA.

Montgomery: Richard Montgomery (1736–75), American general born in Ireland, who led an American invasion of Canada in 1775.

North: Frederick Guilford, Lord North (1732–92), British Prime Minister throughout the American War of Independence and often blamed for the failure of British policy in America.

Sackville: George Sackville (1716–85), later Lord Germain, was British Secretary of State for America, 1775–82, and often blamed for failing to carry out his duties properly.

Howe: William Howe (1729–1814), British general. He defeated the Americans at Breed's Hill (known as the Battle of Bunker Hill, 1775) and recaptured New York in 1776 and Philadelphia in 1777, but he was blamed for not marching north to prevent the surrender at Saratoga of a British army led by John Burgoyne (1722–92).

Clinton: Sir Henry Clinton (1738–95), successor to William Howe as British commander in America, 1778–82. A quarrelsome general, his failure to lift the siege of Yorktown, 1781, was blamed for the British defeat there and the subsequent loss of the American colonies.

Drury lane: a street in London notorious for prostitution in the eighteenth century.

Herod: Herod I (73–4 BC), King of Judæa; in Chapter 2 of Matthew's Gospel he is alleged to have ordered the Massacre of the Innocents, that is, the slaughter of all male children under two years old in Bethlehem, hoping this would include Jesus, but his family, forewarned by a dream, had already fled to Egypt.

Polycrate: Polycrates, ruler of Samos, one of the Greek islands, in the sixth century BC.

Almagro: Diego de Almagro (1475–1538), Spanish conquistador, who accompanied Pizarro in the conquest of Peru, 1532; he later fell out with the Pizarro brothers, who had him executed.

Pizarro: Francisco Pizarro (*c.*1476–1541), Spanish conquistador, conqueror of Peru in 1532, mainly by guile and treachery.

Anno Mundi 5790: that is, 1790 plus 4000, the traditional number of years Bible scholars usually calculated for the period between the Creation and the birth of Christ.

A Dream.

Text: 1786.

Laureate's Ode: it was the duty of the Poet Laureate in the eighteenth century to write an ode for the monarch's birthday; for George III's forty-eighth birthday on 4 June 1786 the ode was written by Thomas Warton (1728–90).

Birth-day dresses: it was traditional to wear one's best and newest clothes on a birthday.

And aiblins ane: probably a reference to Charles Edward Stuart, the Jacobite 'pretender' to the throne.

peace: a sly allusion to the end of the American war, in which George III lost his American colonies.

Willie Pit: William Pitt the Younger (1759–1806), the son of William Pitt the Elder, Earl of Chatham (1708–78), who had led Britain in the successful Seven Years' War, 1756–63.

Queen: Charlotte of Mecklenburg-Strelitz (1744–1818), wife of George III from 1761. She had fifteen children, thirteen of whom survived to adulthood.

Potentate o' W[ales]: George, Prince of Wales (1762–1830), later George IV, was notorious for his lavish life-style and the subject of much scandal.

Diana: the Roman goddess of chastity.

Charlie: Charles James Fox (1749–1806), British Whig politician, usually an opponent of the government and notorious as a gambler and high-liver.

Agincourt: Henry V's famous victory over the French in 1415.

Sir John: Falstaff, the rascally old knight in Shakepeare's *Henry IV* plays who leads the young Prince Hal astray, although on the death of the king his father the prince immediately reforms to become the Henry V who triumphs at Agincourt.

O[snaburg]: Frederick Augustus, Duke of York (1763–1827), George III's second son, whom he made Prince-Bishop of Osnabrück in 1764 when he was six months old.

Tarry-breeks: William Henry (1765–1837), later King William IV, third son of George III, who served in the Royal Navy from 1778 to 1790. Burns's footnote refers to gossip about his relationship with Sarah Martin, daughter of the Commissioner of Portsmouth dockyard.

royal Lasses: George III's daughters, Charlotte, Augusta, Elizabeth, Mary, Sophia and Amelia.

The Brigs of Ayr. *A Poem.*

Text: 1787.

Swiss: Switzerland was a traditional source of mercenary troops up to end of the eighteenth century.

Ballantine: John Ballantine (1743–1812), Ayr merchant and banker, who supported the building of the new bridge, 1786–8, and also encouraged Burns as a poet.

summer-toils: in the earliest editions, this line is linked by a curved bracket with the following two lines, with which it rhymes, to denote that they form a triplet. Other triplets in the poem are similarly marked.

Ayr: the main town of Ayrshire, standing on the river Ayr where it enters the Firth of Clyde.

second-sighted: having the supernatural ability to see things that are invisible to normal sight.

Fays, Spunkies, Kelpies: supernatural beings in Scottish folklore, respectively fairies, will-o-the-wisps, and water-horses, reputed to lure travellers into lakes and rivers.

Pictish, Gothic: some eighteenth-century scholars thought that the Picts, the people of north-eastern Scotland in Roman and early mediaeval times, were not Celts but Goths.

Adams: Robert Adam (1728–92), Scottish architect and designer, was involved in the plans for the new Ayr bridge.

Coil, Lugar, Greenock, Garpal: Ayrshire rivers.

Glenbuck: a place in Ayrshire near the source of the river Ayr.

Ratton-key: the Ratton Quays were part of Ayr harbour; 'ratton' means 'rat'.

second dread command: the second of the Ten Commandments forbids the worship of images (Exodus 20:3).

Proveses, Bailie, Deacons, Conveeners: local government officials: a proves or provost led the burgh council, and was equivalent to an English mayor; a baillie was a town magistrate next in rank to a provost; a deacon was the president of one of the trade incorporations of a town; and a convener was the president of the incorporated trades.

Feal: this couplet is a compliment to the Montgomeries of Coilsfield, on the river Fail, a tributary of the Ayr.

Stair: the home of Mrs Catherine Stewart of Stair (died 1818), an early patron of Burns.

Catrine: the house of the philosopher Dugald Stewart (1753–1823), whom Burns met.

The Northern Lass.

Text: *SMM*, 1788.

Address to Edinburgh.

Text: 1787.

Burnet: Elizabeth Burnet (1765–90), a celebrated Edinburgh beauty.

Sire of Love: Jupiter, Roman sky god and father of Venus, the goddess of love.

Dome: Holyrood Palace, the royal residence in Edinburgh, although never used as such in Burns's time, since no British king visited Edinburgh in the eighteenth century.

Their royal Name low in the dust!: Burns is referring to the replacement on the British throne of the Stuart family, which had ruled Scotland since 1371, by the Hanoverian dynasty in 1714.

bloody lion: the red lion on the Scottish royal standard.

To a Haggis.

Text: 1787.

A Fragment. [There was a Lad]

Text: the manuscript of *Burns's Second Commonplace Book*, begun in 1787, is in the Robert Burns Birthplace and Museum, Alloway (but see notes below).

birkie: later versions replaced this word with 'lad' and the song's title is best known as 'There was a lad'.

Kyle: district of Ayrshire.

Robin: the manuscript has 'Davie' instead of 'Robin' throughout but, since Burns's own footnote shows that he meant the poem to be about himself, 'Davie' has been replaced by this common variation on Burns's own first name, which he himself used elsewhere. The chorus has been changed to the way it appears in R. H. Cromek's *Reliques of Robert Burns* (1808) instead of the version in the manuscript:

> Leeze me on thy curly pow [head],
> Bonie Davie, daintie Davie;
> Leeze me on thy curly pow,
> Thou'se ay my daintie Davie.

Stir: perhaps a mistake for 'Sir'.

[Inscribed around Fergusson's Portrait]

Text: see note below.

Fergusson: Robert Fergusson (1750–74), Edinburgh poet whose poems in Scots inspired Burns. Burns's poem is written on the frontispiece of an edition of Fergusson's poems, reproduced in W. E. Henley and T. F. Henderson, *The Poetry of Robert Burns* (London, 1896–7), vol. II, facing page 416. The first two lines are above and the other five lines underneath an engraving showing Fergusson holding a quill pen. The printed caption reads 'Mr Robert Fergusson Ætat. [aged] xxiv'.

[Lines on Fergusson]

Text: Robert Chambers, *The Life and Works of Robert Burns*, Edinburgh, 1852, vol. III, p. 221.

Written by Somebody on the Window of an Inn at Stirling on Seeing the Royal Palace in Ruins.

Text: a manuscript copy of the poem is in the National Library of Scotland, Edinburgh.

Stirling: a town in central Scotland with an ancient royal castle and palace.

Stewarts: the Stuart dynasty, rulers of Scotland since 1371 and of Britain since 1603, replaced on the British throne by the Hanoverian dynasty, a German family, in 1714.

Ca' the Ewes to the Knowes [First Version]

Text: *SMM*, 1790.

I Love My Jean.

Text: *SMM*, 1790.

O, Were I on Parnassus Hill

Text: *SMM*, 1790

Parnassus, Helicon: both in fact Greek mountains sacred in mythology to the Muses, and both with fountains whose waters gave poetic inspiration, although Burns seems to confuse Mount Helicon, here and in his cantata 'Love and Liberty *or* The Jolly Beggars' (see note above), with Castalia, the fountain of Parnassus.

Nith: a river in Dumfriesshire in whose valley Burns leased the farm of Ellisland in 1788.

Corsincon: a hill in Ayrshire near the source of the river Nith.

Tam Glen.

Text: *SMM*, 1790.

marks: one merk or mark was equivalent to one-third of a pound.

Valentines' dealing: drawing lots on St Valentine's Day to predict future lovers.

Halloween: 'You go out, one or more, for this is a social spell, to a south-running spring or rivulet, where "three Lairds' lands meet," and dip your left shirt-sleeve. Go to bed in sight of a fire, and hang your wet sleeve before it to dry. Ly awake; and sometime near midnight, an apparition, having the exact figure of the grand object in question, will come and turn the sleeve, as if to dry the other side of it' (Burns's note to stanza 24 of his poem 'Halloween').

Auld Lang Syne.

Text: *SMM*, 1796.

Louis What Reck I by Thee.

Text: *SMM*, 1796.

Robin Shure in Hairst.

Text: *SMM*, 1803, with initial capital in line 7.

Dunse: Duns, a town in south-east Scotland.

Nine Inch Will Please a Lady.

Text: *The Merry Muses of Caledonia*, 1799.

Annandale: the valley of the river Annan east of Dumfries.

Afton Water.

Text: *SMM*, 1792.

Afton: a small river that flows into the Nith at New Cumnock in eastern Ayrshire.

[Epistle to Dr Blacklock]

Text: a manuscript is in the Robert Burns Birthplace and Museum, Alloway.

Blacklock: Thomas Blacklock (1721–91), the blind Edinburgh poet, whose enthusiasm for Burns's first book of poems helped persuade Burns to give up his plans to emigrate and try to seek fame in Scotland's capital.

Heron: Robert Heron (1764–1807), assistant to Edinburgh professor Hugh Blair and later author of the first memoir of Burns (1797).

Parnassian: Parnassus is the mountain in Greece sacred in mythology to the Muses.

Castalia: the fountain or spring at the foot of Parnassus whose waters can inspire poets.

brose: oats mixed with boiling water or milk, with added salt and butter.

Ellisland: the farm beside the river Nith north of Dumfries which Burns leased from 1788 to 1791.

On Capt$^{n.}$ Grose's present peregrinations through Scotland collecting the antiquities of that kingdom

Text: a manuscript is in the Robert Burns Birthplace and Museum, Alloway.

Captain Grose: Francis Grose (1731–91), an ex-army officer and artist, who published a number of illustrated volumes on the antiquities of England, Wales and Scotland. He asked Burns for stories about the ruined church at Alloway and received in reply the outline of 'Tam o' Shanter'. The poem itself appeared as a footnote in the second volume of Grose's *Antiquities of Scotland* (1791). Grose also published *A Treatise on Ancient Armour and Weapons* (1785) and *A Classical Dictionary of the Vulgar Tongue* (1785).

Land o' Cakes: Scotland, where oatcakes or bannocks were a staple food.

Maiden-kirk to Johnie Groat's: that is, the length of Scotland, from Maidenkirk, now known as Kirkmaiden, in the Rhins of Galloway in the extreme south-west, to John o' Groats, on the most north-easterly point of the mainland.

Lothians three: East Lothian, Midlothian (including Edinburgh) and West Lothian, all in east-central Scotland

the Flood: Noah's Flood (Genesis 6–9).

Eve: the first woman created by God (Genesis 2:18–24).

Tubal-cain: a descendant of Cain (see note below on Abel) described as 'an instructor of every artificer in brass and iron' (Genesis 4:22).

Balaam's ass: when Balaam beats his ass she speaks to him to complain (Numbers 22); note that the Bible refers to the ass as female.

Witch of Endor: she summons up the dead prophet Samuel to speak to King Saul (1 Samuel 28:7ff.).

Adam: the first man created by God (Genesis 1:26–27).

Abel: son of Adam and brother of Cain, who murdered him (Genesis 4).

My Love She's but a Lassie Yet.

Text: *SMM*, 1790.

My Heart's in the Highlands.

Text: *SMM*, 1790.

John Anderson my Jo.

Text: *SMM*, 1790.

Tam o' Shanter. A Tale.

Text: *Poems, Chiefly in the Scottish Dialect*, Edinburgh, 1793, vol. II, pp 195–208.

Gawin Douglas: Gavin Douglas (1474?–1522), Scottish poet, who translated Vergil's *Aeneid* into Scots. Burns quotes line 18 of Douglas's prologue to the sixth book of his translation; in Book VI Aeneas visits the spirits of the dead in the underworld. 'Brownyis' are goblins, 'Bogillis' are phantoms.

chapmen: later editions replaced this with 'chapman'.

Ayr: the main town of Ayrshire.

Doon: an Ayrshire river.

Aloway: Alloway, the Ayrshire village where Burns was born. It is a short distance from where the River Doon flows through a steep valley, crossed by a bridge, not far from which stand the ruins of Kirk Alloway, the old church where Burns's own father was buried.

Which ev'n to name wad be unlawfu': in early versions of the poem this line was followed by four more:

> Three lawyers' tongues, turn'd inside out,
> Wi' lies seam'd like a beggar's clout; *with; cloth*
> Three priests' hearts, rotten, black as muck,
> Lay stinking, vile, in every neuk. *corner*

They reel'd, they set, they cross'd, they cleekit: standard moves in Scottish country dancing: circling round, dancing face to face, crossing and linking arms (cleekit = hooked).

seventeen hunder linen: linen cloth with seventeen-hundred threads in the warp.

Carrick: the southern part of Ayrshire.

Paisley: a weaving town in central Scotland.

they dare na cross: the 1793 edition misprints 'thy' for 'they'.

The Banks o' Doon.

Text: *SMM*, 1792.

Doon: the river Doon flow north-westwards through south Ayrshire past Alloway to enter the Firth of Clyde a few miles south of Ayr.

Ae Fond Kiss.

Text: *SMM*, 1792.

Such a Parcel of Rogues in a Nation.

Text: *SMM*, 1792.

Sark: the river Sark enters the Solway Firth near Gretna and marks the western end of the border between Scotland and England.

Tweed: the river Tweed marks the border between Scotland and England from Coldstream eastwards to Berwick on the coast of the North Sea (formerly known as the German Ocean).

English gold: a reference to allegations that the union of the parliaments of Scotland and England in 1707 was brought about by bribery.

Bruce: Robert the Bruce (1274–1329), King of Scots from 1306, who led the successful Scottish War of Independence against England, culminating in the victory at Bannockburn near Stirling in 1314.

Wallace: Sir William Wallace (1272–1305), leader of the resistance to the conquest of Scotland by the English king Edward I (1239–1307), who captured Wallace and had him executed in London.

The De'il's Awa wi' th' Exciseman.

Text: *SMM*, 1792.

Exciseman: a government official whose duties included measuring ale and other drinks for their alcoholic content and then imposing the appropriate tax on it; from 1788 until his death Burns worked as an exciseman.

Mahoun: a name for the devil derived from the name Mohammed.

reels: lively Scottish dances, usually involving dancing hand-in-hand in circles.

strathspeys: traditional Scottish dances, slower than reels, named after the valley of the river Spey in the Highlands.

Highland Mary

Text: there is a copy of this song in a letter by Burns in the Pierpont Morgan Library, New York.

Montgomery: possibly better-known as Eglinton Castle, seat of the Clan Montgomery, though the original castle there was replaced in 1796.

The Rights of Woman

Text: a manuscript is in the Robert Burns Birthplace and Museum, Alloway.

Miss Fontenelle: Louisa Fontenelle (1773–99), a London actress who also appeared in Edinburgh, Glasgow and Dumfries, later emigrating to America, where she died. A 'benefit night' was held for her in Dumfries in 1792.

The Rights of Man: the title of a famous book supporting the principles of the French Revolution published in 1791 by Thomas Paine (1737–1809).

In that blest sphere: this line and the following one were omitted from the Alloway manuscript and are supplied from another in Boston Public Library.

When aweful Beauty: this and the following line are very similar to lines 139–140 of Canto I of *The Rape of the Lock* (1712–14) by Alexander Pope (1688–1744).

Ah, ça ira!: the opening words of the most popular song of the French Revolution, literally meaning 'that will go'; looser translations would be 'it'll be all right' or 'we will win'. The rest of the song exists in several versions, all praising the power of the people and some threatening the aristocracy with lynching. For this the song was frequently banned by governments in Britain, France and elsewhere.

Why Should Na Poor People Mow

Text: there is a manuscript of this song in the Huntington Library, California.

Brunswick: Karl Wilhelm Ferdinand, Duke of Brunswick (1735–1806) led an Austro-Prussian army into revolutionary France but retreated after the battle of Valmy, 1792.

Prussia: Frederick William II (1744–97), King of Prussia, accompanied his army during the Duke of Brunswick's unsuccessful invasion of France

Emperor: Francis II (1768–1835), Emperor of Austria, and from 1792 to 1806 also Holy Roman Emperor, the head of the loose confederation of German states known as the Holy Roman Empire.

Kate: Catherine the Great (1729–96), Empress of Russia, who combined with the rulers of Austria and Prussia in seizing territory in Poland in the Partitions of Poland, 1772, 1793 and 1795.

Stanilaus: Stanisław August Poniatowski (1732–1798), the last king of Poland.

George: George III (1738–1820), King of Great Britain and Ireland, whose queen was Charlotte of Mecklenburg-Strelitz (1744–1818).

Whistle & I'll Come to You My Lad.

Text: a manuscript is in the Robert Burns Birthplace and Museum, Alloway.

Ode [for General Washington's Birthday]

Text: a manuscript is in the Rosenbach Museum and Library, Pennsylvania.

Ode [for General Washington's Birthday]: in a letter to Mrs Frances Dunlop dated 25 June 1794, Burns writes that he is framing a poem on liberty: 'I design it an irregular Ode for Gen[l.] Washington's birth-day.— After having mentioned the degeneracy of other kingdoms I come to Scotland thus—', and he quotes from the line 'Thee, Caledonia, thy wild heaths among' to the end of the poem. The manuscript of the complete poem, however, bears only the word 'Ode' as its title; '[for General Washington's Birthday]' has been added here, as in other modern editions, for ease of identification of the poem. Washington's birthday was on 22 February.

Washington: George Washington (1732–99), American general in the War of American Independence and first President of the United States of America.

Spartan tube: the army of Sparta, the most warlike of the ancient Greek city states, marched into battle to the sound of the flute.

Attic shell: Athenian lyre (because the first lyre was supposed to have been made by stringing a tortoise shell).

lyre Eolian; the Eolian harp, a stringed instrument that makes musical sounds when the wind blows on it.

Columbia: a poetic name, derived from that of Christopher Columbus (1451–1506), European discoverer of the Americas, for the United States of America, favoured by those anxious to assert American independence from Britain.

Alfred: king of Wessex from 871 to 899, generally regarded as the first King of England and admired in the eighteenth century as the founder of English law and the freedom associated with it.

England in thunder calls—'The Tyrant's cause is mine!': the passage refers to Britain's joining the First Coalition of European states in war against France in 1793, to the dismay of British sympathizers with French revolutionary ideals.

Wallace: Sir William Wallace (1272–1305); see note to next poem.

Bruce to his Troops on the Eve of the Battle of Bannock-burn.

Text: Currie, 1800.

Wallace: Sir William Wallace (1272–1305), leader of the resistance to the conquest of Scotland by the English king Edward I (1239–1307).

Bruce: Robert the Bruce (1274–1329), King of Scots from 1306, who led the successful Scottish War of Independence against England, culminating in the victory at Bannockburn near Stirling in 1314. The song represents Bruce's speech to the Scottish army before the battle.

Edward: Edward II (1284–1327), son of Edward I, whose attempt to relieve the siege of Stirling led to the battle of Bannockburn.

Act Sederunt o' the Court o' Session.

Text: *The Merry Muses of Caledonia*, 1799.

Act Sederunt o' the Court o' Session: an ordinance drawn up by the judges of the Court of Session, the supreme civil court in Scotland, which usually meets in the capital city, Edinburgh.

A Red Red Rose.

Text: *SMM*, 1796.

Ca' the Yowes to the Knowes [Second Version]

Text: Currie, 1800.

Clouden's tower: some editions add a note from Burns reading 'An old ruin in a sweet situation at the confluence of the Clouden and the Nith'.

For a' that & a' that.

Text: a manuscript copy of this song is in a letter in the Rosenbach Museum and Library, Pennsylvania. Other texts read 'for' instead of 'at' in line 1.

guinea's stamp: the impression on a piece of gold that makes it a coin; a guinea was worth one pound and one shilling.

The Dumfries Volunteers.

Text: *SMM*, 1803.

The Dumfries Volunteers: in 1795 the threat of French invasion led to the setting up of volunteer militia units throughout Britain, including Dumfries, the main town of Dumfriesshire in south-west Scotland, where Burns lived from 1791 until his death. Burns himself joined the Dumfries Volunteers, who provided a military escort at his funeral.

Nith: the river that enters the sea at Dumfries and rises near the hill of Corsincon.

Criffel: a high hill south of Dumfries and within sight of the Solway Firth.

God save the king: the British national anthem.

The Heron Ballads I

Text: a manuscript of the first six stanzas is in the Robert Burns Birthplace and Museum, Alloway; the last stanza is from Allan Cunningham, *The Works of Robert Burns*, London, 1834, vol. III, p. 263.

Galloway: the south-west region of Scotland.

Kirouchtree: Patrick Heron of Kirroughtree (*c.* 1736–1803), in support of whose election to Parliament in 1795 Burns wrote this and several other poems. Kirroughtree House is near Newton Stewart.

Saint Mary's Isle: the mansion, two miles south of Kirkcudbright, of Dunbar Douglas, Earl of Selkirk (1722–99).

A beardless boy: Thomas Gordon of Balmaghie (died 1806), Heron's opponent. He had the support of his wealthy uncle, James Murray of Broughton (1727–99).

Master Dicky: Richard Oswald of Auchencruive (1771–1841).

Stewartry: the Stewartry of Kirkcudbright, the constituency for which the election was held.

Kerroughtree: another spelling of Kirroughtree.

House of Commons: the lower house of the British Parliament.

To the Tooth-Ach.

Text: a manuscript version of the poem, written in a copy of 1786, in *The Definitive Illustrated Companion to Robert Burns*, ed. Peter J. Westwood, Kilmarnock, 2004, vol. 1, p. 19.

cutty-stools: the stools of repentance, the places in each church where those found guilty of misconduct were required to sit as a punishment.

[Oh Wert Thou in the Cauld Blast]

Text: Currie, 1800.

The Solemn League and Covenant

Text: W. E. Henley and T. F. Henderson, *The Poetry of Robert Burns* (London, 1896–7), vol. II, p. 258.

The Solemn League and Covenant: an agreement reached in 1643 between the Protestants of Scotland and the Parliamentarians of England by which the former entered the civil war against Charles I in return for promises that Presbyterianism would be introduced throughout Britain and Ireland. This did not happen and, after the restoration of the monarchy in 1660, those in Scotland who remained faithful to the Covenant were persecuted for their beliefs.

The Selkirk Grace.

Text: Allan Cunningham, *The Works of Robert Burns*, London, 1834, vol. III, p. 311.

Selkirk: Dunbar Douglas, Earl of Selkirk (1722–99), at whose house near Kirkcudbright Burns is supposed to have spoken *ex tempore* this grace before a meal.

Tam Lin.

Text: *SMM*, 1796 (with some re-arrangement of the stanzas).

gowd on your hair: misprinted as 'gowd or your hair' in *The Scots Musical Museum*.

Carterhaugh: a woodland between the confluence of the Ettrick and Yarrow rivers near Selkirk in the Scottish Borders.

Roxbrugh: Roxburgh was an important Scottish royal burgh near the border with England during the Middle Ages but after its castle was destroyed in 1460 the town virtually disappeared; the name remained in the titles of local landowners, various dukes and earls of Roxburgh, and as one of the local government districts of Scotland from 1975 to 1996.

Milescross: not identified; Sir Walter Scott suggested that the name is a corruption of Mary's Cross, which once stood at Bowhill near Carterhaugh.

Comin thro' the Rye.

Text: *SMM*, 1796.

Charlie He's my Darling.

Text: *SMM*, 1796.

Charlie: Charles Edward Stuart (1720–88), who led the Jacobite forces, mainly consisting of Highlanders, in their unsuccessful attempt of 1745–46 to depose George II and replace him on the throne with Charles's father James; Charles was called Bonnie Prince Charlie by his supporters, the Young Pretender by his enemies and the Young Chevalier by those in between. After his father's death in 1766 some gave him the title Charles III. He died in Rome.

The Trogger.

Text: *The Merry Muses of Caledonia*, 1799.

Annan: a river that flows into the Solway Firth through the town of Annan some sixteen miles east of Dumfries in south-west Scotland.

Ecclefechan: a small town five miles north of Annan.

Bonshaw: near Kirtlebridge, a few miles east of Ecclefechan.

The Tree of Liberty.

Text: Robert Chambers, *The Life and Works of Robert Burns* (Edinburgh and London, 1857), Vol. IV, pp. 79–81. Attribution to Burns is disputed by some.

Bastile: the Bastille prison-fortress in Paris whose storming by a mob on 14 July 1789 is the conventional start of the French Revolution.

Frae yont the western waves: that is, from America, where the revolt of the thirteen colonies of the original United States against British rule inspired the revolutionaries in France.

King Loui': Louis XVI (1754–93), King of France, who became the symbol of what the French Revolution opposed, and was imprisoned, tried and executed by the revolutionaries. This brought about war between France and the monarchies of Europe.

Tweed: the river that marks a large part of the border between England and Scotland.

Logie o' Buchan

Text: see note on rediscovered poems.

Buchan: the region of Aberdeenshire north of Aberdeen and bounded by the North Sea and the Moray Firth.

I Courted a Lassie

Text: see note on rediscovered poems. The manuscript marks lines 5 and 6 'Chorus'.

My Steps Fate on a Mad Conjuncture Thrust

Text: see note on rediscovered poems.

Here is to the King, Sir

Text: see note on rediscovered poems.

king: the song equivocates between the rival claimants to the British throne, James and George of the Houses of Stuart and Hanover respectively. This indicates its sympathy with the Jacobite supporters of the Stuarts and one meaning of the refrain is that they are ready to rebel against the Hanoverians once more.

tuti taity: the name of a Scottish marching tune, used by Burns as the setting for 'Bruce to his Troops on the Eve of the Battle of Bannock-burn' or 'Scots, Wha Hae'.

King o' Swedes: supposedly Charles XII (1682–1718), who is reputed to have planned an invasion of England in support of the Stuart cause.

Tho' Life's Gay Scenes Delight No More

Text: see note on rediscovered poems.

Five Extracts from Burns's First Commonplace Book, 1783–85

Text: a facsimile of Burns's manuscript is available in *Robert Burns's Commonplace Book 1783–1785*, first published in 1938 with a transcript and notes by James Cameron Ewing and Davidson Cook, republished in 1965 with an introduction by David Daiches (London: Centaur Press).

Burness: this is how Burns, following his father, at first spelled his surname.

'Stain'd with guilt, and crimson'd o'er with crimes': line 55 of 'Elegy XX: He Compares his Humble Fortune with the Distress of Others' by William Shenstone (1714–63), misquoting 'guilt' for 'blood'.

whose heads are capable: in the manuscript the word 'are' is repeated at the end of one line and the beginning of the next.

Ramsay: Allan Ramsay (1686–1758), Edinburgh poet.

Ferguson: Robert Fergusson (1750–74), Scottish poet who inspired Burns's own poetry.

Carrick, Kyle, & Cunningham: the three districts of Ayrshire.

Wallace: Sir William Wallace (1272–1305), leader of the resistance to the conquest of Scotland by the English king Edward I (1239–1307).

Irvine, Aire, Doon: Ayrshire rivers.

Tay, Forth, Ettrick, Tweed: major Scottish rivers.

The Mill Mill O: a very popular tune to which many verses were set, including some by Ramsay ('Beneath a green shade I fand a fair maid', included in *The Scots Musical Museum*, 1790) and Burns ('When wild war's deadly blast was blawn', 1793, sometimes called 'The Soldier's Return', number 406 in Kinsley's edition) and a bawdy version ('As I came down yon water side') in *The Merry Muses of Caledonia* (1799), page 50f.

Bremner's collection of Scotch Songs: Robert Bremner (1720–89), *Thirty Scots songs adapted for a voice & harpsichord*, two volumes, published in London, probably in 1770. This included many songs by Allan Ramsay. Bremner was a seller of music and musical instruments, first in Edinburgh and then in London.

'To Fanny fair could I impart &c.': another set of verses to the tune 'The Mill, Mill O'; these are in standard English.

This has made me: in the manuscript the word 'made' is repeated.

'buried 'mongst the wreck of things which were': ' . . . Names once fam'd, now dubious or forgot,/And buried 'midst the Wreck of things which were' (Robert Blair (1699–1746), *The Grave* (1743), lines 29f.).

Preface [to *Poems, Chiefly in the Scottish Dialect*, 1786]

Text: 1786.

Theocrites: Theocritus, a Greek pastoral poet of the third century BC.

Virgil: Publius Vergilius Maro (70–19 BC), Roman poet, most famous for the *Aeneid*, an epic poem, but also the author of pastoral poetry in imitation of Theocritus.

'A fountain shut up . . . ': Burns is adapting a verse from the Bible: 'A spring shut up, a fountain sealed' (Song of Solomon 4:12).

Elegies: William Shenstone (1714–63) wrote a number of elegies.

'Humility has depressed . . . ': 'Humility has depressed many a genius into an hermit; but never yet raised one into a poet of eminence' is the final sentence of Shenstone's essay 'On allowing Merit in Others' in *Essays on Men, Manners, and Things* (1764).

Ramsay: Allan Ramsay (1686–1758), the Edinburgh poet.

Ferguson: Robert Fergusson (1750–74), the Scottish poet who, despite his early death, left a body of poems in Scots that inspired Burns's own poetry.

Subscribers: the first edition of Burns's work, *Poems, chiefly in the Scottish Dialect*, was published at Kilmarnock in Ayrshire in 1786 by subscription, that is, buyers paid for copies in advance and the money raised paid for the printing.

Dedication [to *Poems, Chiefly in the Scottish Dialect*, 1787]

Text: 1787.

The Caledonian Hunt: founded in 1777, this was a social club for noblemen and gentlemen, as much interested in drinking as in horse-racing and other sports, but its members subscribed for one hundred copies of the Edinburgh edition of Burns's poems and twelve days after the date of this dedication he himself was made a member.

Elijah, Elisha: when the Old Testament prophet Elijah chooses Elisha as his successor, he does so by throwing his mantle over him while Elisha is ploughing (1 Kings 19:19); a sculpture by Peter Turnerelli (1774–1839) showing the muse throwing her mantle over Burns as he holds a plough was part of the Burns mausoleum put up in Dumfries in 1815–17 and the image became a popular theme for illustration in nineteenth-century editions of his works.

Extract from Burns's Journal of his Border Tour

Text: the manuscript of Burns's tour was acquired by the publisher John Murray.

Captn. Rutherford: John Rutherford (1746–1830), who had been captured by American Indians in his youth and later served as an army officer in North America. He lived at Mossburnford four miles south of Jedburgh.

Jedburgh: a town in the Scottish Borders on the banks of the Jed Water.

Love-lane: not identified.

Blackburn: the Black Burn flows into the Jed Water about eight miles south of Jedburgh.

Mr Potts, Writer: 'writer' means 'lawyer'; nothing more is known of this man.

Mr Somerville: Dr Thomas Somerville (1741–1830), Jedburgh minister and author.

Mrs Fair: Catherine Fair, *née* Lookup, wife of John Fair (died 1796), a lawyer who lived at Langlee south of Jedburgh.

half-ell: an ell was a measurement of length of 45 inches or 1.14 metres.

Miss Hope: all that seems to be known of this lady is that she was one of the Hopes of Cowdenknowes, near Melrose in the Scottish Borders.

Miss Lindsay: Isabella Lindsay (born 1746); she married Adam Armstrong twenty-four days after parting from Burns and went with him to Russia, where she died. Her sister's name was Peggy.

et embonpoint: and stout (French).

un tout ensemble: a whole impression (French).

bonie, strappan . . . sonsie: fine, strapping . . . buxom.

Edinr.: Edinburgh, the starting-point for Burns's tour.

Nota Bene: note well (Latin).

Whiggish: with this word Burns means to insult Miss Lookup as a narrow-minded puritan; although Whig in England meant an adherent of one of the two main political parties (the other being the Tories), in Scotland it referred to the Presbyterian Covenanters, who stood for a traditional austerity of religion.

Dulcinea: the peasant girl Don Quixote treats as his courtly lady in Cervantes's novel.

wanting: missing.

Letter to Dr John Moore, 2 August 1787

Text: the manuscript of the actual letter Burns sent to Moore is in the British Library.

Moore: John Moore (1729–1802), a Scottish doctor who settled in London. He published novels, including *Zeluco* (1786), and travel books, including an account of his stay in revolutionary France in 1792.

Solomon: the Biblical king of Israel, famous for his wisdom.

'Turned my eyes to behold Madness and Folly': 'And I turned myself to behold wisdom, and madness, and folly' (Ecclesiastes 2:12).

Miss Williams: Helen Maria Williams (1762–1827), who was brought up in Berwick-upon-Tweed, was at this time John Moore's amanuensis but in 1790 she moved to Paris, where she lived through most of the French Revolution and spent much of the rest of her life. She wrote poems, novels and books about France, as well as translations of French works.

the pye-coated guardians of escutcheons: the heralds, whose ceremonial dress, then as now, is a multi-coloured tabard decorated with coats of arms. All matters to do with Scottish heraldry and genealogy have been subject to regulation by the Lord Lyon King of Arms since the fourteenth century. Later in his life Burns invented for himself his own coat of arms.

'My ancient but ignoble blood . . . ': Alexander Pope (1688–1744), *An Essay on Man* (1732–4), Epistle IV, lines 211f., with 'my' for 'your'.

gules, purpure, argent: the heraldic terms for the colours red, purple and silver or white.

Kieths of Marshal: the family of Keith were the hereditary Marischals of Scotland from the thirteenth century. The last Earl Marischal, George Keith (*c.* 1693–1778), was a Jacobite who after the risings of 1715 and 1719, with his brother Francis (1696–1758), fled to the continent, where they both had distinguished careers in the service of Frederick the Great of Prussia. Burns's comments suggest that his father's family suffered by association with the Keiths' Jacobitism and that this was a reason for his own sympathy with the House of Stuart.

Club-law: that is, rule by violence.

'Brutus and Cassius are honorable men': in his famous speech in Act III scene 2 of Shakespeare's *Julius Caesar*, Antony does not use the exact words Burns quotes but he does say, with mounting sarcasm, that Brutus and Cassius, the leading assassins of Caesar, are both 'honourable men'.

my father: William Burnes (1721–84) was born in Kincardineshire on the east coast of Scotland but moved to Edinburgh and then to Ayrshire.

'Men, their manners and their ways': line 157 of 'January and May' (1709), a modern version of Geoffrey Chaucer's 'Merchant's Tale' by Alexander Pope.

a worthy gentleman of small estate in the neighbourhood of Ayr: Burns's father worked as a gardener for several Ayshire landowners, including John Crawford at Doonside and William Ferguson (d. 1776) at Doonholm, both near Alloway.

a small farm in his estate: Mount Oliphant, three miles from Ayr, leased by William Burnes from 1765 to 1777.

an old Maid of my Mother's: Betty Davidson, the widow of a cousin of Burns's mother.

spunkies, kelpies, elf-candles, dead-lights . . . cantraips: will-o-the-wisps; water-horses; sparks or flashes of supernatural light; corpse-lights, over graves or dead bodies; magic spells.

The Vision of Mirza: an allegorical fantasy-story by Joseph Addison (1672–1719) published in *The Spectator*, 159, 1 September 1711, and included in Masson's school anthology (see note below).

'How are Thy servants blest, O Lord!': Addison's hymn appeared in *The Spectator*, 489, 20 September 1712, and was included in Masson's school anthology (see next note).

Mason's English Collection: Arthur Masson, *A Collection of Prose and Verse, for the Use of Schools* (the edition of 1764 is described as the fourth). Although Masson was a Scot and his book was published in Edinburgh, its contents were in English and overwhelmingly by English authors, apart from an excerpt from 'Summer' (1727) by James Thomson (1700–48) and three passsages from the tragedy *Douglas* (1756) by John Home (1722–1808).

the life of Hannibal: probably this life of the famous Carthaginian enemy of Rome, victor of the famous battle of Cannae (216 BC), was *The Life of Hannibal. Translated from the French of Mr Dacier* (London, 1737); André Dacier (1651–1722) was a noted French classical scholar.

history of Sir William Wallace: in 1722 William Hamilton of Gilbertfield (1670–1751) published a modernized version of the poem about the life of William Wallace (1272?–1305), the Scottish patriot, by the fifteenth-century poet known as Blind Hary. Hamilton's work became very popular and more widely known that the original.

Calvinism: the austere doctrines of Jean (or John) Calvin (1509–64) became the fundamental theology of the reformed Church of Scotland from the sixteenth century but they were increasingly challenged by more moderate views in the eighteenth century.

Ayr: the main town of Ayrshire, two miles north of Burns's childhood home at Alloway.

'without bounds or limits': this definition of infinity comes not directly from the catechism but from *A Body of Practical Divinity* (1692), a collection of sermons on the Shorter Catechism by Thomas Watson (1620–86), an English puritan, who wrote that 'the Greek word for infinite, signifies, "without bounds or limits"' in his sermon on 'The Being of God'.

Munny Begums: Burns means that the friend who taught him some French, though one of those bound for 'the east . . . Indies', was not likely to be tainted with the sort of corruption alleged against Warren Hastings (1732–1818), Governor-General of India from 1773 to 1785, at his subsequent impeachment (1788–95), when he was accused of accepting bribes from Munny Begum, the former concubine of the Nawab of Bengal.

Factor: the landlord's manager responsible for collecting the rent from tenant farmers. Burns describes the fear such a man could induce in his poem 'The Twa Dogs' (1786), in the present volume.

seven children: the others were Gilbert (1760–1827), Agnes (1762–1834), Annabella (1764–1832), William (1767–90), John (1769–83) and Isabella (1771–1858).

my Partner was a bewitching creature: Nellie Kilpatrick (1760–1820), a miller's daughter who later married a coachman.

bonie . . . sonsie: pretty, jolly.

gin-horse: a horse that works a gin or mill by walking round and round.

Eolian harp: a stringed instrument that makes musical sounds when the wind blows on it.

ratann: drumming noise.

a larger farm: Lochlie or Lochlea, near Tarbolton in Ayrshire, to which the family moved in 1777.

'To where the wicked cease from troubling . . .': Job 3:17, slightly misquoted.

Solitaire: recluse.

Salmon's and Guthrie's geographical grammars: Thomas Salmon (1679–1767), *A New Geographical and Historical Grammar* (London, 1749); William Guthrie (1708–70), *A new geographical, historical, and commercial grammar* (London, 1770).

the Spectator: the literary periodical, mainly written by Joseph Addison (1672–1719) and Sir Richard Steele (1672–1729), first published in London in 1711–12 and 1714, but reprinted many times throughout the eighteenth century.

Pope's works: varous editions of the poems of Alexander Pope (1688–1744) appeared in the eighteenth century.

Tull and Dickson: Jethro Tull (1674–1741), *The New Horse-Houghing Husbandry: or, An Essay on the Principles of Tillage and Vegetation* (London, 1731); Adam Dickson (1721–76), *A Treatise of Agriculture* (Edinburgh, 1762).

The Pantheon: probably the translation by Andrew Tooke (1673–1732) of *Pantheum mythicum seu fabulosa deorum historia* (1659) by Francois Pomey (1618–73), better known as *Tooke's Pantheon of the Heathen Gods and Illustrious Heroes* (1698 and many reprints).

Locke's essay: John Locke (1632–1704), *An Essay concerning Human Understanding* (1690).

Stackhouse: Thomas Stackhouse (1677–1752), *A New History of the Holy Bible* (1737).

Justice: Sir James Justice (1698–1763), *The British gardener's director, chiefly adapted to the climate of the northern countries* (Edinburgh, 1764); Justice was the first person to ripen a pineapple in Scotland.

Boyle's lectures: a series of theological lectures provided for in the will of the scientist Robert Boyle (1627–91).

Allan Ramsay: Scottish poet (1686–1758).

Taylor: John Taylor (1694–1761), *The Scripture-doctrine of Original Sin* (1738); despite its title this book argues against the doctrine of original sin.

select Collection of English songs: though some scholars take this to refer to *A Select Collection of English Songs*, published in three volumes by Joseph Ritson (1752–1803) in London in 1783, this work is too late for the period Burns is describing and probably he means another, cheaper book.

Harvey: James Hervey (1714–58), *Meditations and Contemplations* (1746–7).

vade mecum: a pocket reference book.

Homer's Cyclops: Polyphemus, the one-eyed giant blinded by Odysseus in Homer's *Odyssey*, Book 9.

'where two or three were met together . . . ': a misquotation of Matthew 18:20.

an penchant à l'adorable moitiée du genre humain: 'a liking for the adorable part of humankind' (French, with 'an' a slip of the pen for 'un').

Premier: prime minister.

goosefeather: quill pen.

on a smuggling [coast]: there is a word missing that is usually given as 'coast'; Burns is describing his time at Kirkoswald near Maybole in Ayrshire in 1775 as a pupil of Hugh Rodger (1726–97).

Mensuration: measurement.

Dialling: 'The use of a "dial" or compass in underground surveying' (*OED*).

Fillette: girl (French).

'Like Proserpine gathering flowers, / Herself a fairer flower': John Milton (1608–74), *Paradise Lost* (1667), Book IV, lines 269f., with 'where' changed to 'like'.

Thomson's and Shenstone's works: James Thomson (1700–48), Scottish-born poet, author of *The Seasons* (1726–30); William Shenstone (1714–63), English poet, mentioned by Burns in his 'Preface' to the Kilmarnock edition (see this volume).

the Wits of Queen Ann's reign: the reign of Queen Anne (1702–14) saw the emergence of several writers, including Alexander Pope (1688–1744), Joseph Addison (1672–1719) and Jonathan Swift (1667–1745), whose works set the tone for British literature in the eighteenth century. The collection of letters Burns refers to was probably *Letters on the Most Common, as Well as Important Occasions of Life* (1756) by John Newbery (1713–67), the writer and publisher of books for children.

farthings: the farthing was a small coin worth one quarter of a penny.

Vive l'amour et vive la bagatelle: 'long live love and long live trifling' (French).

Sterne and M'kenzie: Laurence Sterne (1713–68), author of *Tristram Shandy* (1759–67), and Henry Mackenzie (1745–1831), author of *The Man of Feeling* (1771), both novels of the sentimental movement that dwelt on the power of feelings. Mackenzie became a leading figure in Edinburgh literary circles and it was his favourable review of Burns's Kilmarnock edition that marked Burns's acceptance as a poet of significance.

Winter a Dirge, The death of Poor Mailie, John Barleycorn: 'Winter, a Dirge' and 'The death and dying words of Poor Maillie' both appeared in

Burns's 1786 Kilmarnock edition; 'John Barleycorn. A Ballad' appeared in the 1787 Edinburgh edition.

songs first, second and third: Burns presumably means the three songs that appeared together on pages 222–7 of the 1786 Kilmarnock edition: 'It was upon a Lammas night', 'Now westlin winds, and slaught'ring guns' and 'From thee, Eliza, I must go'.

bullition: variant of 'ebullition', meaning a boiling up or effervescence of feeling.

a flax-dresser in a neighbouring town: Burns went to Irvine on the Ayrshire coast in 1781 to learn flax-dressing, the preparation of raw flax in readiness for spinning into linen. Burns first sought instruction from Alexander Peacock but they quarrelled and Burns moved to another instructor whose name is not recorded.

belle fille: 'pretty girl' (French); it is possible that Burns is referring to a girl called Elizabeth Gebbie (born 1761), who may have refused his proposal of marriage, but the evidence is not complete.

mittemus: Burns means 'mittimus', the Latin for 'we send', meaning a warrant sending somebody away, usually to prison, although the word came to mean a death-sentence, or an anticipation of dying.

'Depart from me ye Cursed': Matthew 25:41.

a young fellow: Richard Brown (1753–1833); Burns kept up a correspondence with him for several years and sent him a signed copy of the Kilmarnock edition, but later Brown quarrelled with the poet, apparently after hearing what was said about his attitudes to women in this letter.

Connaught: Connacht, a western province of Ireland.

westindiaman: a ship used for the trade with the West Indies.

the Welcome inclosed: presumably Burns was sending Moore a copy of his poem 'A Poet's Welcome to his Love-begotten Daughter', not published in the poet's lifetime, about the birth of his first child, Elizabeth, born to Elizabeth Paton, a servant at Lochlie, on 22 May 1785.

Pamela: *Pamela, or Virtue Rewarded* (1740), a novel by Samuel Richardson (1689–1761); ironically, in view of the previous note, it is about a servant-girl who resists her master's amorous advances.

Ferdinand Count Fathom: *The Adventures of Ferdinand Count Fathom* (1753), by Tobias Smollett (1721–71).

Fergusson's Scotch Poems: the poems of Robert Fergusson (1750–74) mostly first appeared in Edinburgh newspapers but a collection of them was published in 1773 and there were several later editions that Burns might have seen.

a neighbouring farm: Mossgiel, near Mauchline, leased by Robert and Gilbert in autumn 1783.

'Come, go to I will be wise': only the last four words appear in Ecclesiastes 7:23.

'The devil, the world and the flesh': a phrase used in the baptismal service in *The Book of Common Prayer* (1662 version).

'Like the dog to his vomit, and the sow that was washed to her wallowing in the mire': 2 Peter 2:22, slightly altered.

two revd. Calvinists: Alexander Moodie (1728–99) of Riccarton and John Russel (*c.*1740–1817) of Kilmarnock, whose quarrel over parish boundaries is the subject of Burns's poem 'The Holy Tulzie' (Kinsley's edition number 52; 'tulzie' means a brawl or contest). Both ministers are mentioned in Burns's later poem 'The Holy Fair' (see this volume).

Holy Willie's Prayer: Burns's satirical monologue in the voice of the Presbyterian hypocrite William Fisher (see this volume).

kirk-Session: the committee of church elders, chaired by the minister, that runs a Scottish parish.

The Lament: 'The Lament, occasioned by the unfortunate issue of a friend's amour', published in the Kilmarnock edition, 1786.

Jamaica: Burns booked a passage to Jamaica early in 1786.

pauvre Inconnu: 'poor unknown' (French).

It [was] ever my opinion: the main verb is missing from this sentence and must be supplied.

subscriptions: the cost of printing Burns's poems was met by asking potential buyers to pay in advance.

twenty pounds: compare that with the annual rent of £90 for Mossgiel farm and the statement by Burns's brother Gilbert that the ordinary annual wage for himself and Robert when they worked on that farm was only £7; it is reckoned that from the first Edinburgh edition, 1787, Burns made over eight hundred pounds.

'Hungry wind had me in the wind': clearly the second word is wrong; Burns is adapting line 9, 'Tho' hungry Ruin has me in the Wind', of the paraphrase of Psalm 16 in *A Paraphrase on some Select Psalms* (London, 1722) by Richard Daniel (d. 1739).

the terrors of a Jail: in the summer of 1786 James Armour (d. 1798), the father of Jean Armour (1767–1834), obtained a warrant against Burns to force him to provide maintenance for the child Jean was expecting by him.

Greenock: a port on the Firth of Clyde and a major embarkation point for Atlantic crossings.

'The gloomy night is gathering fast': this song was first published in the Edinburgh edition, 1787.

Blacklock: Thomas Blacklock (1721–91), the blind Scottish poet; Burns addressed a verse letter to him in 1789 (see this volume).

Glencairn: James Cunningham (1749–91), fourteenth Earl of Glencairn, one of the most influential of Burns's supporters in Edinburgh.

'Oublie moi, Grand Dieu, si jamais je l'oublie': 'forget me, God, if ever I forget him' (French); if this is a quotation no source for it has been found, but it may be another example of Burns's displaying his knowledge of French, something he does elsewhere in this letter.

'to catch the manners living as they rise': Alexander Pope (1688–1744), *An Essay on Man* (1732–4), Epistle I, line 14.

Mauchline: the town, about ten miles east of Ayr, nearest to Burns's farm and the place where Jean Armour lived.

Glasgow: the main city in the west of Scotland.

a tour through the Highlands: Burns toured the Scottish Highlands in June and then in August and September 1787.

Letter to Agnes McLehose, 19 January 1788

Text: the manuscript of this letter is in the National Library of Scotland.

Clarinda: Agnes or Nancy McLehose (1759–1841), who had left her husband James and was living in Edinburgh when she met Burns there on 4 December 1787. She invited him to tea but before they could meet again he hurt his knee and was told by his doctor not to go out. Agnes and Burns then began a flirtatious correspondence that lasted for several weeks, even after Burns had recovered enough to meet her personally. It seems to have been the lady who suggested that they adopt the neo-classical pen-names Clarinda and Sylvander. Burns reacted enthusiastically ('I like the idea of Arcadian names in a commerce of this kind', he wrote) and threw himself into the role of a literary lover, in the style of his favourite sentimental novels by Laurence Sterne and Henry Mackenzie.

Thomson: James Thomson (1700–48), Scottish-born poet; the phrase 'Philosophic Melancholy' occurs in line 1005 of 'Autumn' in the 1746 edition of his best-known work, *The Seasons*.

' 'Tis this, my friend, that streaks our morning bright . . . ': Nathaniel Cotton (1705–88), 'To the Rev James Hervey , on his Meditations', lines 39f.

'the dark postern of time long elaps'd': Edward Young (1683–1765), *Night Thoughts on Life, Death, and Immortality* (1742–5), 'Night I. On Life, Death, and Immortality', line 224

'Father, I have sinned against Heaven and in thy sight, and am no more worthy to be called thy son!': Luke 15:21, the words of the Prodigal Son when he returns to his father.

'On Reason build Resolve . . . ': lines 30–31 of 'Night I' of Young's *Night Thoughts* (see note above).

' 'Tis nought to me . . . ': James Thomson, 'A Hymn on The Seasons' (1730).

this time yesternight: in an earlier letter Burns promises to visit Agnes on the evening of Friday, 18 January 1788: 'Friday evening, about eight, expect me.'

'May I be lost, no eye to weep my end . . . ': Francis Beaumont (1584–1616), *Rule a Wife, and Have a Wife* (1624), Act III, sc. i, changed from third person to first.

'Hope, thou Nurse of young Desire . . . ': the opening lines of the first song in *Love in a Village* (1762), a comic opera by Isaac Bickerstaff (1735–1812).

'Innocence/Look'd, gayly smiling on . . . ': not identified; some scholars believe these lines may be by Burns himself.

Letter to Agnes McLehose, 25 January 1788

Text: the manuscript of this letter is in the National Library of Scotland.

Clarinda, Sylvander: see the notes to the first letter to Agnes McLehose in this volume.

make me [do so?]: the manuscript is damaged at this point and, although not strictly needed, editors usually add the words in brackets here.

Ainslie: Robert Ainslie (1766–1838), Edinburgh lawyer and friend of Burns who accompanied him on part of his Border tour in 1787; Burns wrote some of his most uninhibited letters to Ainslie (see the letter of 3 March 1788 in this volume).

Letter to Robert Ainslie, 3 March 1788

Text: *The Merry Muses of Caledonia*, 1872, pp. 85f.

Ainslie: Robert Ainslie (1766–1838), Edinburgh lawyer and friend of Burns who accompanied him on part of his Border tour in 1787.

Mauchline: the town in Ayrshire where Jean Armour and her family lived.

Millar: Patrick Miller of Dalswinton (1731–1815), banker and landowner, who offered Burns the lease of one of his farms, Ellisland, in the valley of the river Nith north of Dumfries.

my old friend: John Tennant (1725–1810) of Glenconner farm, near Ochiltree in Ayrshire; he had previously been a neighbour in Ayrshire. Against Burns's expectations, Tennant approved of Ellisland and Burns was persuaded to take it on, and lived to regret it.

the two plans: that is, to return to farming or to become an exciseman.

scalade: a variant of 'escalade', literally the scaling of a wall, usually as part of an assault on a fortification.

a guid weel-willy pintle: a good well-disposed penis.

the solemn league and covenant: a scurrilous reference to the political and religious agreement of 1643 (see Burns's poem about it in this volume).

Aaron's rod: Aaron is the brother of Moses in the Old Testament of the Bible; his rod or staff displays miraculous properties in the books of Exodus and Numbers, and became a symbol of the power of God.

Jacob's staff: Jacob is one of the Hebrew patriarchs in the book of Genesis in the Bible, but a Jacob's staff is a device for measuring latitude used in navigation and surveying.

Elisha's pot of oil: in 2 Kings 4:1–7 a widow comes to the prophet Elisha asking how to pay a creditor when all she has is a pot of oil; he tells her to pour the oil into other containers and miraculously the pot supplies enough oil to pay the debt.

Ahasuerus' sceptre: in Esther 5:2 Ahasuerus, the king of Persia, holds out his golden sceptre to Esther as a sign of his favour, and she touches the top of it.

Clarinda: Agnes McLehose (1759–1841), with whom Burns had a romantic affair in Edinburgh (see the letters to her in this volume).

Kilmarnock: the main town in Ayrshire.

Cumnoch: Cumnock in Ayrshire, about fifteen miles south-east of Kilmarnock.

Extract from a Letter to Burns from Agnes McLehose

Text: reprinted from *The Burns Chronicle*, Second Series, Volume IV, 1929, pp. 13–15, where the letter is dated 18 March 1788.

before you set out: Burns wrote a short note on the morning of 18 March 1788 to say he was 'just hurrying away to wait on the Great Man'; he was involved at this time in taking up the lease of Ellisland farm and also seeking training, for which he needed official permission, as an exciseman. This is probably the livelihood mentioned later in the letter.

'present in the very lap of Love': James Thomson (1700–48) 'Spring', line 996, in *The Seasons* (1746).

'Feeds the Young Ravens when they cry': Psalm 147:9, from John Patrick, *The Psalms of David in metre* (1694).

Clarinda, Sylvander: the pen-names Agnes McLehose and Burns used in their correspondence.

Mary: Mary Peacock, a friend of Agnes McLehose who later became the second wife of James Gray, a master in the Edinburgh High School.

Bonie: pretty.

Letter to Dr John Moore, 4 January 1789

Text: the manuscript of the actual letter Burns sent to Moore is in the Berg Collection in the New York Public Library.

Moore: the same Dr John Moore Burns wrote to on 2 August 1787 (see this volume); this letter is something of an update to the earlier one.

Ellisland: the farm by the river Nith north of Dumfries that Burns leased in 1788.

Rhodian Colossus: a gigantic statue of Apollo, the Greek god, that straddled the entrance to the harbour on the island of Rhodes in the eastern Mediterranean; it was destroyed in an earthquake in 224 BC.

who forms the secret biass of the soul: 'But God alone . . . Imprints the secret byass of the soul', Mark Akenside (1721–70), *The Pleasures of Imagination* (1744), Book 3, lines 522f.

Epistle addressed to R— G— Esq.: 'To Rob$^{t.}$ Graham of Fintry Esqr, with a request for an Excise Division—' (Kinsley 230), a poem dated 8 September 1788; Burns had been commissioned as an exciseman, a government officer who assessed and collected taxes, particularly on alcoholic drinks, in July 1788 but he had to wait until the following year before he was appointed to a tax-district, or division.

Creech: William Creech (1745–1815), Edinburgh bookseller and publisher. He was notorious for his meanness and at first, as Burns says, the poet had difficulty getting money from him, although Burns later said Creech had been 'amicable and fair with me'.

'I could' not a 'tale' but a detail 'unfold': Burns is varying line 15 of Act I, scene 5, of Shakespeare's *Hamlet*, when the ghost tells Hamlet 'I could a tale unfold'.

Bailie: a bailie was a local magistrate; Creech became one in Edinburgh in 1788 and Lord Provost of the city in 1811.

My Jean: Jean Armour (1767–1834), Burns's wife.

taken a farm: Ellisland (see above).

younger brother: Gilbert Burns (1760–1827), who, with the rest of the family, stayed on at Mossgiel, near Mauchline in Ayrshire, until 1798; Burns's mother, born Agnes Broun or Brown in 1732, died in 1820.

Commiss: abbreviation of 'Commissioners'.

to thee sweet Poetry, delightful maid: 'And thou, sweet Poetry, thou loveliest maid', Oliver Goldsmith (1730?–1774), *The Deserted Village* (1770), line 407.

Extract from a Letter to Mrs Frances Dunlop of Dunlop, 12 January 1795

Text: the manuscript of this letter is in the Robert Burns Birthplace Museum, Alloway.

Frances Dunlop: Mrs Frances Dunlop (1730–1815) of Dunlop in Ayrshire was a widow who began a correspondence with Burns in 1786 that lasted until this letter, whose comments on the execution of the king and queen of France outraged Mrs Dunlop. Burns seems not to have realized how sensitive the political issue of the French Revolution was to a woman who had sons and grandsons in the army and daughters married to French royalist exiles. He wrote several times after this letter to ask why Mrs Dunlop had not replied, but it was not until the last days of his life that she relented enough to respond and he may not have lived long enough to see her final communications to him.

the Doctor: John Moore (1729–1802); see the notes to the letters Burns sent him included in this volume.

'View of Society & Manners': Moore published both *A view of society and manners in France, Switzerland, and Germany* in 1779 and *A View of Society and Manners in Italy* in 1781.

Addison: Joseph Addison (1672–1719), English essayist, best known for his contributions to *The Spectator* (1711–12 and 1714).

Swift: Jonathan Swift (1667–1745), Anglo-Irish satirist, author of *Gulliver's Travels* (1726).

Sterne: Laurence Sterne (1713–68), English novelist, author of *Tristram Shandy* (1760–67).

Zeluco: a novel by John Moore, published in 1786.

in his last Publication: Moore quotes 'Tam o' Shanter', lines 61 to 66, on page 459 of the second volume of *A Journal during a Residence in France* (1793).

Entre nous: 'between ourselves' (French).

a certain pair of personages: Louis XVI, king of France, executed 21 January 1793, and his queen, Marie Antoinette, executed 16 October 1793.

Roscoe: William Roscoe (1753–1831), English historian, writer and politician; Burns quotes lines 23 and 24 of his poem 'O'er the vine-cover'd hills and gay regions of France' (1791) effusively welcoming the French Revolution.

London trials: in a series of trials in 1792, 1793 and 1794, leading British radical politicians were tried for sedition and treason as the government attempted to repress agitation for reform in the aftermath of the French Revolution; although the trials were largely a failure for the government, they were followed in late 1795 by laws that stifled the reform movement by restricting public meetings.

Billy Pit: William Pitt the Younger (1759–1806), Prime Minister, 1783–1801 and 1804–06, led Britain during the French Revolution and the wars that followed.

Letter to James Armour, 10 July 1796

Text: the manuscript of this letter is in the Robert Burns Birthplace Museum, Alloway.

James Armour: Burns's father-in-law (d. 1798) was a mason in Mauchline, Ayrshire.

Fife: an eastern county of Scotland; Mrs Armour was on a visit there when Burns wrote.

when her hour comes: Jean Armour Burns gave birth to Maxwell (d. 1799), her ninth child by Robert, on the day of the poet's funeral, 25 July 1796.

friend: Burns may mean 'family relation', a common eighteenth-century usage.

Index of Titles

Index of First Lines of Poems